# God Is My Spinach

## Robert Pickering Sr.

# July is hot... quotables from a sizzling book.

**Are there unwholesome thoughts imbedded in my subconscious?** Or simply was it too darn much sugar in that hot fudge sundae I ate after dinner!
—July DAY 20

**In the case of Moses, he was not passive.** He took on an Egyptian overseer, stood up to Pharaoh and hiked the desert for forty years. It is hard to see him as a wimp.
—July DAY 21

**I do not necessarily believe that the Lord helps me with my golf game...** [but I remember to] "always be thankful" when I am lining up a fourth putt!
—July DAY 27

# But wait. Read what the Reverands say:

Good reading, Mr. Pickering.
—Rev. Jim McChesney,

Always, it provides a positive moment to begin each day.
—Rev. Richard Ireland

From the ground up, Bob helps us to see how God is at work in the stew of our daily lives...
—Rev. Michael Miller

...you will see how Bob can write about his faith. I want you to know that Bob lives his faith just as well.

—Rev. Ed Dubose

Printed in the United States of America

First Printing, 2012

ISBN 978-0-9883074-0-7

BSM Publishers
12000 Marion Lane, 1101
Minnetonka, MN 55305

# God Is My Spinach

## Robert Pickering Sr.

## Acknowledgements

There are many people who have contributed to this book since it was started in 1999. First is my Good News buddy Tim from Mountain Iron, Minnesota. He suggested that I write my own devotionals rather than distributing one that I had read. My wife June has tolerated and contributed her devotion and love to the equation while putting up with my early morning ramblings.

The Good News messages went to a group of over 150 people of various denominations. Each person is special to me as a friend in Christ. Each message resulted in replies from different individuals and encouraged me to keep on writing.

There are several clergy who have encouraged me including Rick Ireland who had them added to the church web site; Mike Miller, Lyle Christianson and Jim McChesney who have often commented and shared thoughts about the writings.

My editor and friend, Steve, has supported my Good News messages since 2000 when we started posting them on the Spirit of Hope website. He helped me grow them into Spinach. Without his advice and efforts this devotional may not have happened.

# Contents Page 1

# Contents Page 2

# Contents Page 3

# Contents Page 4

# Contents Page 6

# Contents Page 7

# Contents Page 8

## November

## December

# **Contents** Page 9

# Happy New Year

Happy New Year. For the next few weeks the athletic clubs will be filled with "New Years resolutionists."

Diet programs will come and go, self improvement books will be purchased or at least the dust will be blown from last year's cover! Does that sound familiar? Yes, we all have had a few resolutions fall by the wayside.

I do not know if Paul wrote this passage on New Year's Eve but it is appropriate. Many of us have new goals today: weight, fitness, financial goals etc. Paul is asking us to look at our spiritual goals, "... Forgetting what is behind and straining toward what is ahead, I press on toward the goal to win the prize." Hold that thought as

**Not** that I have already obtained all this,
or have already been made perfect,
but I press on to take hold of that
for which Christ Jesus took hold of me.
Brothers, I do not consider myself yet to have taken hold of it.
But one thing I do:
Forgetting what is behind and straining toward what is ahead, I press on toward the goal to win the prize for which God has called me heavenward in Christ Jesus.
—Philippians 3, verses 12–14

you proceed through the New Year.

**Thought for Today**: Let us look ahead rather than behind. Let us look ahead at the opportunities in our lives. This year let us practice Christian ethics and life style in all phases of our lives and by all means share our faith with others.

**Prayer for Today**:
Heavenly Father, as this New Year begins please hear our prayer for serenity:

God grant me the serenity
to accept the things that I cannot change.
The courage to change the things I can.
And the wisdom to know the difference. Amen

Hear this for all the world's people so that your love and peace may dominate this New Year. Amen

# Our Task For a New Year

Happy New Year! We all say it and think it. However, we do not always live it. There are problems in our lives: illnesses, financial issues, family stress, etc., that do not roll over at midnight on December 31st.

However, we have control of "Happy New Year" in our heads. If we are the light of the world, then we need to be happy and allow the light to shine.

> **"Then** was our mouth filled with laughter,
>
> and our tongue with rejoicing:
>
> then said they among the nations,
>
> Jehovah hath done great things for them.
>
> Jehovah hath done great things for us;
>
> and we are joyful."
>
> —Psalm 126, verse 2

When we hear or read the news there is a lot in there to be depressed about. Many of the things that are going on in the world are tragic. As Christians we do need to care and be concerned. However, we also need to pray and give thanks to the Lord for the good news side of the coin. Overall, our focus needs to be on the positive side. There is always more right than wrong and more good than bad.

In a recent TV sermon, Joel Osteen asked, "The bible says we are the light of the world. Have you got your light shining out?" We need to focus on that with our smiles and our laughter. We need to be the warm glow and the light of the world.

**Thought for Today**: Today will be a great day. Yes, all of the normal things will occur. There will be illness, stress, cranky kids, bad weather, too much to do, etc. So what? There will also be great friends and family, fresh air, good food and other positives. We need to keep our light shining so others may see it.

**Prayer for Today**: Dear God we give thanks for the warmth and joy that you give us in our hearts and our Christian love for others. We thank you for all the happiness in our lives and the ability to share that joy and laughter with the world. Amen

# Agape Love?

Do you remember the bracelets WWJD, "What would Jesus do?" There is no doubt about it, He would love you and if somehow he wanted to kill you he would try to love you to death!

That's a bad analogy, one of my many but not my worst! Jesus was blessed with the ability to love completely, agape love. That term is used over 200 times in scripture and I am not sure that it is humanly possible to get to that point.

> **"Of** all the commandments, which is the most important?"
>
> "The most important one," answered Jesus, "is this: 'Hear, O Israel: The Lord our God, the Lord is one. Love the Lord your God with all your heart and with all your soul and with all your mind and with all your strength.' The second is this: 'Love your neighbor as yourself.' There is no commandment greater than these."
>
> —Mark 12, verses 28–31

Real love, for your neighbor, enemies, bosses, etc., is a very personal issue. The secret is separating behavior from the individual self. At the core, all people are loveable and we need to love them.

**Thought for Today**: For today let us make a special effort to search inside ourselves and feel affection and love for everyone we meet.

**Prayer for Today**: Dear Lord and Father, today we pray for the ability to care deeply for all of those around us. Please help us flush our conscious and unconscious prejudice and dislikes from our minds; help us be more like Jesus. Amen

Unfortunately there are times when I seem to put conditions on my love; times when I travel and deal with strangers in an airport and there are certain races and nationalities that concern me. I have put some subconscious conditions on my love for them.

In the new and diverse community where we have lived for several years, I caught myself introducing myself to some but not others. Oops, was I being discriminatory? I sure was—unwittingly—and had to change my behavior. So today everyone I meet gets an introduction. Ah, but do they get my love?

# Persistence

> **Then** Jesus told his disciples...that they should always pray and not give up.
>
> —Luke 18, verse 1

Last year several friends were forced to live these words. They were cut from their jobs due to staff reductions at their workplace and were hurt very badly financially and emotionally. There is a single mom who had to seek a whole new career. Another family lost the wife's job after 29 years while the husband took a twenty percent pay cut. These similar and devastating stories are too common in America and around the world.

In the two specific instances mentioned, June and I know them both well and they were good disciples. Through twelve months of rejection and hard times they never gave up and never lost faith.

Through the holiday season each seemed at peace and doing better than I would have done under the same circumstances. They had not given up hope and were still plugging away, interviewing and prayerfully seeking. I thought of them on New Year's Eve and wondered if they could even begin to say Happy New Year, out with the old and in with the new. We prayed for them and the many others in the same position.

There is a Bob Dylan phrase "Times are a-changing..." and maybe not for the better. In fact one of life's only constants is change! I have said many times that life is similar to an endurance event. It takes persistence to get to the end. There will be ups and downs. We must keep our eyes on the prize. We need to "...always pray and not give up."

**Thought for Today**: Let us pray for people in need; people dealing with tough life issue: health, family, financial, or others. Oh yes, like charity begins at home, it is a given that prayer does also.

**Prayer for Today**: Heavenly father today we pray for smooth sailing through the rough seas of life. We pray for ourselves and others who are in need. We pray that we will do better and seek a way to do your will here on earth. Amen

# Serenity Prayer

As we get into the New Year, peace and tranquility always seem to be part of our New Year's goals. Last year we did too much. One more committee at church, the kids need a coach, how can we get everyone to every game, lesson, class, etc? Oh, the boss wants us 50 hours a week too!

It takes faith and courage to let go and let God play a role in our lives.

> I... will have sufficient courage so that now, as always, Christ will be exalted in my body..."
> —Philippians 1, verse 20

At work and in our daily lives, we often fail to take the risk of allowing God to take control. Often we do not accept the spiritual help available. We will handle it all. Where is our humility when we try to do it all?

> ... humbly accept the word planted in you, which can save you.

> God grant me the serenity to accept the things I cannot change, the courage to change the things I can, and the wisdom to know the difference.

—James 2, verse 1
We tend to forget the basic rules taught to us by our faith. When we are taking control, adding stress to ourselves, do we ask for the help available?

> If any of you lacks wisdom, ask God...and it will be given to you.
> —James 1, verse 5

We are told to keep God at the forefront in our search for this inner peace.

> And the peace of God, which transcends all understanding, will guard your hearts and minds in Christ Jesus.
> —Philippians 4, verse 7

The serenity prayer is simple. We all know that simple is good. Let us start the new year with this thought in mind.

**Thought for Today**: Let us focus on peace and tranquility in our lives; with our families, neighbors, and coworkers.

**Prayer for Today**: Let's use the serenity prayer, today and for the year, especially when over stressed. Amen

# Kindness

One of the greatest feelings happens when someone treats us kindly. It may be as simple as when they open a door when we are carrying something, when someone lets us into a traffic lane, or offers to help in any other way. We get the wonderful feeling of gratitude and thankfulness. A few of these feelings each day contributes to a great day.

I feel strongly that being on the giving end, the door opener, courteous driver etc., is an even better feeling. Contributing to others in such small ways seems to make the day go by smoother. The warmth of their smiles

**But** the fruit of the Spirit is love, joy, peace, patience, kindness,
goodness and self control. Against such things there is no law.
—Galatians 5, verse 22

and the thank yous... make my day and it will make yours also.

**Thought for Today**: Today let us enjoy ourselves by smiling to show appreciation when others show kindness as well as when they acknowledge ours.

**Prayer for Today**: Dear Lord, today we pray that we can contribute to others in a kind and considerate manner. We pray that when we interact with people they will be glad; that they will feel Jesus through our actions. Amen

# 23rd Psalm

In the '40s and '50s, public school in Massachusetts always started with the 23rd Psalm, the Lord's prayer and the salute to the flag. Wow, by today's standards, that is powerful stuff. Let us take a look at this and see if we can apply it to our lives today.

> **The** Lord is my shepherd,
> I shall not want.
> He makes me lie down
> in green pastures,
> he leads me beside
> still waters...
> —Psalms 23, verses 1–2

The first two lines above lead us to tranquility. Faith will take care of our wants and lead us to that inner peace we desire and lead us to the restful place beside still waters.

> He refreshes and restores my life;
> He leads in the paths of righteousness for His name's sake
> —Psalm 23, verse 3

There are always periods when things in our lives need rebuilding. There are temptations to take the easy way. These verses point out that the way to get out of the "dumps" is to follow Him.

> Yes, though I walk through the valley of the shadow of death,
> I will fear no evil, for You are with me;
> Your rod and Your staff to comfort me.
> —Psalm 23, verse 4

In the biblical context, the rod is an instrument used for guiding, rescuing and protecting (sheep) and the staff is an instrument of support. The Psalm points out that the Lord is with us and will guide and support us throughout our lives.

Yes, today our lives get filled with stress. As Christians we are given wonderful tools to work with in our daily lives. The more we let God lead us, the more we will be at peace.

**Thought for Today:** Let us reflect on this New Year and all of our goals and resolutions.

Read the 23rd Psalm and accept the help that God has available to us. It will be a big help in locating those still waters we all seek.

**Prayer for Today:** Heavenly Father, many times stress builds up in our lives. It is a combination of hurts, anger and resentments kept hidden inside of ourselves. I pray that when this occurs, I find a way to let you help and can accept the guidance, protection and support promised through our Christian faith. Amen

# Trust

Trust is an interesting concept. There are camps and seminars where trust in others is emphasized. They take you on rope and cable courses in trees, sliding down zip lines at breakneck speeds—but the one I like best is standing straight up and falling backwards knowing that the team will catch you. Yes, that takes trust.

In our lives our catcher is always with us but somehow we need to trigger the catch! Does that confuse you? I hope so. Often we get caught once a week on Sunday morning. Yes, we allow the Lord in for a bit. In fact I remember one spring in Massachusetts when our four children were small and we skipped several Sundays because of the stress of getting to church. That did not work very well.

Certainly all that we do is necessary: it is on the calendar, we made the commitments, etc. OK, so here we are at midday, over stressed, the boss just dumped a big job on us and there is no relief in sight. Now is the time to count to ten, take a deep breath and focus. It is

> **Trust** in the Lord with all your heart and lean not on your own understanding; in all your ways acknowledge Him and He will make your paths straight.
> —Proverbs 3, verses 5 and 6

time for meditation even if only for a few minutes.

"…He will make your paths straight."

**Thought for Today:** Today, this week or even this hour will not be stress free. Today and this week let's remember to stop and pray. Take a break.

**Prayer for Today:** Dear Lord, today we will be dealing with our full and busy lives. We may not have the time to acknowledge your presence in our lives. We give thanks today for your being here with us and pray that we take the time to allow you to help us through the day. Amen

# Confidence

Folks, we are starting a new year and for once I did not make any New Year's resolutions. That means I have decided to accept my faults! In the past, mine involved weight and fitness, and statistically that made me average. But after the two triathlons this summer neither weight nor fitness seemed important this year.

The Psalmist above gives us a strong message for the new year and clearly demonstrates that through our faith we can find confidence and trust. The newspapers, the TV journalists and media all want to sell us on negativity. They are after ratings and, for whatever reason, they think focusing on the negative is the way to sell their time. That is not a good service to the world. OK, we do read the news but we also need to read the good news of Jesus to balance the books. His good news can overcome all the news media's negativity.

> **For** you are my hope;
> O Lord God, you are my trust…
> And the source of my confidence.
> —Psalm 71, verse 5

This Psalmist also said:

> But as for me I will always have hope
> —Psalm 72, verse 14

and

> You will increase my honor
> And comfort me once again
> —Psalm 71, verse 21

You can see that the good news needs to be our resolution for the next year. Through the good news of Jesus Christ we will all have a better life and live in a better world.

**Thought for Today:** Happy New Year to all. It will be as we grow in confidence and trust in those around us. It will be when we share the good news with those around us. It will be as we grow together in our faith.

**Prayer for Today:** Dear Lord and Father, we are coming to the end of a year and are faced with the opportunities that present themselves each January 1st. As always we want to do better in every way. This year we pray that we can discover the spiritual maturity and growth to be better at being a disciple and worker for You. We pray that we may find a clear vision of what we can do for you. Amen

# God's Help Wanted

When reading the news paper, do you ever take a quick look at the help wanted section? Many of us do for a variety of reasons- some are searching for an improvement in their career position, some for new careers, salesmen sometimes spot new companies as prospects; there are many reasons. In hard times and slow economies, the section grows thinner than normal, but probably gets a closer review by the readers.

Many of us attend church services weekly. We hear a message. Sometimes we listen and absorb and come away enthusiastic about the subject, other times we are pleasantly soothed and calmed and even sometimes we are disinterested. I think it is OK to be in any one of those moods after hearing a message. Because we are all different, even God can't send us a message on Sunday that affects all of us uniformly.

What does it mean when we are enthusiastic about a message? When it inspires us to think about action? Perhaps there is an opportunity to serve, help out, increase our time or cash commitments. Whatever it may be, we

**For** by the grace given me I say to every one of you:
Do not think of yourself more highly than you ought,
but rather think of yourself with sober judgment,
in accordance with the measure of faith God has given you.
Just as each of us has one body with many members, and these members do not all have the same function, so in Christ we who are many form one body, and each member belongs to all the others."
—Romans 12, verse 3

have heard God's "Help Wanted" and it is our choice to apply for the job. It is our opportunity to allow God's will to be done through us here on earth.

**Thought for Today:** Today let us focus on our daily activities. Let us search our planners and calendars for the Godly reasons to be busy. Let us allow some time to do God's will as we move through our busy schedules.

**Prayer for Today:** Heavenly Father, the world is a confusing place. Wars and conflict abound, hunger and poverty seem excessive and there is violence on the streets. All of this seems inconsistent with your will. We pray that we find a message, a way to contribute, a way to serve society in your name; a way to understand and respond to your "Help Wanted" section. Amen

# Perfection

In twelve-step programs, there is a reading called "How It Works." It recognizes that the program is to develop "spiritual growth not perfection." We all tend to get into that perfect mode: perfect mom, perfect dad, perfect employee and the list goes on. Obviously, each of us falls short of perfection.

In our daily lives, we make mistakes. We could count them weekly and judge ourselves as failures. The only one of us that does not make mistakes probably does nothing. Many people work their way into depression by counting their failures.

In our spiritual lives it is not any different. We all have made mistakes and will continue to be less than perfect. We may feel bad or judge ourselves rather severely. However, "God is not unjust; he will not forget your work and the love you have shown...." We must remember that as we walk the walk.

> **God** is not unjust; he will not forget your work and the love you have shown him as you have helped his people and continue to help them. We want each of you to show this same diligence to the very end, in order to make your hope sure. We do not want you to become lazy, but to imitate those who through faith and patience inherit what has been promised.
> —Hebrews 6, verses 10–12

**Thought for Today**: Today we will fail again at being perfect. Let us try to focus on the good that we do, the encouragement that we give others and the love we have in our hearts. That will help us have a great day.

**Prayer for Today**: Dear Lord and Father, there is scary and awful news every day. Often we forget your love because of worry and concern. Today we pray that we may focus on your understanding and caring love. We pray for the opportunity to demonstrate and share your love with others. Amen

# Soar Like Eagles

Growing up in the '50s, a bald eagle was a rare sight. In fact, I do not think I ever saw one. Now 60 years later they are soaring over shopping centers, eating fish out of the local lakes and generally hanging out with us. Now that we see them more often, it is easy to see why our founders selected it as a national symbol. They are big, majestic and beautiful birds. Their revival as a species shows us how humans can contribute to God's creations and the world we live in. We changed a few rules, respected the Lord's way and the bald eagle is now a common sight.

> ...**those** who hope in the Lord will renew their strength.
> They will soar on wings like eagles;
> they will run and not grow weary,
> they will walk and not be faint.
> —Isaiah 40, verse 31

We are always searching for ways to make a better world, a way to soar. In my early years working in engineering for a very large company, many of the rules seemed restrictive and bureaucratic. The younger engineers in the department, including myself, thought we were going to change the world, right *now!* That was not the way big company systems worked. When frustration with the system came to the surface our trainer and mentor often advised us to "Rise above it and move on." Eagles do that.

There is a story about eagles rising above storms. They sense the storm coming and use the wind to rise above the dangerous winds and ride out the storm. In many instances in life we need to keep our faith while staring at negativity, the storms of life. We count to ten, punch a pillow, and when we are smart we ask the Lord for support. When we involve our faith to handle our personal storms we minimize our stress and greatly improve our quality of life.

## Eagles in a Storm

Did you know that an eagle knows when a storm is approaching long before it breaks? The eagle will fly to some high spot and wait for the winds to come. When the storm hits, it sets its wings so that the wind will pick it up and lift it above the storm. While the storm rages below, the eagle is soaring above it.

The eagle does not escape the storm. It simply uses the storm to lift it higher. It rises on the winds that bring the storm.

When the storms of life come upon us—and all of us will experience them— we can rise above them by setting our minds and our beliefs toward God. The storms do not have to overcome us. We can allow God's power to lift us above them.

God enables us to ride the winds of the storm that bring sickness, tragedy, failure and disappointment in our lives. We can soar above the storm.

Remember, it is not the burdens of life that weigh us down, it is how we handle them. The Bible says, "Those who hope in the Lord will renew their strength. They will soar on wings like eagles."

**Thought For Today:** Let us use our faith in the Lord to rise above the problems of every day life.

**Prayer For Today:** As our country moves forward with a new adminstration, let us pray that as a country we can find a way to serve "God's will" rather than "our will." Amen

# Bring Love Home

We are all having concerns regarding our financial futures. It seems that institutions we trusted are letting us down. We are changing our style of operation and the way we live our lives.

> **Love** bears up under anything and everything that comes, is ever ready to believe the best of every person, its hopes are fadeless under all circumstances.
> —1 Corinthians 13, verse 7

There are businesses laying people off, those that continue working are doing more for either less or the same. In short form, our lives have become more stressful and in many cases the stress has grown into frustration and then anger. Sometimes it is hard to focus on the benefits brought to us through the Lord and our faith through Jesus Christ.

One of the reasons that "Good News" exists is exactly that. Meditation works and helps bring us back to reality. There is a Good News recipient whose wife has had chronic degenerative back problems for over 15 years. She is tired of pain killers and muscle relaxants. A few years ago she started meditation classes and learned to meditate to the point of self hypnosis. She reduced her drugs to one quarter of her previous dosage. The stress and worry about her disease was causing the tension and many problems that added to her symptoms.

Many of us bring our daily problems into the home at night and bring our frustrations in to our family life. Children bring home their frustrations from school, mom and dad from their jobs (or from a bad round of golf) or from the evening traffic. What for? Tonight when you go home, try sitting in the driveway and read this message and leave the stress behind. Pray that you can go into the house in a loving and caring mood and contribute to the peaceful and loving environment called home.

**Thought for Today:** Someone once said that at times we are all salesmen. My example of preparing for a meeting is a serious part of business life and success. Let us all focus on "preparing for the meeting" with our families and with God. Let us contribute to peace and tranquility rather than helping increase stress.

**Prayer for Today:** Dear Lord and Father, today I pray for peace, peace in my family, my relationships and throughout the world. Amen

# Breaking Rules

Is the Law the Law? Do we always obey the Law? Man's common law and the Ten Commandments are broken every day all around us. Just try driving the speed limit on a busy road. Someone will pass you. I read last week that 56 percent of the people surveyed answered that it was OK to cheat on their taxes. Remember the "Fuzz Buster" radar detector? I suspect that everyone reading this today is guilty of breaking a rule in the last 24 hours.

As a 50,000 mile per year salesman in the '70s, I was asked many times why I did not have a "Fuzz Buster." My answer was always the same. I did not want to demonstrate to my children that it was OK to speed or that I could choose a rule to break. After all, if I could choose which rules I would follow, then my children would be apt to think that was the way to deal with our family rules. We teach by example. (I did break a few speed limits.)

**We** will not hide them from their children; we will tell the next generation the praiseworthy deeds of the LORD, His power, and the wonders He has done. He decreed statutes for Jacob and established the law in Israel, which he commanded our forefathers to teach their children, so the next generation would know them, even the children yet to be born, and they in turn would tell their children. Then they would put their trust in God and would not forget his deeds but would keep his commands.
—Psalm 78, verses 5–7

The Psalmist talks about "...commanding our forefathers to teach their children...." The facts are simple, we must teach our children and the best way to do that is to live a Godly example for them to follow. That is a tough order.

**Thought for Today**: Let us focus on our habits regarding both God's and common laws. Let's think about them in regards to honesty and integrity. Let's observe where we may do a better job—and patch up a few holes.

**Prayer for Today**: Heavenly Father, our children are loved by you as much as by ourselves. We pray that we are doing them justice; that they are learning your laws and ways from our teachings and our example. We pray for your guidance so that our children will follow and experience the peace comes from loving you. Amen

# MLK Day

There are many quotes from the great Martin Luther King and when I researched them I picked the one above because I had not heard it before. It does not make a great philosophical statement, there is not a spiritual or social justice meaning; it is a simple truth. Living and having the right to pursue freedom always needs to be protected.

Other quotes by MLK have deeper meaning, spiritually and are more often used. Below are the ones that seem to be popular in the media:

> Darkness cannot drive out darkness; only light can do that. Hate cannot drive out hate; only love can do that. Hate multiplies hate, violence multiplies violence, and toughness multiplies toughness in a descending spiral of destruction.
> —Strength To Love, Martin Luther King, Jr.

**It** may be true that the law cannot make a man love me, but it can keep him from lynching me, and I think that's pretty important.
—Rev. Dr. Martin Luther King, Jr.

One that I personally like is:

> Faith is taking the first step even when you don't see the whole staircase.

And as Christians we need to demonstrate that we have the faith, we need to always take the first step.

**Thought for Today**: This is the day the Lord has made and He made it for all humankind. We need to remember and promote equality, always.

**Prayer for Today**: Dear Lord, today we do not pray for forgiveness of the past discrimination and separatist social acts of our forefathers. We need to accept them and move forward. Today we pray for the guidance and will to contribute to peace and acceptance through Jesus' love. Amen

# Win-Win

In America there seems to be a win lose philosophy running rampant through out our society. There is a lot of hero worship devoted to overpaid athletes. We seem to have adopted Vince Lombardi's attitude "Winning isn't everything, it's the only thing." Well, that may be our world, but it is not God's world.

> ...**what** is man that you are mindful of him,
> the son of man that you care for him?
> You made him a little lower than the heavenly beings and crowned him with glory and honor.
> —Psalm 8, verses 4 and 5

The Psalmist above clearly demonstrates that we were created a little lower than the angels and crowned with glory. There is plenty of God's love for each of us. There are world wide resources that when shared in God's way will do for all. We live in a great world with great people and somehow we taint it with our own un-Godly behaviors.

As a young athlete in the '40s, I remember the expression "It's not whether you win or lose, it is how you play the game that counts." Somehow that has stuck with me through out my life. It is an expression of a win-win philosophy. I think that is what God had in mind.

**Thought for Today**: Today let us focus on creating win-win situations in our lives. Observe our surroundings and lighten them up a bit. Slow for the other drivers, merge rather than block. Open a door and allow a few people through. Sit forward in church and leave some room in the back for late comers. Let's show everyone that we all can win.

**Prayer for Today**: Heavenly Father, last week there were war protests. Many nations are eyeing each other with cross intentions. Anger seems to be the rule of the day. We pray for some guidance. We pray for understanding. We desire peace and fellowship with our fellow man rather than anger and violence.

# The Light

Have you ever had a person take unfair advantage of you? Lie about a deal? Sell you something that did not meet expectations? Perhaps a neighbor encroaching on a property line? Doing something opportunistic or unnecessarily aggressive?

**The** eye is the lamp of the body.
If your eyes are good, your whole body will be full of light.
But if your eyes are bad, your whole body will be full of darkness.
If then the light within you is darkness, how great is that darkness!
—Matthew 6, verses 22–23

Well, I think that if the aggressive (dark) side exists, it is God's place to do the judging. However, in our lives, June and I have concluded that being God-like and following the Golden Rule is the only way to pursue goals.

Opportunistic behavior is one of my pet peeves. However, we live in a free market society. Let the buyer beware, competition for resources is a way of life. That is the American way! Or is the American way the Golden Rule?

June and I have often met someone in a church environment who was very aggressive in business. In fact, some out and out crooks! (OK so we should not judge, but that's another Good News) The question we often ask is, "Can a person be an opportunistic shark in one part of his life, deal with a dark side, and be a Christian on Sunday?"

**Thought for Today:** Today let us consider how much darkness exists inside of our lives. Let us make a conscious choice to let the light in and share it with others. Let us light up other people's lives in the name of Christ.

**Prayer for Today:** Heavenly Father, we offer prayers for peace. There are nuclear threats in Korea, alleged chemical weapons in the Mid East and extremely harmful biological material was found in London. It makes us ask, where is the world going? We pray that sharing the light brings common sense and tranquility to the world. Amen

# Let the Glory Be God's

The "Super Bowl" takes place this weekend and there are big numbers associated with it. Numbers like 150 million people watching on TV, 3 million dollars for a 30 second ad, 250 million added to the area economy—Oh yes, a number I do not have but tried to find: there are a number of competitors and coaches from both teams who will attend a prayer meeting and bible study Sunday before the game. They are members of the Fellowship of Christian Athletes.

My sports history goes back to age six as a YMCA swimmer and my 60-plus years of associating with athletes has convinced me that they are overall not a group to be proud to know. For the most part, their years of competition and winning-is-everything attitude has influenced them in a negative manner. Frankly, I don't like them and avoid them.

The athletes that surprise me the most were the Olympians that I have been blessed to know. My brother Wayne and I competed against several that swam in 1956 and 1960. My conclusion in regard to them is that they focused so much on their game that they did not develop very good social skills. For the record, that's being very kind.

> **Praise** be to the Lord,
> for He has heard my cry
> for Mercy.
> The LORD is my strength
> and shield;
> My heart trusts in Him and
> I am helped.
> —Psalm 28, verses 6 and 7

On Super Sunday there will be members of the "Fellowship" who have kept a balance in their life. In sports I find them a pleasing and great minority. They represent what I feel every Christian and person needs to be: the best they can be with an appreciation of the Lord and Jesus Christ. Below is the last paragraph of their Competitors Creed.

> I give my all, all of the time.
> I do not give up. I do not
> give in. I do not give out.
> I am the Lord's warrior—a
> competitor by conviction and
> a disciple of determnination.
> I am confident beyond
> reason because my
> confidence lies in Christ.
> The results of my efforts
> must result in His glory.
> Let the competition begin.
> Let the glory be God's.

**Thought for the Day**: Let us enjoy the day by being the best we can be while keeping the Lord in the forefront.

**Prayer for Today**: Dear Lord, today let us be cool and relaxed, patient and observing, caring and loving as we deal with others. Let us shine your light so others will recognize we are at peace. Amen

# Friendships

Intimacy is not only a marriage or "significant other" issue. In my business world, several of us, many on the Good News list, have met the evening prior to a sales meeting for a prayer dinner. There is a closeness that exists within that group.

Another business man in the Good News group once shared with me that his small company starts each week with a prayer breakfast. You can feel something special when dealing with those guys, even when you do not know exactly why.

Several years ago I came to realize the intimacy of a group of men who gather to share while dining. The reading that day dealt with "The Intimacy of the Table" and how often we share while dining with others. This time of gathering, whether it be with family or friends, is special to us.

However, within a relationship, husband-wife, parent-child, good friends or in other instances, intimacy makes a partnership.

> **Husbands**, love your wives, just as Christ loved the church and gave himself to her.
> —Ephesians 5, verse 25

**Thought for Today:** We all like to feel comfortable and intimacy within a group creates a warmth that we all love. However, we are often guarded with our feelings when in groups. We are conservative and hold back. Let us think more about letting our inner selves be seen by others. Let us share our Christian love and create more intimacy with our friends and associates.

**Prayer for Today:** Heavenly father, we seem to be living in a world with hate and revenge common place. Young mothers as human bombs, nations terrorizing other nations and in business there are too many lose-lose negotiations. We of faith are searching for your will in all of this. Today we pray that we can understand and contribute to friendships and world wide Godly solutions. Amen

# Perfect Will

In other Good News we have discussed the whole person: spirit, mind and body. In Paul's message to the Romans there is an emphasis on the mind. If you are reading this you probably don't need it.

When growing up in the late '40s and '50s, we would spend a lot of time reading. There were whole groups of us kids, reading and trading books. Yes, sometimes comic books, but also everything from Uncle Wiggly to Sherlock Holmes. As we grew older the books changed to National Geographic and Mickey Spillane. It was a period of intellectual and physical growth.

Personally, in the '60s my reading habit was broken and I went years without reading a book. The ability to imagine myself in a story, to fantasize about being the great Sherlock Holmes, Huck Finn or Superman passed me by. Surely my intellectual growth was stagnant or at least slowed down. I fit the pattern of the new television world, visual rather than intellectual.

> **Do** not conform any longer to the pattern of this world, but be transformed by the renewing of your mind. Then you will be able to test and approve what God's will is—his good, pleasing and perfect will.
> —Romans 12, verse 2

A career change to sales saved me from being stagnant. Engineers need to work on their skills to become salesmen. The best source of information was reading books. So, after a fifteen year drought, my reading habit was initiated out of necessity. Reading again became part of my life and it spread to both growth and recreational works. I feel blessed by this today.

**Thought for Today:** Let us ask, "What may we choose to do differently to...be transformed by the renewing of our mind?" Let us take the time to renew our commitment to intellectual growth.

**Prayer for Today:** Dear Lord and Heavenly Father, we pray for guidance regarding love and peace. We are a nation and world community out of control. We as Christians pray for our leaders and the leaders of the world to find a solution. We pray they do your will, follow your path and resolve our problems through love, peace and understanding. Amen

# Good Feelings

Good feelings are great. Throughout our lives there are those special moments that burn into our memories, the warm fuzzies. They vary in many ways. Often, at a funeral, family and friends recall those feelings about a loved one who has passed. They make a great celebration of life.

As an athlete, I have experienced a lot of self induced memories. A hole in one, championship swimming races and a 1991 Triathlon with my daughter Karen are my favorites. This type of memory is good, but the ones that set me on fire and bring tears to my eyes are the ones I have from helping other people. The smile on the face of a nursing home patient when you visit them or seeing progress or success in another person after assisting or mentoring generates feelings that exceed personal memories.

> **There** are different kinds of gifts,
> But the same spirit.
> There are different kinds of service,
> but the same Lord.
> —1 Corinthians 12, verse 5

Service to others not only brings them joy, but a great feeling of satisfaction within the server. We all have been given gifts by the Lord. Real satisfaction in life can be accomplished through the sharing of these gifts with others.

**Thought for Today:** Today let's take some time and do some serious thought about our past service. Let us enjoy the memories, the reward given to us by God for our service. Yes, we deserve the "warm fuzzies" given to us for sharing our gifts. Enjoy the moment and today with His blessings.

**Prayer for Today:** Heavenly Father, we thank you for the many gifts that you have given us, the feelings that we have when we use these gifts in our daily lives and the opportunity to use them to serve humanity. We pray for the wisdom to discern what you want us to do and the will to do it faithfully and well. Amen.

# A Place To Hide

In the '80s there was a speaker, Ty Boyd, on the business speaking circuit that was a very good Christian, business man and TV ad man who introduced me to the National Speakers Association. Ty taught that to be successful you had to be happy. Also, to be happy you had to have a "life plan" that included all phases of life. It is early in the New Year and we all have our resolutions and goals; that is a good thing in my mind. However, what is our plan to accomplish those goals?

Frankly, I do not really care about the plan to lose weight or get fit, the resolution to be a better employee, etc. My reason for writing this is to share some thoughts on using what has been given to us through Jesus to be successful and happy. This will be a year of change and we all will need to use the Lord as a refuge, a place to seek peace.

> **The** boundary lines have fallen for me in pleasant places;
> …You have made known to me the path of life;
> …you will fill me with joy in your presence, with eternal pleasures at your right hand.
> —Psalm 16, verses 6, 11 and 12

The expression "When the going gets tough the tough get going" is sportsy and cute. My thoughts are that when the going gets tough spiritual people will recognize the pleasant boundaries given them by the Lord and be at peace. They will see the path of life made available to them through faith and experience; the joy of following the path, the will of God. The closer we stay to the Lord and His plan, the happier and more successful we will become.

**Thought for Today** (Week or Year!): There are many challenges as we move forward. Today let us focus on staying close to God. If we have not put this closeness in our life plan, let's do it now. Let's set ourselves up for success and happiness.

**Prayer for Today:** Dear Heavenly Father, we are scared and concerned as we move forward through a changing world. We pray that we may hear your call and find refuge in your love. We pray that throughout life we may follow a plan to be close to you and do your will here on earth. Amen

# God's Seven Gifts

Paul's message to the Romans lists seven specific gifts. Each of us has been blessed with some of them and has the opportunity to use them in our every day lives. We are bombarded with opportunities. God's "HELP WANTED" asks us to use our gifts to do His work. We are therefore facing two challenges. One is to recognize the gifts given to us. The other is sharing these gifts with others in our daily lives.

It is the sharing of these gifts in a loving Christian way that brings us peace.

**We** have different gifts, according to the grace given us.
If a man's gift is prophesying, let him use it in proportion to his faith.
If it is serving, let him serve; if it is teaching, let him teach;
if it is encouraging, let him encourage;
if it is contributing to the needs of others, let him give generously;
if it is leadership, let him govern diligently;
if it is showing mercy, let him do it cheerfully.
—Romans 12, verses 6 and 7

**Thought for Today:** Today let us focus on our gifts. Let us understand them and how to use them to help ourselves and others.

**Prayer for Today:** Dear Lord, again we pray for peace and justice in a seemingly troubled world. We are trying to understand what everything means and our piece in it all. Often, many of us feel too small to help. Since "...we are one body in Christ" we pray that we may recognize our gifts and use them. Amen

# Service

I like the term "measure of faith" in any context. It causes us to stop and wonder exactly what scale we would measure it with, yards or meters? Euro vs. dollars? Pounds vs. kilograms? Faith, of course, can not be measured in such easily quantified terms. The measure that probably matters is probably how well we use God's gifts.

> For by the grace given me, I say to every one of you: Do not think of yourself more highly than you ought, but rather think of yourself with sober judgment, in accordance with the measure of faith God has given you.
> —Romans 12, verse 3

> We have different gifts, according to the grace given us.
> If a person's gift is … serving, let him serve.
> —Romans 12, verses 6 and 7

When serving others is done as a passion it is truly a gift from God. The warm feeling of having helped is always worth the efforts. Many people are famous because of this gift and some have been raised to sainthood. In our generation, Mother Theresa was certainly blessed with it. The best part of the gift of service is we all have it and can feel it at some level. We all at some time will have the opportunity to be the "Good Samaritan." We need to use this gift when we can and enjoy the feeling that God gives us as His reward.

**Thought for Today**: Today let us think about how we may help. Is there someone with an ill family member that could use a visit? Can we make time for coffee with a friend? If we can't plan an opportunity to serve, let us look during the week for a chance to use this gift.

**Prayer for Today**: Dear Lord, service to you is important to us but we are confused.

Violence seems to invade our lives at all levels. World wide there are terrorist threats, locally there are too many assaults on others. We need and want to help. We need and desire to serve our families, others around us and somehow contribute to Your will here on earth. We pray for an opportunity to help others in a way that will benefit all. Amen

# Leadership

Leadership is one of God's greatest gifts. The world has experienced great leaders in many different forms. The ability to have a passion and develop followers that believe and follow the lead is truly a gift from God. In this regard, Jesus is, was and will be the "King of Kings." Leadership and followers without greed, win-win, love abounds, etc. make Him different from all others.

On a more human scale, we have leaders within our society. Many of us are leaders of our families; some of us are managers in business, youth sports or at church. Often when in these "leadership roles" decisions are made that are different than Christ would have made them.

Several years ago the bracelet with "WWJD" engraved on it was popular. Those letters stood for "What would Jesus do?" The bracelet served as a reminder that when we are making a decision, it is always a good idea to

**We** have different gifts, according to the grace given us.
If a man's gift is prophesying, let him use it in proportion to his faith. If it is serving, let him serve; if it is teaching, let him teach;
if it is encouraging, let him encourage;
if it is contributing to the needs of others, let him give generously; if it is leadership, let him govern diligently; if it is showing mercy, let him do it cheerfully.
—Romans 12, verses 6 and 7

consider our faith and our leader. As normal humans we will not achieve perfection. We can however strive toward it with every decision we make when we are asked to lead.

**Thought for Today:** We need to again review the gifts that we received from God. We need to recognize and utilize them. When we are placed in a decision-making role, we need to consider "What would Jesus do?"

**Prayer for Today:** Heavenly Father, we are all called on to make decisions. Financial pressure, personal prejudices and many other factors often cause us to drift from your will when making choices. Today we pray that throughout the New Year we may all make decisions that fit your plan; that would be as Jesus would do. Amen

# Teaching

Webster says that a teacher is someone who "... gives knowledge or insight to another." Yes that is part of it all and if that is the case we are all part-time teachers. I do not think that we can get through a day without sharing part of a personal knowledge base with someone. The scary piece is that we do not always know when we are teaching.

The formal teacher, the professional, whether it is a Sunday school teacher or K-12, is someone that very intentionally shares knowledge. Often there comes a magical attachment between them and their students. Most of us have a strong memory from our early days about a teacher that was special.

We are often teaching others through our public actions. Yes, others observe us and we unknowingly share. One Sunday morning in church, I observed an older gentleman holding hands with his wife.

> **We** have different gifts, according to the grace given us.
> If a man's gift is prophesying, let him use it in proportion to his faith. If it is serving, let him serve; if it is teaching, let him teach…
> —Romans 12, verses 6–8

Later he had his arm around her like a teenager on a Friday night date. Let me share with you that this guy and I had a very negative business relationship. That day however, he and his wife set an example for me and for those all around them. I grew to know them better and use his "behavioral teaching" often to improve my own relationship.

As my family has grown up, June and I have observed a lot of behaviors in our children that make us proud. Also, we often observe something that we wish they had not learned from us. Yes, we often teach our children the wrong stuff! Wouldn't it be great if they only saw us at our best? My dad used to say "Do as I say, not as I do." *Oops*, that is not reality. Within our families, parents are always teachers.

**Thought for Today:** Let us recognize our God-given roles as teachers. We did not ask for it, we can not avoid it, so let us do it well. Each day let us share through our behaviors, words and actions, teachings that will make us proud.

**Prayer for Today:** Heavenly Father, today we ask that we feel your spirit so that we may act like a disciple of Christ. Let our behavior teach those around us that there is good in the world. Amen

# Contributing

When are we contributing to the needs of others? Every day in some way we contribute. We rarely risk physical harm or sacrifice but contribute in lesser ways. Sometimes our contributions are intentional and planned. Often they are reactionary and just something that we do.

Through our Church we often help serve at shelters, contribute to transients in the neighborhood and in many other ways. At home many of us jump in when neighbors have projects or problems. Even the simple act of preparing food for someone who is ill is a serious contribution, a spiritual act. As Christians we were all given this gift at some level. As Christians we get a great feeling, a gift from God when we contribute to others.

**We** have different gifts, according to the grace given us.
If a man's gift is prophesying, let him use it in proportion to his faith. ...If it is contributing to the needs of others, let him give generously...
—Romans 12, verses 6 and 8

**Thought for Today:** This week let us contribute. No I do not mean put some coins in the tip tray at a fast food restaurant (but go ahead anyway). I mean let us look for and find someone that we can help. Each day we walk past opportunities to contribute to someone in need. Let us search them out and contribute to their tranquility.

**Prayer for Today:** Heavenly Father, often the balance in our lives seems tipped toward being selfish. The immediate needs of ourselves and family occupy too much mind-share. We tend to forget to reach out to others. Today we pray for improved focus on Your work. We pray for simpler lives in which we can put "Your will" on our "to do" lists and calendars. Amen

# Encouraging

Another gift mentioned in Romans 12 is "encouraging." As leaders and teachers we need to recognize that those around us often need encouragement. As heads of a family, the old school was often critical. Walk softly and carry a big stick. Let's go out behind the woodshed! Parenting had yet to be enlightened.

Just yesterday while jogging around a soccer field during a game I listened to opposing coaches with different approaches. One encouraging the players to do things, the other advising them what not to do; one encouraging, one scolding. The encouraged team had a totally different look. The "don't do this" team had the negatives fresh in their minds and showed it. Guess who won!

In business management, many schools and teachers coach that the annual review is the one time each year that management can encourage, inspire and coach an employee. Wow, that is often not the case. Unenlightened managers tend to give unbalanced reviews, "yes-but" style. When that happens, it leaves the employee flat

> **We** have different gifts, according to the grace given us.
> If a man's gift is prophesying, let him use it in proportion to his faith.
> …If it is contributing to the needs of others, let him give generously…
> —Romans 12, verses 6 and 8

regardless of the pay increase and the company loses its big chance to pump up an asset.

People that have the gift of encouragement are blessed and I hope many of you have it.

**Thought for Today**: Like teaching and leadership, this week we will all have an opportunity to encourage someone. To some it will be a natural gift, to many it will be a chore. Let us recognize where we fit and utilize God's gifts in our lives to make God's world a better place.

**Prayer for Today**: Heavenly Father, we are often confused. The book says, "There are different kinds of working, but the same God works all of them in all men." However, faith is used by many as a reason for terror and war. We pray that we can understand this; we pray that all persons can come to understand this. We pray that the entire world come to understand your many gifts and use them to lead to common good. Amen

# Mercy

The gift of mercy is a hard one to define but an easy one to see. In a recent book I read on the American Civil War there was a chapter about Clara Barton and how she and her nurses risked their lives tending to soldiers in the field. That is a true gift of mercy.

Often we are listening to a speaker who presents his case with great emotion as opposed to using logic. They demonstrate empathy, compassion and sympathy rather than addressing things logically. Often these speakers have the gift of mercy.

People with this gift pick up on the emotional response of others. They want harmony in their lives, at home and work. Physical contact is highly valued and they seem to understand the body language of others very well. As with other gifts there are limitations.

> **We** have different gifts, according to the grace given us.
> If a man's gift is prophesying, let him use it in proportion to his faith. …If it is contributing to the needs of others, let him give generously…
> —Romans 12, verses 6 and 8

Webster says mercy means to "to console or to succor one afflicted" and the Amplified Bible says "He who does acts of mercy, with genuine cheerful eagerness." Mercy leaps from the heart and there is no resistance to caring. Mercy is a gift from God to those who can keep on giving!

**Thought for the Day:** Let us think about who we are and what gifts God has given us. Let us learn to use these gifts in our lives and in the lives of others better.

**Prayer for the Day:** Heavenly Father, today I give thanks for gifts that show mercy for others. They are gifts that the world needs. Amen

# Prophesy

We look at prophets as old-time geniuses, people with wisdom who spoke their minds and often worked to correct society's ills. They were different from most because they spoke their minds and were often controversial. They were rarely in doubt but not often considered correct; many were martyred.

Speaking out on controversial matters and society's ills is gutsy at the best of times. In our world today our population seems to be split down the middle. Most votes are close to a 50/50 split. Today's prophets offend almost half the people when they speak.

> **We** have different gifts, according to the grace given us.
> If a man's gift is prophesying, let him use it in proportion to his faith.
> …If it is contributing to the needs of others, let him give generously…
> —Romans 12, verses 6 and 8

I believe that we are all given the gift of having prophetic ideas, but that only a few have received the gift as Paul meant it in his message. Those few are the outspoken leaders and supporters of change in the world. They are still around and will be recognized by future generations.

**Thought for Today:** Let us try to recognize our gifts and how we apply them in our personal lives, within our community and our business lives.

**Prayer for Today:** Let us pray that the prophets in our society continue doing the Lord's work. They have a real gift that needs to be heard and not forgotten. Amen

# Gifts

For a week we have thought about our gifts from God. It is early in the year and He wants us to use them. Paul talked about them in Rome and Corinth. None of us have received all of the gifts and we need to recognize which ones we have and apply them to doing God's work here on earth.

Here are some thought provoking questions about the gifts God gave to each of us:

Have we developed an understanding of the gifts we each received?

Do we use them in our daily lives?

Do we have an obligation to use them to help others?

**We** have different gifts, according to the grace given us.
If a man's gift is prophesying, let him use it in proportion to his faith. …If it is contributing to the needs of others, let him give generously…
—Romans 12, verses 6 and 8

We need to think about our gifts and how we use them in our lives.

**Thought for Today**: Today let us all recognize our gifts as we put them to use in every day activities. Let us give thanks to the Lord for them.

**Prayer for Today**: Dear Lord, we are living in a confusing world of negativity and frustration. Hate seems to dominate our news. Terror and war abound around the World. Senseless violence seems to dominate our local news. Today we pray that we can recognize our gifts and skills while we pray for your guidance so that we may contribute to expanding your love here on earth. Amen

# Confidence Through Trust

Sometimes I take credit for original comments that my friend Alan calls Pickeringisms. One of my favorites is "All days are not created equal." That is very true in all areas of our lives. In our marriages each day can be different when one or the other spouse feels moody or a bit off. The same happens in the workplace where there are more interactions and opportunities for stress. That's what makes life interesting and challenging.

In the book "I'm OK, You're OK" the four states of every two-person relationship are reviewed. The four states are summarized as "I'm OK, you're not OK": when one person has some stress or discomfort with the moment. That same position is reversed with the second condition, "I'm not OK, you're OK." Then of course the whole relationship may be a mess with the condition "I'm not OK, you're not OK." A great place to be is home when all is well, and comfortable, "I'm OK, you're OK;" the state of wedded bliss; live happily ever after. (Wow is that optimistic!)

> **One** who trusts in the Lord is secure.
> —Proverbs 29, verse 25

There is a constant, a power of one, that works for us on any day, in any condition; that power is our faith. In the long run my Pickeringism can be totally negated with faith and the knowledge that God is with us. There is the old expression, "When the going gets tough the tough get going." I would prefer to think that when the going gets tough, the smart ones are praying!

**Thought for Today**: Today let's be secure in the knowledge that the Lord is with us and will help us through—no matter what state we are in!

**Prayer for Today**: Dear Lord, today we give thanks for your support in our everyday lives. We are thankful that no matter how the world around us changes you will be there when we need you. We are thankful for your blessings. Amen

# Punxsutawney Phil

On Groundhog Day every year in Pennsylvania they forecast the end of winter. This year Phil's shadow was seen and it was declared that winter will end in six weeks. Well, you see Phil is never wrong because somewhere in the world in six weeks it will be warm; probably not here at my home in Minnesota.

Phil is a character, not even a legend. He is no Paul Bunyan, Johnny Appleseed or Ichabod Crane. He is just a groundhog being disturbed for a group of people in Pennsylvania to have fun. Frankly he is not a very good idol!

**We** know that "An idol is nothing at all in the world" and that "There is no God but one."
For even if there are so-called gods, whether in heaven or on earth…
…for us there is but one God,
—1 Corinthians 8, verses 4 and 5

I would love to see them open Phil's den next year and have Jesus step out in a white robe, the sun beating down on him in a heavenly glow, and have the crowd speechless. Imagine Jesus saying something like, "Sorry folks but even I refuse to do a long range forecast. There will be more bad weather here in the north country but do not fear for the Lord will be with you." He would then give is his blessing and arise toward the heavens.

Bless you all and may we have an early Spring!

**Thought for Today:** The Lord blesses us and keeps us 365 days a year.

**Prayer for Today:** Dear Lord and Father, we pray for those in the north that deal with fire and ice. May they take the time to appreciate the seasons and the beauty of it all.

# Peacemakers

A peacemaker is not a person who avoids issues but a person who resolves issues; one that will go where others avoid. Some do it because it is their job, some because it is their passion. I view a peacemaker as one who stirs the pot! That is generally a negative saying but it also is the way to solve problems and bring good (peace) by generating a deeper discussion.

**Now** when Jesus saw the crowds,
He went up on a mountainside and sat down.
His disciples came to him, and he began to teach them.
…Blessed are the peacemakers,
for they will be called children of God.
—Mathew 5, verses 1, 2 and 9

peacemaker does not allow that to happen; peacemakers are aware of the sound bites but stir the pot in an attempt to make a tolerable and acceptable brew. They have a tough job.

In our church we have a lady who I have grown to love. She is a thinker, a pot stirrer, a cook of issues and a value to us all. In the last ten years I sat in several

In out very busy world we have become a society of sound bites. It is thought that if you can't get someone's attention in ten seconds you can forget them. What I find really confusing is that often I agree with the sound bites on both sides of an issue. Some examples are in health care; I agree that something needs to be available for all and on the other side that we should take care of ourselves; I agree that we should not hand out our tax dollars to private businesses but that we can't afford to lose jobs; I feel that the Sabbath needs to be honored (bring back blue laws) but that would cost jobs; … and my list goes on.

Please do not consider this political; I just want to point out the conundrum of our times. My point is that when we lower ourselves to becoming a sound bite society we become polarized. The

meetings where she contributed in moving a polarized team to successful conclusion. Several times I was the team leader and she saved my bacon; we got great results. She is a good cook; a peacemaker and politician.

My point is that Jesus wants us to contribute, to stir the pot for acceptable solutions. Paul advised the Romans:

"Let us therefore make every effort to do what leads to peace and to mutual edification." —Romans 14, verse 19

**Thought for the Day:** For today let us realize that we will be blasted by sound bites, snippets of reality that can polarize our thinking. For today, let us ask what Jesus would do with that snippet!

**Prayer for the Day:** Dear Lord and Father, today we pray for the ability to think and ponder what is between the sound bites of our society. We pray for the ability to follow Jesus and understand your will here on earth. Amen

# Self Respect

God made us in His image but one of humanities significant problems is people suffering from low self esteem and a lack of self respect. It manifests itself in a myriad of problems including substance abuse and depression. It is lousy way to go through life.

Twelve Step programs have been very useful in dealing with self esteem issues. They work because they have people admit there is a power greater then themselves (God) and their goal is spiritual growth. Basically, low self respect occurs when someone loses touch with the Lord and has trouble recognizing His presence in their lives.

Spirituality, self respect and confidence go hand in hand. Understanding that the Lord is with us every day makes for a satisfactory life style. If you are reading this, you probably have life under control. Meditation is one way of recharging our spiritual batteries. We need to do that for

**Then** God said, "Let us make man in our image, in our likeness,
And let them rule over the fish of the sea and the birds of the air,
over the livestock, over all the earth,
and over all the creatures that move along the ground."
So God created man in his own image.
—Geneses 1, verses 26 and 27

our selves, our families and others around us.

When we have respect for ourselves, self esteem, others will want what we have. That is when we can help.

**Thought for Today**: When we look in the mirror, let's look past the visual image of ourselves. Let's look into our own eyes and try to see inside where our heart and soul reside. Take that thought out and display to others our pride, self respect and our faith in the Lord.

**Prayer for Today**: Dear Lord and Father we live in a wonderful place surrounded by beautiful people. Some let differences separate us and come between us. We pray that we can contribute to dissolving and understanding those differences. We pray that with our strength through you we find a way to do your will and take a step toward acceptance of spiritual differences by respecting others. Amen

# It's Only Money

Several weeks ago, my pastor and I were having coffee at his request. His concern was due to some business stresses that were effecting June's and my lives. During this session we talked about money, law suits and tough decisions that often have to be made. Often these decisions are made to minimize financial risk. We surely all do that. This was without me having remembered today's passage.

As we talked about my life strategy, he was challenging some of my decisions based on normal financial logic. My comments made Pastor Rick laugh harder than I had ever heard him laugh in our seven year relationship. They were that "June and I felt that God had a plan that we had not yet seen and that somehow we were serving His needs." Then I made a slight error and slipped into some studio language, "After all, it is only #@^%#

> **Therefore** I tell you, do not worry about your life, what you will eat or drink; or about your body, what you will wear.
> Is not life more important than food, and the body more important than clothes?
> Look at the birds of the air; they do not sow or reap or store away in barns, and yet your heavenly Father feeds them.
> Are you not much more valuable than they?
> Who of you by worrying can add a single hour to his life?
> —Matthew 6, verses 25–27

money." Pastor Rick almost fell out of his chair in laughter.

There is a message there somewhere. Matthew 6, verse 27 asks what "worry" will do for us. But we still worry. What will worry accomplish? Higher blood pressure? Broken relationships? Jealousies? Just maybe we should pray more than we worry. After all, our faith says that God is with us at all times.

**Thought for Today**: Today let us think about Matthew 6, verses 25–27, and try harder to enjoy the day. Think about how great it would be to get through without "worry." Let's "Let go and let God."

**Prayer for Today**: Heavenly Father, there are many reasons for us to be concerned about our future. There is war and conflict in the world; many of us are unemployed or concerned about our future; our children are exposed to dangers that were not around when we grew up. It seems that there are endless reasons to worry. Today we pray for the faith and good judgment to let you help us. We pray rather than worry. Amen

# Excellence

Earlier I wrote about my "Pickeringism" that all days are not created equal. Here is another example. There are days that we are full of boundless energy and others when we are as flat as pancakes. However, these feelings are mental, physical and emotional states. They do not have an effect on our hearts, just on our performance or output.

As a long term weekend athlete, there have been too many days when only the heart showed up for the workout; the arms, legs and head wanted to go back to bed. There were also many days when that's how the day started but when it ended, the performance was in the excellent range.

One of my best friends and four-time Olympic athlete relates to this. Pat has trained every day of his life and he can

**Whatever** you do, work at it with all your heart, as working for the Lord, not for men, since you know that you will receive an inheritance from the Lord as a reward. It is the Lord Christ you are serving.
—Colossians 3, verses 23–24

relate to the fact that the heart and head lead the body often, "...work at it with all your heart, as working for the Lord," and you will be rewarded with excellence. Excellence starts with belief in yourself and in the Lord. The rest will follow.

**Thought for Today**: Today let us remember that "All days are not created equal." On the day that we want to go back to bed, let us trust our heart and move out. Let us take the leap of faith and give ourselves the chance to exhibit the excellence that God wants us to share.

**Prayer for Today**: Dear Lord we give you thanks for your ongoing presence in our lives. When we are physically worn you help us recover. When emotionally drained you recharge our spirits. We give thanks that you are always with us. Amen

# Rule Number 1

It is nice to be what I call "somewhat retired." That is to be busy but to have more choices than I used to have (e..g., my choice this morning is to write and go to bible study (with great carmel rolls!) instead of swimming laps. This morning I choose to work for the big boss, later I will be in some business meetings.

Early in my engineering career I had a boss who had the following sign on his wall:

> Rule number One: The boss is always right.
> Rule number 2: When the boss is wrong, see rule number one.

Exactly who did he think he was? I will share that he was a real controller and task master. I want to apply his words to our lives because I believe the sign was right on when we consider our God the boss!

Many of our Good News buddies have young families, two careers and an activities schedule for the family. In one of my family units my daughter has two jobs, the husband one and two middle school students. Life seemed easier when June and I had our four, or maybe we were younger and could juggle more balls in the air. Either way, there was more than once that we lost track of the real boss. There were coaches, sales

**Whatever** you do, work at it with all your heart, as working for the Lord, not for men, since you know that you will receive an inheritance from the Lord as a reward. It is the Lord Christ you are serving.
—Colossians 3, verses 23–24

managers, the tax man and the list seems endless. Somehow it all fell into place.

In our history and in your future and especially today, the *boss* is always right! It is our choice on a daily basis to decide who is boss; "…as working for the Lord."

**Thought for Today**: Today will be what we golfers call a "gimmie." A total violation of the rules of golf, not putting the ball in the hole. Life really does not give us many gimmies either so I am wrong. There will be challenges; stress and we will run out of time. Today let us meet the challenges and remember who we are and what we are working for through Jesus.

**Prayer for Today**: Today we give thanks for all of our blessings. We pray for a simple day of peace and joy with a minimum of stress. Amen

# Trust and Faith

We all experience times in our lives, certain situations when our trust level is down. These are usually times when we must let a situation be under someone else's control.

> **When** I am afraid,
> I will trust in you.
> In God whose word I praise,
> in God I trust.
> —Psalm 56, verse 3

A teenager spending a weekend away with friends, away at camp or going off to school. We fear what they may find to do.

A family member not home at an expected time. We fear an accident or other harm.

Consider a simple four way stop sign with all drivers arriving at the same time. Often no one trusts enough to go first.

Reading this, it would be easy to think that the subject was fear, but it is trust.

> The Lord is my light and salvation–Whom shall I fear?"
> —Psalm 27, verse 1

There is a direct link between a weak faith and trust in the Lord, and high levels of anxiety and stress. Yes, there are days when we are strong and have no fear, then there are days when we are weak.

On the weak days, we need to meditate. Leave the news turned off, put down the newspaper and get closer to God.

> Call upon me in the day of trouble; I will deliver you, and you will honor me.
> —Psalm 50, verse 15

**Thought for Today**: When we have doubts, let us stop, take a deep breath and try to place our faith in God. If we can do that, our reactions to doubtful situations will be less stressful.

**Prayer for Today**: Heavenly Father, as we go through our busy schedules, it is easy to forget you. We try to control, manipulate and alter our lives to fit "our will" and lose sight of "your will." We seem not to trust you. We pray that we can slow down, consider your will for us and increase our trust in you. Amen

# Intimacy

I want to update the above to "It is not good for a person to be alone" because loneliness is a problem for everyone and faith and godly interaction is a great help. We all appreciate intimacy and being close.

But what does it mean to be close and how do we get there? What is our personal responsibility in the equation? First, comes openness followed closely by honesty! We need to be open with the other person and straight up honest. When two people can be that way with one another intimacy has a fighting chance.

Recently at a Friday breakfast, our friend Don tearfully shared with us his feelings of personal loss. His Golden Retriever, who walked with him twice a day had passed. The love around that table shared with Don was very special and unfortunately rare for a group of guys. It was intimacy at its best.

> **Then** the Lord God said, "It is not good for the man to be alone."
> —Genesis 2, verse 18

My observations are that when we are very young we are often too impetuous to allow intimacy. Relationships seem to stay on the surface and interaction is activity-based which is rarely heartfelt. The middle age, say, 30 to 60, seems when people have the most confidence and are willing to be close. Unfortunately, I see a retraction as people age.

As a summary, I do not think we can help the youth become intimate; that is a growing thing greatly helped by wisdom and spiritually. I have great concerns and prayers for us as we grow older. We lose capabilities and want to hide the losses. We often lose intimacy and become more distant from our loved ones as we age. That is sad and worth praying about.

**Thought for Today:** For today let us focus on our open and intimate relationships. Let's be sure that they are intact and growing. Let us involve the holy spirit in our lives.

**Prayer for Today:** Today we pray for the lonely, those that cannot open up their hearts to others; share their fears and wishes. We pray that they find the spirit of intimacy through our Lord Jesus. Amen

# Intimacy, Marriage

I want to alter Paul's message here to "Love your spouse just as Christ loved the church and gave himself" because a relationship is a two way street. This morning as I write this I have said two prayers: One giving thanks for a safe trip home from our annual UK vacation; the other for my wife who is still asleep and blessed with less jet lag than I. It is important to love and pray for each other in a relationship.

In early years, what I call my dark period, June's and my relationship was more one sided, on the surface. My business schedule, parenting four children, endurance training, tennis and several other items caused our interactions to be out of balance. June was more of a support person than a partner. There was deep love on both sides but not intimacy.

During my dark period June was my light at the end of the tunnel and through the grace of God, I saw that it was not a train coming from the other end! Today our relationship is more balanced and giving; perhaps too much so if that is possible.

> **Husbands**, love your wives, just as Christ loved the church and gave himself to her.
> —Ephesians 5, verse 25

The Lord gives us an unlimited supply of love when we are born. It is never ending, always available to give and we have a chance to share it with our spouses every minute of the day. As my favorite philosopher NIKE says, "Just Do It!"

**Thought for Today**: Today let us each tell someone close, friend or family, how much their relationship means to us.

**Prayer for Today**: Dear Lord, today I give thanks for those people in my life that are close to me; spouses, friends or relatives. May I share my love for them as Christ did for the church. Amen

# Strengthening

We male animals are strange; we don't ask directions, fail to speak up and hide our feelings.

Our egos seem to have a negative effect on our lives. We unnecessarily challenge ourselves. On the other side, women will ask for help or directions, admit when they don't know something, and try to learn.

It is like we guys are trying to hide our inequities, but we cannot hide them from God and he will support us even when we do not know, ask or want Him to. We can hide weakness and inequities from each other and often do. One of my life goals is to let them through, show them off and pray they go away.

Recently we headed out to a visit at a hospital we had not been to in the past. As the driver I had checked Google maps, my old map book and written all the contact information down on paper; I had it all. Sure enough, we got to the freeway exit and followed the signs all the way into the parking lot and then into the lobby! You see, Bob the guy wasn't going to have to ask directions!

> **For** the eyes of the LORD range throughout the earth to strengthen those whose hearts are fully committed to him.
> —2 Chronicles 16, verse 9

Fortunately throughout my life, I have been willing to ask for and take spiritual direction. Oh, sometimes I wandered around a bit lost, but eventually figured out where to get help. It seems that the eyes of the Lord have always been on me as they are on you. He sees and strengthens us all.

**Thought for Today**: Today there will be times when we need more strength. Let us find it through Him; through prayer and meditation.

**Prayer for Today**: Dear Lord and Father, today is a day that you have made for me to enjoy. Today is a day where stress and problems are waiting for me. Today I give thanks for the wonderful day, the people around me and the strength to deal with whatever happens. I am blessed through You. Amen

# Lincoln

President Lincoln presided over a war that was the bloodiest in the history of our country. He could not have done what he did without his extremely strong faith. His bible was often at his side in meetings and had dog-eared pages from continual use. It reinforced his belief that he and the union were doing the right thing.

It brings to my mind the old joke about disagreements in church congregations. It says that the arguments are often fierce because both sides feel that they have God on their team! Well, in church politics we are not making decisions that cause battles where 10,000 plus soldiers die, people get assassinated, brothers fight brothers and the freedom of a race are at stake. Still somehow we do the Lord's will.

When Lincoln felt badly, which happened after a traumatic field report, he would lean on the Biblical hope offered to him (and to all of us). Today's

> **But** the wisdom that comes from heaven is first of all pure; then peace-loving, considerate, submissive, full of mercy and good fruit, impartial and sincere. Peacemakers who sow in peace reap a harvest of righteousness."
> —James 3, verses 17 and 18

verse was one he used often when he was in need of reassurance.

He would say to his cabinet and all who would listen, "Let us renew our trust in God and go forward without fear and with manly hearts."

**Happy Birthday Abe.**

**Thought for Today:** Today is the birthday of America's most loved president. His faith is a strong example to us. We are commanded to be happy Christians, to be the light of the world, to share and contribute through our faith. Today let us shine our light brightly.

**Prayer for Today:** Dear Lord and Father we give thanks today for those great men who have gone before us and contributed to our world. We pray that we are contributing in some small way to accomplishing your will and spreading a world of peace and love. Amen

# Respect

Earning respect is an on-going challenge throughout our lives. Communication, according to the book of Proverbs, will make other people want to connect with us. Proverbs 15, verse 22 talks about the benefits of good council, good advice.

Many of you have heard me say " Two heads are four times better than the best of the two alone! Also, three heads are nine times better than the best of the three working alone!" Well, there are no scientific studies to confirm what my friends call a "Pickeringism," but it is true at some level. Sharing our thoughts and advice makes us all stronger.

To earn respect be a willing advisor. Share your experiences, your knowledge and good will with those in need. Share that precious intellectual property that God has allowed you to accumulate. Earn respect through sharing.

> **Plans** fail for lack of counsel, but with many advisers they succeed.
> —Proverbs 15, verse 22

**Thought for Today:** Today let us think about helping others through our experienced advice. Let us also try hard to let others help us. Let us listen and share as Proverbs advises us and observe how much better we are when we practice sharing.

**Prayer for Today:** Dear Lord, today we pray for peace and tranquility for those around us and throughout the world. We pray that somehow our life's experiences may be shared and used as an example of your will. Amen

# Be My Valentine

"Love one another" is a great idea. It does not include any qualifiers or reasons to separate people from the group; it means all, every day and every moment. That is our Christian charge and it means everyone, every day.

> **Finally**, all of you, be like-minded, be sympathetic, love one another, be compassionate and humble.
> —1 Peter 3, verse 8

This is a day that in America has become a symbol of romantic love where symbols seem to replace the real thing. It is good to have a day when we symbolize our love, caring and dedication. It is good to focus on those around and dear to us. It is kind of fun.

I can remember in grades 1–6 in the '40s, each of us gave each other a valentine. The distribution was quite a process and was long and had a bit of mayhem to it. There was a tremendous amount of excitement and energy expended in the process. It took the teacher and two or three mothers to contain the enthusiasm. That's a great example of how challenging it is to truly love one another. There are a lot of people in our lives to love.

As Christians we believe that we were made in God's image. To love everyone we need to have God's heart and capacity to care. Happy Valentine's Day!

**Thought for Today:** Today we will focus our love on those closest to us; our families, significant others, moms and dads, etc. That is great but let's also try to care for everyone!

**Prayer for Today:** Dear Lord, today we give thanks for our ever expanding hearts that seem to have enough love in them for everyone. We give thanks for the ability to understand and care for all.

# Also Ran?

Being an also-ran is a way of life. We rarely finish first. As many of you know I detest the famous Vince Lombardi quote, "Winning isn't everything it is the only thing." Here are some examples: My friend Pat McNamara qualified in four different Olympics and did not win a medal; my brother Wayne swam for years and was a national top ten in four events but never had a national championship; Ted Williams and Carl Yastrzemski played years for the Red Sox and never received a world series ring; and the list goes on! None of the above is a loser and all are proud of their accomplishments.

In my personal instance, I have two triathlon trophies out of 25 races; a second and a third. There was always someone faster. Did I lose? Never. In each Triathlon that I did, in the last mile of the run I would well up with tears of joy from the shear pride in my accomplishment. The pain experienced during the run would go away, the legs would seem fresh again and the finishing sprint would feel and look great. Second, Third or twentieth did not matter; I was winning inside!

Clint Purvis, the team chaplain for Florida State Universtiy's football team under Bobby Bowden put it like this after a

> **Then** the LORD said to Joshua, "Do not be afraid; do not be discouraged."
> —Joshua 8, verse 1

tough loss to Miami, "There is a huge difference between getting beat in a game and being a loser." Clint reminded the team of the characteristics of being a winner:

1. A winner still remembers that God never forsakes his own.
2. A winner must remember that it is always painful and costly to claim victory again.
3. A winner will always remember the source of all his blessings.

—from Bobby Bowden's Called to Coach, Howard Books, 2010

We rarely are number one but since God is always with us, we are always winners.

**Thought for Today:** Today we will have battles we do not expect. With God's help, let us be winners no matter which way the battle turns out!

**Prayer for Today:** Dear Lord and Father, today we thank you for being with us at all times in every place. We thank you because when you are al... winners. Amen

# Marriage

Many of you that know me have heard me discuss the many wonderful benefits of a good marriage. The great mutual support, the care when illness arrives, the mutual celebrations of the many events that occur. Yes, marriage is truly a great institution when things are well and blessed by God.

Many times it has been stated that marriage is the world's toughest job. Let me quote from The Mystery of Marriage by Mike Mason.

> Marriage, even under the best of circumstances, is a crises; one of the major crises of life. It is a dangerous thing not to be aware of this. Whether it turns out to be a healthy, challenging and constructive crises or a disastrous nightmare depends largely upon how willing the partners are to be changed, how malleable they are.

**A** wife of noble character who can find? She is worth far more than rubies. Her husband has full confidence in her and lacks nothing of value.
—Proverbs 31, verses 10 and 11

"Crises" seems a bit extreme to me, but certainly marriage is a great opportunity for the fulfillment of life and it certainly is not without its "opportunities" for either success or failure. A marriage blessed by God, one in which the partners have allowed God's love to grow in their relationship, is one of the worlds greatest experiences.

**Thought for Today**: We are facing many distractions in our daily lives; work, busy schedules, terrorism, war, deficits and many more. Let us look at our primary relationships. Let us focus introspectively, up close. Let us understand that when things are fine in our relationships, the outside problems seem less intense. Basically, let's focus on our loves.

**Prayer for Today**: Heavenly Father, we are in a world of hurting people, a world of fear. Fear of job loss, fear of not finding a job, fear of terrorism, fear of financial ruin and many others. Many of us are growing uncomfortable. Today we pray for love within our lives. We pray that somehow we can feel your presence in all of the fear and overcome our doubts. Somehow we pray that through your love the fears will dissipate. Amen

# Let's Talk

The city of Boston has a public area called Boston Commons. It is a central park that was set up as a common grazing ground for city-owned livestock. I believe that even today, all Boston residents have the legal right to graze their cow on "the common."

"The Common" is now and always was a meeting place for people to discuss the issues of the day. It still serves that function today. There are people on every corner, some literally standing on soap boxes, discussing everything from gay issues to the Mid East. In fact, you can generally find a "talker" that is representing your ideas no matter what you feel.

The most common subjects the talkers address are issues of faith. There will be conservatives on one corner and liberals on the next using the same Bible passages to reinforce their beliefs. Often, they engage their audience in debates that may be very intense. "The Boston Common Talkers" represent America's free speech at its finest.

> **You** must go to everyone I send you to and say whatever I command you.
> —Jeremiah 1, verse 7

Most of us shy away from publicly sharing our faith with others. Jesus clearly wants us to share but we generally do not have the confidence to speak out in public. We need to realize that we need to share and "…say whatever I command you."

**Thought for Today**: Today, let us all look for a chance to tell someone about our faith. Let us invite some one to share, someone we may help and possibly even invite them to join us at a service.

**Prayer for Today**: Heavenly Father today I pray for the strength to do your will here on earth. I pray that I may share my story of my life with You with someone. Amen

# Love Each Other

In our diverse society today there are many different cultures. God is adding ingredients to America's melting pot. We are constantly challenged by a change in the brew. There are growing populations of various nationalities and religions that seem foreign to us. Yes, some of these make us uncomfortable. Must we accept and love them all?

Picture yourself leaving a movie tonight and walking through a parking lot. You see a group of youths of your race coming toward you. They could be a street gang or a church youth group or your friends going to the next show. At first there is some doubt, then recognition and then, hopefully, comfort.

Sometimes we are uncomfortable with who is approaching. We get nervous. When that occurs, it can be justified as a safety precaution. Often it can be a sign of sub conscious or even a conscious prejudice. Yes, often our prejudices show up in this way. As Christians we need to recognize this when it happens.

**Help** us accept each other as Christ accepted us; teach us as sister, brother, each person to embrace; Be present , Lord, among us, and bring us to believe we are ourselves accepted and meant to love and live."
—Fred Kaan, *Help Us Accept Each Other,* UMC Hymnal, number 560, 1974

To get back to the question, "Must we accept and love them all?" the answer is clear. John quotes Jesus in chapter 15, verse 17, " This is my command: Love each other." Jesus left no one off the list.

**Thought for Today:** Today let us look at our fears, our prejudices and the way we view the diverse elements of our society. Let us ask if we can learn to exhibit Christian love toward these elements. We will learn that we can when we try.

**Prayer for Today:** Dear Lord, help me reach out to people. Help me understand the undesirable. There is still terror and the threat of war throughout the world. We are confused and have difficulty loving our enemies. We pray for the ability to understand and follow Jesus' command for love. Amen

# Forgiven

We are our worst enemies when it comes to forgiveness. We will forgive others and hold on to our own feelings of remorse for years. In twelve step programs the eighth and ninth steps are about making amends to people. Often these amends are greeted with a curious look because the offended person had forgotten the incident.

It is the sixth week of the New Year and statistically 90 percent of New Year's resolutions have fallen by the wayside. Most of resolutionists are disappointed in themselves and sometimes remorseful because they did not make it! Why?

We all need to think about that. It is honorable to try to improve and make resolutions. It is not dishonorable to not succeed. We need to accept forgiveness and grant it to ourselves; Jesus would.

> **You** forgave the iniquity of your people and covered all their sins.
> You set aside all your wrath and turned from your fierce anger.
> —Psalm 85, verses 2 and 3

**Thought for Today**: For today let us forgive ourselves for our perceived short comings and look forward to our future successes.

**Prayer for Today:** Heavenly Father, today we pray for our future success. We do your work and do not seem to succeed but know you are with us. We thank you for your patience and forgiveness. Amen

# Don't Give Up

With my son in the music business, we have seen a lot of young people try to live their dreams of fame. To some it comes fast and they go from teenager to a star. But to others they need time to grow into their dream.

Barry Manilow used to play piano in the bars of New York and write jingles for advertising agencies. He applied himself, developed his skills and then his God-given talents prevailed. He never gave up.

Remember Barney Miller, the cop played by Hal Linden? Very few people watching knew that this very funny cop was a future Broadway star. He was a patient man with a strong faith that was following a path to success. Eventually, partially because of his TV fame, he got a chance to live his dream. Now he is at the top of his game and living his dream on Broadway.

While writing this today, a Good News friend emailed me to tell me how he and his family are doing. We fought the battles of life together back in the '60s. He found his way to California; we are in Minnesota. Here is a quote from his text, "Jesus had it all planned, all I had to do was show up when he summoned me. It's sweet."

> **Then** Jesus told his disciples...that they should always pray and not give up.
> —Luke 18, verse 1

All of our lives need to start someplace. We often do not control our destiny and just need to keep on plugging. Joel Osteen uses the term "...keeps on keeping on." I like "Today is the first day of the rest of my life." Jesus said "...always pray and not give up."

**Thought for Today:** Today let us focus on what we want to be when we grow up. Not because we are young but because we have a future. Our lives are always changing; we always need to have our faith in hand. Through our faith we can always find ways to grow, to solve issues and be better.

**Prayer for Today:** Heavenly Father, we are learning that life is an endurance event, not a sprint. Today I pray for stamina, guidance and the patience to keep at it until you deliver me to your place. Amen

# Thanks For the Memories

Today our pastor preached about a recent trip to Israel. He told of conflict about where the holy places are and who deserves to control them. His message was that God may be found everywhere by everyone who is open to Him. The following is a personal story that may relate to that.

We recently had the opportunity to have lunch at a seaside restaurant in my home town of Saugus that meant a lot to us. We had our first date there in July of 1967! My son, his wife and their new baby joined us. This place had a family history, my aunt Virginia was a waitress there in the '40s, my uncle Ken played guitar in a group there, it was an after the ball game hang out for the old gang in the '60s. It was a place with memories for us.

In the '60s, my friend and Good News recipient Ralph and I carried too many drunks home. There was Larry, Dave, Pierre and others. Oh yes, Ralph and I are programmed reformers today. Those are some of the growing pains of the past.

> **In** the name of our Lord Jesus, Always give thanks for everything to God the Father."
> —Ephesians 5, verse 20

The place was also the start of a great experience; my life with June. I do not think she was very impressed at first. The place smelled of fish, it had uncovered Formica tables, the crowd did not even come close to that of an English pub, and the Melody Ramblers were a loud country band. However, the baked stuffed lobster for $3.75 and the 25-cent beers were impressive! It was not a place where one would normally go in search of the Lord. Unknowingly, we started our journey with Him that evening. You see, we were not looking, we were not in search of God but we were open willing suspects. In Paul's message to the Ephesians he says "…Always give thanks for everything to God the Father." We do.

**Thought for Today**: Today let us pause when we are stressed out. Take a break from the bad weather, the office stress, the youth sports playoffs and think back to our blessings, Let us take a time out each day to thank the Lord for who we are.

**Prayer for Today**: Today Lord I give thanks for your presence in my life and the many gifts that you have given me. Amen

# Washington

Today is George Washington's Birthday. There are many stories and fables about his life. There is the Cherry tree that he allegedly chopped down and the silver dollar he threw across the Potomac. These are unproven myths but great folklore.

He was a man of great vision. He envisioned that his ragtag army could defeat the British. He realized when he was wrong and smart enough to involve the French as allies. It takes a great man to recognize a weak position and make the proper corrections.

The quote above expresses his dreams for America. It is also the stated Christian dream delivered through Jesus. My question today is how can we accomplish the justice and equality that these two great men dreamed about? That's easy; we all need to do a little every day!

> **As** Mankind becomes more liberal, they will be more apt to allow that all those who conduct themselves as worthy members of the community are equally entitled to the protections of civil government.
> I hope ever to see America among the foremost nations of justice and liberality.
> —George Washington

**Thought for Today:** Today let's take a step toward bringing equality and justice to our world.

**Prayer for Today:** Today dear Lord, we pray for equality and the opportunity to contribute to creating a just and equal society. Amen

# Giving?

There is an interesting feature of retirement that I call "The *all I am ever going to have* syndrome." Please don't try to look that up because it is just another Pickeringism! I see it all the time in retirees and am fighting it every day in my own life. In a recent article I quoted Dr. Joyce Meyer stating that you cannot be selfish and happy. The syndrome tends to close retirees in and they stop giving and not listening to their hearts.

In our hearts we would like to give everything away, help people when we can, but in practice I am afraid we have a bit of the syndrome! That throws a bit of a wet blanket on our lives. As a former financial chair at our church I need to share two stories with you. The first was a lady who came forward with a three year gift that put her at double the next largest contributor. It was a significant blessing to the church but an even greater blessing for her. Another year a widow called me in December as we were trying to balance the budget and wanted to talk. I had

> **"Each** of you should give what you have decided in your heart to give, not reluctantly or under compulsion…
> And God is able to bless you abundantly, so that in all things at all times, having all that you need, you will abound in every good work."
> —2 Corinthians 9, verses 8 and 9

some concern because although she was a nice lady we were not close and she was not the easiest person to approach. We had coffee and she offered to balance the budget for us with a five figure check.

Both of these blessed ladies insisted on absolute confidentiality and we honored that even down to masking the donations in the accounting system so they could not be traced. However, we could never mask the feeling that these generous people felt, their smiles and their enthusiasm. You see, they gave from their hearts and did not hold back.

The message today is that money is important, we need our cash. However, listening to our heart is also important if we are going to be happy and satisfied with our lives.

**Thought for Today:** Today let us focus on giving to someone!

**Prayer for Today:** Heavenly Father, today we pray for those in need. We pray that we may recognize that need and contribute to them in some meaningful way. Amen

# Let God Lead

God works in many ways when we allow Him to help us. Yes, He is always there, but not always present in our minds. We have a way of being self centered, focusing on business issues, personal problems etc... We want to be in control. We can deal with it ourselves.

Many years ago, June came home with a big orange refrigerator magnet that had the message "Let go and let God" written across it. She did it because we were, and still are, control freaks. Often we get into the "control mode" when we can not help or do anything about the problem. Trying to control things beyond our sphere of influence made us "tired...weak...and worn."

It is easy to become frustrated when things are beyond our control. It is normal to try to control. It is better to recognize our place and let God take our hand, lead us home.

**Precious** Lord,
take my hand
lead me on, let me stand,
I am tired, I am weak,
I am worn;
through the storm,
through the night,
lead me on to the light,
take my hand
precious Lord,
lead me home."
—Thomas A. Dorsey,
*Precious Lord, Take My Hand,* UMC Hymnal number 474, 1932

**Thought for Today:** Today is the first day of the rest of our lives. We do not have to function the same way as we did yesterday. Let's take a look at God's influence in our decisions. Let's let some of it go and allow Him to help us.

**Prayer for Today:** Heavenly Father, we thank you for our many blessings and the many wonderful things that we enjoy. We are concerned about others in our society that have less; some without food, housing or a job. We are concerned about the many people that are afraid they will lose their jobs and their security. There seems to be a growing acceptance that this is OK here on earth, as long as it is the other guy. Today we pray for our society in general. We pray that somehow everyone can be at peace, that everyone may find enough, that all children have food and that our riches are shared as You would have us share them. Amen

# Let Go

This week a Good News recipient talked to me about some resentment that was bothering him. This individual has an extreme amount of integrity and was an officer of a corporation. Unfortunately, he was let go for taking a stand on the side of ethical and legal corporate behavior. He is having a problem with forgiving his former associates and is wondering where God is in this equation.

The term legal and ethical corporate behavior is one that is unchallengeable for us that practice Christian ethics in our lives. We need to settle for nothing less, especially in the work place. Insisting on ethical behavior sometimes will cost us in the short term. Forgiving those that have wronged us in this way is always difficult, but necessary if we are to protect ourselves and our family long term.

We all need to practice letting go and let God deal with offenders. For our own sake and the sake of our families, we need to have God deal with our

> **Cast** your cares on the LORD
> and he will sustain you;
> he will never let the righteous fall."
> —Psalm 55, verse 22

resentments while we look ahead to our future. Keeping resentments inside, holding ill will within us causes an accumulative effect that hurts those around us. Resentments manifest themselves into anger, sometimes paranoia and lack of trust.

In most cases as Christians, when a negative situation occurs, the Lord will open doors of opportunity. We need to pray and remember that things happen for a reason that we do not often understand. Remember that "…He will never let the righteous fall."

**Thought for Today:** Today let us all look toward the future and leave our worries behind. Leave resentments and hurts in the hands of the Lord and focus on taking our lives to a higher level through faith.

**Prayer for Today:** Today Lord we pray for all who are pressured by people of influence to perform in an un-Christian manner. May they find a way to keep their Christian ethics and their career. Amen

# Gods Love and Grace

June and I have been blessed by being close to people of varied faiths. Through our association with each, we have come to a strong belief that we all worship the same God in different ways and we all experience God's grace.

Several years ago we became good friends with the family of an executive from Pakistan. It was our first real close relationship with a Muslim family. We were close to them in 2001 and observed the frustration that a true Muslim felt in regard to September 11.

Recently a Jewish friend that I have known and liked for years shared with me that he does bible studies so he can learn about the Christian perspective. His strong family values, general positive personality and strong ethical standards make him someone I am glad to know.

We have spent many Sundays with my family in Unitarian Meeting Houses when we return to Massachusetts. We are learning more about my mom's grand parents who were Unitarian ministers.

To avoid making this a 10,000 word essay, let me summarize some of our other relationships: A son in law who is a Southern Baptist, a brother in law who

> **Know** therefore that the LORD your God is God; He is the faithful God.
> —Deuteronomy 7, verse 9

is a Catholic priest in the UK, a Buddhist sister in law, a Mormon best friend who lost touch with his faith, a Native American friend who has involved us in some spiritual activities, and the list goes on.

In each instance mentioned, June and I have experienced good friendships and observed strong Godly values in our friends. In most instances, we have observed God working in our friends' lives and seen God's grace at work in many ways. Most importantly, we have experienced God's grace through our friends.

**Thought for the Day:** Let us recognize those around us that are different and try to befriend someone new. Let us seek out someone that looks at God in a different way. The Lord blesses them also.

**Prayer for the Day:** Dear faithful Lord and Father, the world is a great and wonderful creation. There are many peoples of all colors and beliefs. There are generation gaps, social differences, and economic separations. Often the differences get in the way of social graces. Today we pray the ability to bring unity to the world. Amen

# Commitment

One of the ways to be successful in life is to keep all of your commitments. If you say it, make sure you do it; even after having second thoughts. Become known as one hundred percent reliable. It is probably impossible to be 100% but the closer you are the more you will benefit.

I have a friend who coached youth soccer and had never played. He told the league that he was unqualified but would be available if they could not find someone else. They called and he managed a team and, with the help of two assistants that could teach skills, they worked things out. He managed the team rather than coached and the kids had fun. This same guy also managed a youth hockey team and could not skate. You see, the people with the skills did not (or could not) make the time commitment.

In the business world one of my jobs was training people new to sales. Trainees working with me heard the word commitment a lot. Fortunately, in sales, most of the competition lacked the passion or desire to be fully committed.

> **Whatever** your lips utter you must be sure to do…
> —Deuteronomy 23, verse 23

If you were the one that got back to the customer first, if the customer trusted you would be prompt, if your information was reliable, you would get the first call and the most orders. It was a simple task and the most important.

At some time in your life you made a commitment to God. These messages are an opportunity to review that commitment and recharge your batteries; a way to keep committed and stay on track in a world of distractions.

**Thought for Today:** Today let us be committed. First to God and then to ourselves by being the best we can be!

**Prayer for Today:** Dear Lord and Father, today we give thanks for our many blessings. Our families, friends and people that we do not know yet. We give thanks for being Godly people that will be accepted and liked by others. Amen

# He Comes Through

Grand events are wonderful. Yesterday June and I took three octogenarians out to lunch; my mom for her 89th birthday and two aunts from her generation. It is always great to hear them reminisce about old times.

All three have gone through good times and bad. They were all widows, there were new knees and hips at the table and a lot of arthritis. But wow, that was not the conversation. There was an attitude of joy and pleasure, smiles all around. The good times were the focus.

I am sure that there was anxiety amongst us. There had to be concern about my brother's cancer, about growing arthritis issues and, by the way, it was snowing and the roads were bad. But for the moment, all anxieties were cast away, joy

> **Humble** yourselves ...
> under God's mighty hand,
> that he may lift you up in
> due time.
> Cast all your anxiety
> on him
> because he cares for you.
> —1 Peter 5, verses 6 and 7

and love abounded. Great moments of joy are a gift from God. We need to enjoy them.

**Thought for Today:** Today let us focus on casting away our angst and turning our lives over to the Lord. Let us especially focus on the older generation. Let us reach out to them with love and share the good times.

**Prayer for Today:** Heavenly Father we pray for ourselves, our friends and loved ones. Many are ill and experiencing fear, uncertainty, loneliness or hurt. Many need You in their lives and have not found You. We pray that we may help be the conduit that strengthens their faith and eases their anxieties. We pray for a way to do your will in this way. Amen

# Paul's Sales Training

Last year our Pastor Ed had each of us in bible study pick a "Faith Verse," a verse or more that we feel we try to live by; one that means a lot to us. The above was one of several selections that I made. There is a lot to it and it is a good way to live your life.

I want to talk about my sales mentor and trainer, George. In the years he spent training me he sounded just like Paul in his message to the Romans. He would not tolerate sales bluster—he always was sincere and expected the same from me.

George did not like evil, like late deliveries, bad product or cheating on pricing—he liked what was good: fair deals, integrity and ethics. He taught me to respect and honor both the manufacturer and the customer and that they had to come before me—that was not always easy.

Verses eleven and twelve have to do with keeping a positive attitude; a difficult thing in life, especially in sales. You see, no salesman has more than half of the market share, so by definition they lose more than they win. In my business we had about a ten percent share so we lost nine out of ten. George taught me to always be upbeat and positive, "Never be

> **Love** must be sincere. Hate what is evil;
> cling to what is good.
> Be devoted to one another in brotherly love.
> Honor one another above yourselves.
> Never be lacking in zeal, but keep your spiritual fervor, serving the Lord.
> Be joyful in hope, patient in affliction, faithful in prayer.
> Share with God's people who are in need.
> Practice hospitality.
> —Romans 12, verses 9–13

lacking in zeal... Be joyful in hope, patient in affliction."

During those years, George was not a church person; just a great guy sent to me from God to be my mentor. We now have a different relationship, friends of each other, of the Lord and of Jesus. He is a Good News Buddy. I will hear from him when he reads this.

**Thought for Today**: Today let's focus Paul's important message in verses 11 and 12. Let us use them to keep our attitude positive so that we may have a positive effect on those around us. "Never be lacking in zeal... Be joyful in hope, patient in affliction."

**Prayer for Today**: Dear Lord and Father, today we give thanks to our mentors; those who have influenced our lives. That includes Jesus, Paul and the others that you sent to guide us. Amen

# Still Place

The world is a busy place and this Good News is not for June and me any more, but it applied for all the years we were raising our children, running three businesses, active in our church, etc. I believe it is one of the reasons we made it through it all and the reason we are not overbooked seniors. (Note that I did not describe us as retirees!)

Many Americans are overbooked; families are tied up every day with career and children's activities; empty nesters seem to have filled the time with commitments; retirees often do not know how they ever had time to work! That leads to a lot of stress, tension and, often, family failures. That's correct; the family that plays too much together just may not have enough quality time to survive. They do not have time to call for help.

In his book *Bread for the Table*, Henry Nouwen says it this way:

> These are words to take with us in our busy lives. We may think about stillness in

> **Be** still and acknowledge that I am God
> —Psalm 46, verse 10

contrast to our noisy world. But perhaps we can go further and keep an inner stillness even while we carry on … It is important to keep a still place in the "marketplace." This still place is where God can dwell and speak to us. … with that stillness God can be our gentle guide in everything we think and do.

**Thought for Today**: As our economy changes and adjusts to market conditions, many of our friends and neighbors are undergoing unplanned changes in their lives. Let us pray that God will be a presence in their lives as they pursue the opportunities presented to them through these changes.

**Prayer for Today**: Heavenly Father, the world around us is confusing, sometimes cruel and always difficult to understand. Please allow us time to step aside from our busyness and dwell upon "your will" rather than "our needs." Let us find the peace or stillness to allow "thy will to be done on earth as it is in heaven." Amen

# Raising Expectations

We have talked a bit about how the head and heart lead our bodies. How often our thoughts may be negative and they can lead us into depression. Let's face it, when we read or listen to the news, they talk mostly about negative events. However, most of what goes on in the world is positive. We need to focus on that!

Remember the words to the old song, "When you're down and out, lift up your head and shout, It's going to be a great day." We are often confronted with the local curmudgeon, the person who finds fault with everything. Let's face it, they are right, it is always too hot or too cold! Too rainy or their lawn needs watering! Things are too expensive! Coffee is too weak or strong! Pray for them, they need us.

We will have negative influences in our lives. As we move through our daily lives, we are blessed with the tools to

**Since**, then, you have been raised with Christ, set your hearts on things above, where Christ is seated at the right hand of God. Set your minds on things above, not on earthly things.
—Colossians 3, verses 1 and 2

deal with the negative side. I read this on a sign in front of a local church recently, "The Lord does not guarantee us smooth passage, just a safe landing." It is up to us to use our Christian tools to stay positive and be happy.

**Thought for Today:** Today we will have to deal with negative issues. Let us turn them into a positive experience by dealing with them promptly. When we encounter some that seem to linger and not go away, let us remember to turn those over to God through prayer.

**Prayer for Today:** Today is the day you have made for us. Unfortunately the roads have bumps and there are unknown troubles out there awaiting us. Today we pray that your presence will guide us through the tough moments and that we may accomplish our goals in Your name. Amen

# Life of Victory

Often when June and I are working with older people we find them remorseful. Sometimes we even find them angry and focused on what life was like rather than focusing on the joys that they have now. We have seen this so much that we have resolved to make sure that our grandchildren will remember us as happy and content. That is a lofty goal as we grow older.

Recently we spent a weekend with four octogenarian widows; my mom, her older sister, my dad's sister and mom's sister in law. Each has faced the challenges in their lives; the loss of a spouse, ill health at some level, the loss of certain capabilities that accompany ageing. It could have been a long day, full

...I will proclaim your righteousness, yours alone. Since my youth, O God, you have taught me, and to this day I declare your marvelous deeds. Even when I am old and gray, do not forsake me, O God, till I declare your power to the next generation, your might to all who are to come.
—Psalm 71, verses 16–18

of talk of what they have lost or what they wish they were. *It was not.* It was a day full of laughter and fond memories.

These women had persevered. They have paid their dues but are dedicated to enjoying their lives to the fullest. One of my favorite television evangelists, Joel Osteen, likes to say, "Keep on keeping on!" They sure are and are blessed because of it.

**Thought for Today:** Today let there will negative influences that occur. We can either dwell on them or deal with them. Today let us focus on moving on with our lives and our faith.

**Prayer for Today:** Dear Lord and Father, the world is full of confusion. There is trouble in the Mid East, deranged people shooting up our sacred institutions and some awful winter weather. We pray for the ability to understand it all and put it into the context of your plan. We offer special prayers for the older generation as they move onward. We pray for peace, understanding of our place in your world and the opportunity to do your will here on earth. Amen

# Faithfulness

Spring is a great time of the year. In the north we enjoy transition from winter wonderland to green. In the desert the transition is from rainy season to a dry desert in bloom. The longer days bring brightness to our lives. In its simplest form, the kids can play outside after dinner in the daylight! (So can mom and dad!)

Somehow in spring, we become affected with positive energy. There are more smiles on people's faces and more interaction with neighbors. It is a time when we can see the hand of the Lord at work and appreciate His blessings. This is a time when our faith is renewed.

**Great** is thy faithfulness
Morning by morning new mercies I see
All I have needed thy hand has provided
Great is thy faithfulness
Lord unto me
—Thomas Chisholm, William Runyon, *Great is Thy Faithfulness* 1923

**Thought for Today:** Today let us all observe and enjoy the wonders of spring. Let us appreciate the many things being reborn and feed off of the Lord's energy and the beauty of spring.

**Prayer for Today:** Dear Lord and Father, today we give thanks for the rebirth of spring flowers, green grasses and the blessings of warmer weather. We give thanks for these reminders of your love and power. We thank you for always being with us. Amen

# Persistence

In the '40s and '50s there was a Boston announcer that used to say, "A quitter never wins and a winner never quits." Today we live in a fast-paced society that seems to demand instant gratification. In the business world everyone is looking for the proverbial "low hanging fruit"; the diet fads are advertising fast weight reduction; if a trip is more than 400 yards we drive to save time. We want what we want when we want it and often fail to be diligent, persistent and patient.

In the '80s at a sales meeting Ty Boyd did a presentation called "The Life Plan" in which he talked about making a plan for life like we do for business. He preached that we needed to set goals for life and keep our focus on attaining those goals. We all start out with a plan, but many let it go and start reacting to life's situations rather than implementing the plan.

A strong factor in keeping a life plan in order is spirituality. Spirituality gives us the ability to focus on the good rather than reacting to the negative. Having the

> **The** plans of the diligent lead to profit
> as surely as haste leads to poverty.
> —Proverbs 21, verse 5

ability to forgive and to pray helps get through the tough days and keep our focus on the plan. In Paul's message to the Romans in verse twelve he advised, "Never be lacking in zeal, but keep your spiritual fervor, serving the Lord. Be joyful in hope, patient in affliction, faithful in prayer." We need that to be a part of our life plan.

**Thought for Today**: Today let us remember where we want to go. There will be both positive and negative distractions. Today let us focus on our spirituality in both celebration and under stress. Let us give thanks when things go as planned and pray when they do not.

**Prayer for Today**: Dear Lord we are busy working our plan every day. Today we pray for success, positive memories and that our plan fits your plan. Amen

# Friend, Spouse?

Years ago in a Methodist Youth Fellowship meeting, we were asked to write out what characteristics we valued in a friend. The discussion that followed demonstrated that we all had similar values. The characteristics of honesty, integrity, sense of humor and spirituality were most commonly mentioned. The differences were mostly activity based. The card players wanted a partner, runners a training partner, travelers a travel partner etc. I wanted to meet an Olympic swimmer.

The point of the exercise was to lead into a discussion on marriage. The facilitator pointed out that the same characteristics would be desirable in a future spouse. At that age most of us had not thought much about potential spouses. We were still in the Charlie Brown era, dreaming about the cute little red-haired girl. (I do not know who the girls thought about but I don't think it was me!)

> **How** good and pleasant it is when brothers (people) live together in unity!
> —Psalm 133, verse 1

The facilitator then had us look in a mirror. You see, the goal of the meeting was not about finding a perfect friend or spouse. It got turned around. We had to ask ourselves if we fit our own model. In the weeks that followed we had discussions about growth; about becoming the person we specified. For most of us at that age, it was the first time we thought about what others saw in us. It was scary and enlightening.

I am not sure if the Psalmist was thinking about blood brothers, sisters, spouses or whomever. However, we need to live in harmony with each other and focus on being a good friend to make that happen.

**Thought for Today:** Today let us focus on working on being a good friend; in the work place, the neighborhood, at church and at home. Let us focus on sharing our space with others in unity.

**Prayer for Today:** Dear Lord today we pray that you help us become better friends to those around us. You are with us and we pray that your light shine through us and on our friends. Amen

# Hope through Prayer

Hold on to your faith, keep holding on. When the going gets tough, when choices are hard, when the stress builds, pray about it; turn it over to God. Paul's letters repeat that time and time again and often we are not hearing it. Our faith is not always strong and we can be confused.

In his message , he is talking about a great way to get through a day, week or month. He is preaching a way of life through faith that leads to confidence and peace.

Memorize this one, try it and you will like it!

> **Never** be lacking in zeal, but keep your spiritual fervor, serving the Lord. Be joyful in hope, patient in affliction, and faithful in prayer.
> —Romans 12, verses 11 and 12

**Thought for Today:** Let's attack today with "fervor," being "joyful" and by all means prayerfully.

**Prayer for Today:** Dear Lord we give thanks for the day you have made for us to have. We thank you for the opportunity to do your will and contribute to each other's peace. Amen

# Motivation

A recent Facebook posting from my daughter stated, "worked 15 hours today with another 12 on the docket for tomorrow..." She is a dedicated professional making her living educating 10 and 11 year olds. She feels that her job is a gift from God that allows her to contribute to the lives of others. She is not going to get rich doing it.

As a 40-year sales professional I have stated many times that no long-term sales person is in it for the money. The stresses of sales, the treatment received from the public, dealing with supplier's failure to meet the customer's expectations are just not worth the money. The only long-term overachieving sales people somehow believe they are helping others. Many believe that they are blessed by God for the opportunity to contribute.

With all that stated, *greed* can slide into the equation and when it does the situation will get ugly; every single time!

> I saw that there is nothing better than that all should enjoy their work, for that is their lot; who can bring them to see what will be after them?
> —Ecclesiastes 3, verse 22

When we allow our lives to get out of balance our lives spin out of control. Like a wheel on a car, we thump along out of sync with the system. If we don't re-align ourselves, we will wear out quickly just like that tire does. Oh, and the vibration from the out-of-balance tire damages other parts of the car. In the case of our personal lives, we do damage to our families.

Democracy and free enterprise encourage competition and overwork. Motivation is good, working hard is the American way but we also need balance. Jesus' words in Luke 12, verse 15, state "Take care! Be on guard against all kinds of greed..." Motivation is good when it is pure; balance always needs to be at the forefront.

**Thought for Today:** Today, this week and this month, let us focus on our balance. Let's communicate with our loved ones and be sure that our lives are running without unnecessary bumps. Let's keep our spirit, mind and body in sync.

**Prayer for Today:** Dear Lord and Father, today we give thanks for all that we have received and have. We pray that you will guide us through the maze of life so that we will contribute to doing your will here on earth. Amen

# Endurance and Life

In our seemingly endless search for tranquility, we always seem to "want what we want, when we want it." Waiting seems like an impossible task. We seem to want our victories to come via the easy route. That is rarely a reality of life. Life is not a sprint; it is an endurance event, a marathon.

Many of you know of my amateur career as an endurance athlete, a triathlete (swim, bike and run). Just to get to the starting line in a race takes hours of practice, mostly alone; sometimes in pain; often in bad weather conditions. However, in most races there are over thousands of participants! That's correct, thousands. This is generally true of most endurance events. What for? Why do people do that?

Let me summarize the feelings that occur during a typical triathlete. There is anticipation and excitement standing on the beach during the national anthem. There is generally a feeling of spirituality during the blessing. In all my races, there was a period of fear at sometime during the swim. Boredom, pain, doubt and an entire array of other feelings occur during the bike ride and run. Then comes good time; the approach to the finish line.

The finish line of an endurance event generally has a crowd of 10,000 to 50,000 spectators. Enthusiasm and positive energy seem to radiate out of the crowd to be absorbed by the competitors. Most of my fellow racers agree that the feeling of finishing, the pride, and the

> **Blessed** is the man who perseveres under trial, because when he has stood the test, he will receive the crown of life that God has promised to those who love him.
> —James 1, verse 12

accomplishment and of course, just being done, is very special. Many of us have never crossed the finish line without tears of joy in our eyes.

As a grandfather and senior citizen, I can look back over the years and see the parallels between racing and life. Life is full of challenges, fears and excitement. Consider what James said in his twelfth verse:

> Consider it pure joy, my brothers, whenever you face trials of many kinds, because you know that the testing of your faith develops perseverance.
> Perseverance must finish its work so that you may be mature and complete, not lacking anything.

Let's remember to live our lives as Christians, be patient, meet our challenges and look forward to receiving our "crown of life."

**Thought for Today:** We are all living through trying times. There is too much to do, too much work, not enough play time. However, we have God and through Him we have our Christian friends. Today let's look toward the future knowing that patience and perseverance will bring us tranquility and happiness.

**Prayer for Today:** Heavenly father, as Christians we are not perfect. We seem to want immediate gratification throughout our lives. Today we pray for patience to discover your will, the courage to implement it and the knowledge to recognize your presence in our lives. Amen

# Draw Nearer to God

We often slip into moods that weaken our spirituality and faith. In life, fear, anger, lack of trust (doubt) often get more attention than they deserve. It is normal for humans to let them dominate their thoughts but it is also not a healthy way to live.

At a meeting recently, the subject of "angry unhappy people" was being discussed. There are unfortunate people who have not forgiven enough. They have hung on to so many resentments that they have become cynical, angry, unhappy or all of the above. It almost seems that this is a penance for not practicing forgiveness.

We need to somehow live closer to Jesus' example; to forgive and to believe that out of this life will come peace. Draw nearer to God. Spirituality and faith are works in progress. Let God take our hand to find peace and tranquility and continued spiritual growth.

> **Therefore**, brothers, since we have confidence to enter the Most Holy Place by the blood of Jesus, by a new and living way opened for us through the curtain, that is, his body, and since we have a great priest over the house of God, let us draw near to God with a sincere heart in full assurance of faith...
> —Hebrews 10, verses 9–22

**Thought for Today:** Today let us selfishly think about ourselves. Focus on our own faith. Certainly we will have opportunity to be angry and frustrated. We need to recognize when that occurs, act more like Jesus and "draw near to God with a sincere heart in full assurance of faith..."

**Prayer for Today:** Heavenly Father, today we pray for the world leaders. We pray for the innocent victims of violent acts. We especially pray for two special sets of children. Those that are taught to be human bombs (martyrs) in the Mid East and the children in terrorist (war) zones. We pray that the world will draw near to you and that peace will prevail. Amen

# Fitness 1

We are a wonderful machine/animal, born with feelings, the intellect to apply logic to our lives and without sin. For most of us it is all downhill from there. Society gives us the opportunity to pursue pleasure through wealth, eating great foods and entertaining ourselves while sitting down. The pure hearts that we were born with become hidden by our pursuit of worldly materials and "…the delicate, inner parts…" become hidden with excess weight. Today I want to address the body rather than the mind.

There are three people that have meant a lot to me in my life that have taken care of what God gave them better than most. One is my dad's sister, the others are personal friends that I met when I relocated to Minnesota. They have contributed subliminally and outwardly to who I am today, have a high level of faith following in very different theologies and are similar in other ways.

> **You** made all the delicate, inner parts of my body and knit them together in my mother's womb.
> Thank you for making me so wonderfully complex… Your workmanship is marvelous.
> —Psalm 139, verses 13 and 14

The aunt I have written about before. She is a yoga instructor and in the '60s she started talking about changing our diets to decrease fat content. Our family was a roast beef every Sunday type of family that trended toward obesity. She broke the family trend and started a life of both physical and mental fitness. Today, in her 80s she is still a teacher and role model in her community.

We will talk about the other two tomorrow!

**Thought for Today:** Today let us focus on our physical selves. Let's park a bit further from the door, say no thanks to the desert tray, walk the stairs as we are able. Let us be as good as we can be.

**Prayer for Today:** Father, today we give thanks for who and what we are and the many helpers that you have sent us along the way. Amen

# Fitness 2

Following on from yesterday:

The second is a friend in Christ that I met in my years of excessive training for triathlons and running. He once had a business career but that went away and he became a personal trainer.

There was a very difficult transition from a commercial cash flow to that of a club trainer. His strength and faith have kept him a positive role model and he has contributed to people as both a social and physical example. In the challenging financial times we are experiencing today people who can emulate his example will be better for it in spirit, mind and body. Winning the battle has a lot to do with having a strong faith and keeping it in focus.

The third person is a church associate who impressed me when we started attending church here in Minnesota. Early on, I remember sitting in an annual meeting when he was talking and hoping that someday I could

**You** made all the delicate, inner parts of my body and knit them together in my mother's womb.
Thank you for making me so wonderfully complex...
Your workmanship is marvelous.
—Psalm 139, verses13 and 14

contribute as much to the church. He was a leader that I wanted to emulate. Oh, his name is George and he turns 80 today. He has been a blessing in my and June's life.

In summary, we are what we are; born in a state of near perfection, we spend a lifetime trying to mess it up. The Lord gave us some marvelous equipment and a marvelous opportunity and he supplies ongoing help. It is a wonderful life and we need to take care of our spirit, mind and body in His name.

**Thought for Today:** Today let us focus on our physical selves. Let's park a bit further from the door, say no thanks to the desert tray, walk the stairs as we are able. Let us be as good as we can be.

**Prayer for Today:** Father, today we give thanks for who and what we are and the many helpers that you have sent us along the way. Amen

# Judgments

We often judge others by our own personal standards. As Christians that usually means that we are very trusting. We expect others to be honorable. In some instances, however, we make negative judgments of others based on an impression that did not fit our personal model. Yes, admit it, you have done this!

Often we observe an impression of others that generates doubt in our minds. It may be their dress, a display of anger or aggression or something they said. We make judgments without drilling into and knowing the inner self of the person. Clearly we are making an error when we judge others this way.

In the world today there is violence, terror and way too many negative judgments based on generalizations. Are Muslims bad from the Christian perspective? How about the other way around? People try to judge movies as anti-Semitic or in other racist ways rather than as entertainment. Are they using their entertainment medium as a justification for their own feelings? We will never know.

> **Do** not judge, or you too will be judged. For in the same way you judge others, you will be judged, and with the measure you use, it will be measured to you.
> —Matthew 7, verses 1–3

What we know as Christians is that it is not our place to judge. It is our place to accept and forgive. When someone or something in our lives is unacceptable and needs to be changed we need to change it in a Christian manner. That means with love, compassion and often prayer.

**Thought for Today:** We will need to make many choices as we go through the day. We will be given the opportunity to interact with people. Let us try not to judge those around us. Let us work with them, help them when we can and accept them for who they are.

**Prayer for Today:** Dear Lord, we are again concerned about terrorist attacks around the world. We have governments making judgments and creating conflict. We do not always understand it all. Today we pray that we, the people, may find a way to support your ways rather than the ways of governments and terrorists. We search for solutions through prayer and meditation. Amen

# Reinforcement

In my high school years of football, our coach was a negative motivator. It seemed that everything we did was wrong. The best complement we ever received was a "good job, but...." The criticism after the "but" was all that most of us ever remembered. None of us believed that we were very good and we were not having any fun. In 1956, three of us quit the team to go to private schools for a variety of reasons. There was a large article in the local paper about how significant a loss it was to the local high school team because they lost some great players. All three of us were really surprised at the compliments given to us by the coach.

At my new school, I found my way to a swim coach named Al Houston. Al was a caring man, a positive motivator and would have two or three swimmers at each Olympic games. Receiving positive motivation was a wonderful experience.

> ...**let** us be self-controlled, putting on faith and love as a breastplate, and the hope of salvation as a helmet. ...Therefore encourage one another and build each other up, just as in fact you are doing.
> —1 Thessalonians, verses 8–11

The team all felt good, worked hard; we liked Al and each other. We were also the best team in the northeast. We learned to care about excellence, not letting each other down and generally caring about each other.

This is a strong message. We are in challenging economic times right now and there is a lot of negativity in the world. Each day we read and see bad news. To stay positive we need to follow the lead of Christ and demonstrate our love and caring. We need to show our fellowship toward others.

**Thought for Today**: Today we will have the opportunity to be negative. School teachers will have a mischievous child, salesmen will lose an order, the weather may not be good—and we will want to whine. When that happens, stop and meditate, "Therefore encourage one another and build each other up." Let us all have a positively great day.

**Prayer for Today**: Heavenly Father, today we pray for those with negative ideas, those with aggression toward humanity and their victims. We pray for them and the opportunity to influence them in a positive way. Amen

# Thankfulness

It is sometimes hard to be thankful and gracious. Often, we have a problem seeing reasons to be thankful. The human animal has a wonderful way of focusing on the negative and not remembering the Lord's gifts.

When my brother Wayne had cancer that had metastasized into his bones, he was not enjoying life. June and I visited him. We delivered a gift to him from the Tuft's university athletic department. It was a very special memento done specially for him by the long-standing swim coach. The athletic department honored him as their best swimmer of his era.

Wayne, who is not the most talkative guy in the world, spent the whole afternoon praising the givers. He even thanked June and me for our efforts. It was the

**Give** thanks
with a grateful heart,
Give thanks
to the holy one;
…and now let the weak say
"I am strong"
and the poor say
"I am rich."
because of what the Lord
has done for us.
Give thanks.
—Henry Smith,
*Give Thanks,* 1978

highlight of our trip. In fact, he wouldn't shut up! It was a blessing for us to hear him.

When things are bleak, we need to focus on our blessings. God is with us and wants us happy under all conditions. "Let us then approach the throne of grace with confidence, so that we may receive mercy and find grace to help us in our time of need.
—Hebrews 4, verse 16

"Give thanks… because of what the Lord has done for us."

**Thought for Today:** Today let us acknowledge and recognize our blessings. Things will not go perfectly, something will surely go wrong. Let us make a choice to turn the negativity over to God and thank the Lord for the good times.

**Prayer for Today:** Dear Lord, today we ask for special prayers for those who have serious illness and their care givers. We pray for their peace and tranquility and the ability to support them with your help. Amen

# Live in Peace

Each week our pastor starts out with similar words. Something like, "We gather together to celebrate what we know is true; Our God is a loving and caring God who loves all humanity." Hold that thought and realize that we were made in his image.

If we accept those statements as truths, then why are we sometimes resentful, angry, depressed and concerned? Certainly, none of us is perfect and we have these emotions and thoughts. Truly, if we could "...Live in peace with each other... be patient with everyone," we would be meeting God's expectations and free ourselves of many of the anxieties of life. Peter in his letter tells us how. "...Be joyful always; pray continually; give thanks in all circumstances..."

**Now** we ask you, brothers, to respect those who work hard among you, who are over you in the Lord and who admonish you. Hold them in the highest regard in love because of their work. Live in peace with each other. ...be patient with everyone. Make sure that nobody pays back wrong for wrong, but always try to be kind to each other and to everyone else. Be joyful always; pray continually; give thanks in all circumstances, for this is God's will for you in Christ Jesus.
—1 Thessalonians 5, verses 12–18

**Thought for Today:** Today things will not always go in our favor. We will have opportunities to be resentful or angry. We must choose to be thankful, caring and joyful. In the words of Nike, "Just do it!"

**Prayer for Today:** Dear Lord, our world seems to have slipped into a hate-driven society. Around the world there are wars, terrorism and discrimination based on too many issues. We are confused by it all. Today we pray for some understanding, for knowledge of your role in this and insight on how we should react.

We pray that each of us may find a way to contribute to a joyful and peaceful society. Amen

# St Patrick's Day

Growing up in Boston there was always a very large St Patrick's Day parade and celebration. There were stories about a saint who drove the snakes out of Ireland, green beer and buttons that said everyone was Irish for today. It was great fun; mythical fun without a grain of truth to it!

St Patrick was an Irish saint and lived from 387 to 461. He is credited with bringing Christianity to Ireland. Wow, I never heard that growing up. Wikipedia does not mention green beer or parades. He was a great man who converted a country. He allowed the Irish to become free of their demons (maybe snakes?) and experience the grace of Christ. We need to honor him for that today!

> **It** is for freedom that Christ has set us free. Stand firm, then, and do not let yourselves be burdened again by a yoke of slavery.
> —Galatians 5, verse 1

**Thought for Today**: Today let us honor a person who spread our faith and the grace of Jesus to a heathen population. Ok, let's do it by drinking a toast with green beer!

**Prayer for Today**: Dear Lord and Father, today we give thanks to Saint Patrick and the many saints of the first millennium. They brought the grace of Christ to the world and made our lives special. We pray that in some way we are guided to carry on their work. Amen

# Old Salt

We know that the Romans used salt as money; it was life giving, necessary for survival and needed by everyone. So when Matthew called us the salt of the earth it is a high compliment; praise in its highest form. It was one of my grandfather's favorite expressions but he used it sparingly. You really had to do something well to hear it.

I considered leaving out the "no longer good" thought but changed my mind. There is in my thoughts no person who should be "thrown out and trampled." Somehow we all have hope and as Christians a part of our task on earth is helping people, preventing them from being "trampled." Our task is first to be strong in our spirituality, strong in our

> **You** are the salt of the earth. But if the salt loses its saltiness, how can it be made salty again? It is no longer good for anything, except to be thrown out and trampled underfoot.
> —Matthew 5, verse 13

faith and offer it to others through invitation. Demonstrate publically that we are at peace and invite people to join us.

Unlike commercial and sea salt, a person can be infected with the spirit and be made salty again.

**Thought for Today:** Today we will meet someone who is down spiritually. We will have a choice to talk and invite or turn the other cheek and do our own thing. For today and every day, let's try to help through invitation.

**Prayer for Today:** Heavenly Father, today is a great day, you made it for us and we will use it for you. Today we give thanks for the opportunity to help others, to recharge their saltiness. Amen

# Hope

There must be some lucky guy out there married to a woman named Hope. Isn't that a great thought; awakening every morning with hope; drinking morning coffee with hope; never being too far from thinking about hope. I like that analogy and the reality is we can be all of those things because the Lord is always with us and through Him hope abounds.

One day last winter I sat down to write my message and nothing was happening. So I did exactly the wrong thing; I filled my coffee cup, read the paper and watched the local news. My mom was snowed in, there were several murders reported and of course some political issues. There was nothing there to inspire hope but plenty to pray about. I commented to June when she awakened that it was a long time since I started my day that way and I hope it is longer next time.

> **God**, fill them with all hope, joy and peace that they may abound in hope by the power of the Holy Spirit...
> —Romans 15, verse 13

One of the greatest things about being a Christian is having hope. When we look toward the future we must remember Proverbs 23, verse 18, "There is surely a future hope for you, and your hope will not be cut off."

**Thought for Today:** Let today be a day of hope and light!

**Prayer for Today:** Dear Lord and Father, today we give thanks for our everlasting hope and joy available to us through Jesus. We look forward to a day that we can contribute by showing others the way by example through our hope and light. Amen

# Good Things Happen

Yesterday we looked at the start of a new day and the great opportunities that each day has for us. As Paul said to the Romans, "God works for the good of those who love him." Well, maybe that's what I really meant. Yes, each morning we choose from our many options. There is the TV news, the newspaper, (sports section or business?), daily meditation or prayer, and exercise are all classic options. Each of us needs to choose every day or go back to bed.

The sun will rise tomorrow and every other day. How we greet it is our choice. Not all days will go our way. If they did, Rabbi Kushner's book about bad things happening to good people never would have been written. Just maybe each day

> **And** we know that in all things God works for the good of those who love him, who have been called according to his purpose.
> —Romans 8, verse 28

when we wake up, before the newspaper and TV, before the exercise, perhaps we need to remind the Lord we love Him.

The song *"Morning has Broken"* finishes with "Praise with elation, praise every morning, God's re-creation of the new day." Yes, tomorrow shows promise through God's love. We need to accept it and move ahead.

**Thought for Today:** Today, let us look forward to the sunrise and the opportunity of each new day. Let's bring the Lord with us, let Him support us and let us give thanks for His presence in our lives.

**Prayer for Today:** Dear Lord and Father, today we are blessed with another day. We pray that we may use it to spread your word and blessings. Amen

# New Beginnings

Those of you that have known me long enough understand that on March 21, 1977, my family and I started a true "New Beginning." That was the year of treatment for alcohol abuse and the adoption of the slogan "This is the first day of the rest of your life." They supported me as did my friends and business associates. Each year I am reminded that through faith and friendship there is a good life. I thank all of you that have been my friends and associates since then.

The story of recovery is repeated in our society every day with the grace of God ever present in the process. Often as Christians we see a need and get a chance to help. One of the beauties of being Christian is the act of helping.

**This** is a day of new beginnings, time to remember and move on, time to believe what love is bringing, laying to rest the pain that's gone.
Christ is alive and goes before us, to show and share what love can do.
This is a day of new beginnings; our God is making all things new.
—Brian Wren, *This Is a Day of New Beginnings*, verses 1 and 4, Methodist Hymnal, number 383, 1978

**Thought for Today**: Today we will be out in the world interacting with friends and business associates. We may see a need to help. Many people will back away. Let us recognize needs in others and step forward with God's support and offer the Christian assistance that is needed.

**Prayer for Today**—The Serenity Prayer:

God Grant me
the serenity
to accept the things that I
cannot change.
The courage to change
the things I can.
And the wisdom to know
the difference. Amen

My blessings to all of you.

# Worst Enemy

My worst characteristic is holding on to my transgressions and errors. I still feel bad about things that happened 50 years ago! I believe that most people are that way but I pray that they are not. Self forgiveness is always a challenge.

In twelve step recovery programs, making amends to people who you may have harmed is part of the process. Working with people over the years has shown me that at least half of those contacted do not remember the offense! That has always intrigued me. If my first statement is fact, at least half of our internal remorse is totally unnecessary. We hang on to things that just do not matter; we are our own worst enemy.

That is not the case written by the Psalmist above. David is talking about his affair with Bathsheba and his conscience is bothering him deeply. He is praying for cleansing and forgiveness. The good part is that he will receive it. The question is, can he accept it?

> **Wash** away all my iniquity and cleanse me from my sin. For I know my transgressions, and my sin is always before me.
> —Psalm 51, verses 2 and 3

In our human world, we are very hard on ourselves and need to develop a stronger spiritual growth to find acceptance.

**Thought for Today:** Today let's move on with our activities unencumbered by our internal memories. Let's leave remorse behind and generate some positive memories!

**Prayer for Today:** Dear Lord and Father, like David we have been holding on to past transgressions. We know you will forgive us and that is not our issue. Today we pray that we may let them go, let them escape so that they do not affect the work we can do for you in the future. Amen

# Harvest? Invitation?

We are in the spring of the year and our fields are softening from the winter frost and it is getting close to planting time. Harvest will be in the fall. That is how the world works in my upper Midwest mentality. We till, plant, weed, water, prune and when we are lucky, we harvest. Along the way there is wind, rain, hail, heat and all the forces of nature that we have no control over. June and I had beautiful gardens for over twenty years and miss it a bit every spring.

Jesus is not talking about a food harvest. Jesus is talking about making converts, telling the story, inviting people to worship. To that task there are no seasons. Hold on to that thought because there just may be times of harvest in our churches; times when we are more invitational than others.

There are times when we are fairly open to inviting people to worship, Easter, Christmas, Rally Sunday and many special events throughout the year. It is fairly easy and most of us feel comfortable inviting people to join us at those special times. However, there are 52 weeks a year and most of us hold on to our invitations to worship way too much.

> **Don't you** have a saying, 'It's still four months until harvest'? I tell you, open your eyes and look at the fields! They are ripe for harvest.
> —John 4, verse 35

We are all proud of our faith, our congregations, and our church and are willing to share on special occasions. We are asked to "…open your eyes and look at the fields!" Let's ask a friend to join us soon.

Open your eyes and look at the fields!

**Thought for Today**: Many of us are members of declining Christian churches. Today let's think about why.

**Prayer for Today**: Dear Lord and Father, our troubled world seems to often take control of our lives. Trouble seems to supersede your will. Today we give thanks that in our personal world we have a choice to follow you. We pray that we can choose to contribute to doing your will here on earth by following Jesus' teachings. Amen

# Tradition

As a sales and marketing person for over thirty years I saw markets change in many ways. In the old days we drove a lot of miles selling trinkets and gadgets that met customer needs. We often brought new technology and served as an educational force and consultant.

Through technology the products evolved as did the communication. The advent of email and the internet minimized personal visits. In today's world, the customer has reviewed my products and others online and our challenge is to assist in his selection process. Rather than driving around all day, I sit online with the customer reviewing our products and applying them. Our style is totally different but our message is the same. We can meet your needs.

We have a project in our church trying to adjust to 2000 years of a changing market. We need to TWEET, POST,

> **Now**, brothers and sisters, I want to remind you of the gospel I preached to you, which you received and on which you have taken your stand.
> By this gospel you are saved, if you hold firmly to the word I preached to you.
> —1 Corinthians 15, verses 1 and 2

email and use the latest technology to give out a 2000 year old message to an ever changing population. Our worship services are overhauled so we refer to them as traditional, combined and contemporary. We are challenged.

However, even though our communication has changed, the message has not and cannot. Over these new mediums and through the different styles we must hold firmly to the word. The new market will find the help they need in a very old message.

**Thought for Today**: For today let's marvel at the message; never changing, always true. The Lord is with us.

**Prayer for Today**: Heavenly Father, today we are in a hurry. Our calendars are full and technology gives us very little time to meditate. Today we pray for your guidance through it all. We pray for grace and solitude through Jesus. Amen

# Letters?

Wow, it sure is scary to think that we are a letter from Christ. Are we really qualified to represent Jesus in our everyday lives? That is certainly a challenging thought and Paul was certainly challenging the people of Corinth. Was he challenging us or can we discount his word here as too ancient?

I really want to talk today about the difference between qualified and certified—two words that are not interchangeable but are often used in the same context. In the world of the spirit, when it comes to representatives of the Lord, there is a strong difference. Ordained pastors are certified to give communion, baptize and, I am sure, many other things that I do not even know about. However, we are all ministers of the gospel and through our spirituality; we are the light, the message and the Spirit. We are qualified through our covenant to shine that light.

> **You** yourselves are our letter, written on our hearts, known and read by everyone. You show that you are a letter from Christ, the result of our ministry, written not with ink but with the Spirit of the living God, not on tablets of stone but on tablets of human hearts.
> —2 Corinthians 3, verses 2 and 3

**Thought for Today:** Today I recognize my qualifications given to me by my covenant to my faith. I will share them and use them through the spirit given to me.

**Prayer for Today:** Heavenly Father, for today help me live as an example of you, as a window into the spirit. For today let others see you through my eyes. Amen

# Righteousness

When we strive to align our lives with the Lord's commandments we are striving for righteousness. We are trying to be the best we can be and it is a daily battle. When I entered a twelve step program in 1977 the slogan was "one day at a time." Often it was an hour or even a minute at a time. That's what it takes to be filled. There needs to be a hunger and thirst (a bad word in AA!). But that is a good thought in life.

Every day is a new day made by the Lord. Every day we will make choices that are both good and bad. By having a hunger and thirst for being good or righteous, we will make mostly the right decisions. However, we will mess up; that's human! Our faith is about forgiveness when we do but our humanness wants to hold on to the guilt. That's what Sundays are for; to recharge our spiritual batteries and be at peace.

**Blessed** are those who hunger and thirst for righteousness,
for they will be filled.
—Matthew 5, verse 6

**Thought for Today:** Today let us go out and feed our hunger and thirst. Let's finish the day fulfilled.

**Prayer for Today:** Dear Lord, today we give thanks for being part of your team. We go forth with thoughts of righteousness and doing your will here on earth. We pray for your guidance in our daily efforts. Amen

# Character

What a wonderful world it would be! We are all aware of the rules and will have a chance to break them daily, weekly, etc. Temptation is always around and I frankly succumb to it too often. I guess each morning I need to pray "Dear Lord, for today I pray to be perfect." No coveting, jealousies, anger, aggressiveness toward others (that must mean complete stops at the stop signs!). Ok, when I am done writing this I will try again!

There are only ten rules to obey for a great life and a great world. Most of us try; many of us fail. That's why we go to church on Sunday and pray daily. Somehow we end the day wishing we were better—that we were perfect.

Each day we strive for perfection; that is we try to build character. We attend church and pray and that generates spiritual growth. Building character is slightly different, but parallels it. The closer we are to the spirit, the easier it is to have that perfect character we all desire.

> **Now** all has been heard; here is the conclusion of the matter:
> … keep his commandments, for this is the duty of all mankind.
> —Ecclesiastes 12, verse 13

Persistence is the word, perfection is the goal. Pray daily, obey the commandments daily and life will be good. Never give up being the best you can be.

**Thoughts for Today**: For today let us be aware of the commandments in all of our activities.

**Prayer for Today**: Dear Lord and Father, today we give thanks for our wonderful lives and the hope we have for the future through our belief in Jesus. For today we pray for the strength and judgment to be obedient and of the highest character. Amen

# Relationships

Paul's message sure says it all and it would lead us to a perfect society. Unfortunately, we have not quite arrived at the point of grace. Our society and our world is competitive by design. Now we are in what they call a world economy and nations are competing for resources. Can it be that Paul was wrong? Should Paul have said something like "Grab the brass ring before the other guy gets it." Or maybe just "Do unto others" and leave of the finish of the golden rule. I do not think so.

Our competitive world works best when people team up and work together. People working together as a team can do more good that working as a group or individuals. Certainly the same is true of nations working together.

Paul's message may describe utopia or world at peace; truly a wonderful thought that we just cannot ever forget. Perhaps it will start with us as individuals, spread through congregations and then through nations.

That has to be the dream if not the goal.

> **Do** nothing out of selfish ambition or vain conceit. Rather, in humility value others above yourselves, not looking to your own interests but each of you to the interests of the others. In your relationships with one another, have the same mindset as Christ Jesus.
> —Philippians 3, verses 3–5

**Thought for Today:** For today let's simply be totally unselfish and humble in our activities.

**Prayer for Today:** Dear heavenly Father, today we give thanks for the many blessings we have. Today we pray that somehow through our actions we may bring our surroundings and maybe the world closer to peace. Amen

# Becoming Like Him

"Becoming like Him" is a great goal. It speaks of faith, hope and charity; three wonderful assets. Fortunately, we all have them; we all experience them, Just not one hundred percent of the time. Sometimes we are not faithful; we occasionally let our minds drift away. There are times when disappointment or depression lead us to lose sight of the hope we need. And charity often takes a back seat to perceived necessity.

Ok, this is not Sunday and I do not do sermons. None of us are perfect and we will probably never attain anything like perfection. However if you are reading this you are doing the right thing at this moment; meditating, enjoying a quiet moment, hopefully drinking your favorite beverage and thinking about "What Would Jesus Do today!"

As Christians, our lot in life is to strive for perfection, work daily on our spiritual growth and be comfortable in our lives through Jesus.

> **I** want to know Christ—yes, to know the power of his resurrection and participation in his sufferings, becoming like him…
> —Philippians 3, verses 10 and 11

**Thought for Today:** Today let us take a look at our calendars for the next 24 hours and ask ourselves the question, "What would Jesus do today?"

**Prayer for Today:** Dear Lord and Father, today we want to give thanks for resurrection. It is spring and the message is all around us; holy week speaks about the roots of our faith and the coming of spring reminds us of the wonder of your powers. We are blessed and give thanks. Amen

# One for All

My former pastor used to say that we invite a guest to church every twelve years or so! He blamed our lack of invitation for not having congregational growth. A second pastor came along and tried to motivate us with a sermon about our style and referred to us as "the frozen chosen!" Neither pastor grew the congregation during their tenure.

Several years ago a new guy showed up and started talking about having an invitational ministry. That was a new term and he invited us to join him in that task. So we did and the church grew! What a concept.

You see, when Jesus was talking to his disciples, even he said that he needed to get out and talk to others. We are supposed to have open doors, open hearts and open minds but need to remember that without an invitation there may not be anyone coming through the opening!

> **I** have other sheep that are not of this sheep pen.
> I must bring them also.
> They too will listen to my voice, and there shall be one flock and one shepherd.
> —John 10, verse 16

**Thought for Today:** Today let's go about our business with our hearts and minds open and receptive to the needs of others.

**Prayer for Today:** Heavenly Father, thank you for the many friends and the fellowship we have together. We pray for the opportunity to help others with their spiritual needs and growth in your name. Amen

# Human Judgments

When our faith is strong we are comfortable in our beliefs. Then our lives are good. That is the time when we make decisions easily without stress and doubt. In our lives we make hundreds of decisions and judgments every day just to get through life. Most are easy and automatic. Some are not.

Many of the decisions we make are not spiritual in nature. Where to get coffee on the way to work, what to make for dinner, will we go to church; all seem to be done on auto-pilot. They are often established out of our everyday habit.

In counseling training we are taught that it takes an average of six weeks to change a habit and establish a new one. That's why we have such difficulty with self improvement. In the old comic books Captain Marvel used to shout "shazam" and everything around him would fall into place. Our lives are not like that; not comic-book-simple!

I have a close friend who has recently found his way into a twelve step program for gambling and alcohol abuse. It has been a year now and we talk often. A few weeks ago he commented that he wishes someone had put him in touch with his "higher power" years ago. Well, I will share that many of us had tried.

> **The** person with the Spirit makes judgments about all things, but such a person is not subject to merely human judgments.
> —2 Corinthians 2, verse 15

The important issue is that he has found contentment, probably happiness, and it came through spiritual growth, starting with a belief system. His judgments are now spiritual and based in a God. His Judgment about all things has been changed and become Godly.

It is always great to see someone grow spiritually.

**Thought for Today**: Today let's continue to be on auto pilot and do the simple things we always do. When we get to the tough ones, let us turn them over to the Lord and be sure He is our actual pilot.

**Prayer for the Today**: Dear God, today we give thanks for our routines, the things we do stress-free and on auto-pilot. We pray that your presence in our lives leads us to Godly decisions and we have a positive impact on those around us. Amen

# **B**oldness

April Fools' Day is a day of practical jokes, misleading emails and general tomfoolery! Ok, so let's skip reading our devotional, forget the Holy Spirit and our Lord so that we may participate. That will not work because we cannot hide from the God we all believe in.

Today the comics in the newspaper will have Fools' Day jokes, the news and sports programs will be full of them and there will be a few bogus press releases to get your attention. If I were to write a press release for today it would be "Bob shoots par at St. Andrews!" or "…donates a million towards the church mortgage."

People would recognize immediately that these were jokes and some would know they were my fantasies.

Today like all days I hope this devotional puts you on track to recognize the Holy Spirit in your life and the role it plays for you. While others are playing the jokes, we need to be sure that we are bold in our faith.

Blessings to you all and enjoy the start of April.

> **Almighty** God, may they be filled with the Holy Spirit and speak the Word of God with boldness...
> —Acts 4, verse 31

**Thought for Today**: For today we will be bold in our faith and remember that it is ok to be a joker also!

**Prayer for Today**: Father, we give thanks for all that we are and have. We thank you for having the freedom to enjoy a good joke, a great laugh and the faith to know the real truth. We thank you for being with us and meeting our needs. Amen

# Security?

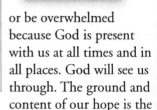

Recently while writing, a news flash came across my computer screen that there was a shootout on a local highway that had shut down the road. So what? I am here safe in my home. Well, I live within a half mile of the spot and they had put all the local schools on lock down until the situation was resolved. I did not feel very secure at all.

When a crime occurs in "our neighborhood," we ask, "How could this happen here?" The truth is that tragedy and violence can happen anywhere. None of us is immune. June and I have said for years that anything can happen at any time. We are always wary when we travel but not so wary when we are at home.

The author of the 23rd Psalm wrote these familiar words, "Even though I walk through the valley of the shadow of death, I will fear no evil, for you are with me." The psalmist does not say that we will not have to walk through the darkest valley or that evil does not exist. Rather, the psalmist reminds us that we need not fear

> **The** Lord Almighty is with us; the God of Jacob is our fortress.
> —Psalm 46, verse 7

or be overwhelmed because God is present with us at all times and in all places. God will see us through. The ground and content of our hope is the promise that nothing in all creation can separate us from God's love.

Real security cannot come from walls and fences; real security comes from having a relationship with God.

**Thought for Today:** Today let us feel secure in our faith, our neighborhood and in all of our relationships.

**Prayer for Today:** Heavenly Father, when the foundations of our lives are shaken, hold us close to you and remind us that you will never leave or forsake us. You alone are our hope and security. Amen

# Don't Forget To Call

It is easy to go through a busy day without acknowledging the presence of God in our lives. In fact, sometimes when we get to the end of a day and look back, the day seemed out and out un-Godly. That is our own fault. When that happens, we have not done the best job of caring for ourselves.

We will have busy and stressful days. Whether working or playing, bad things happen to all of us. Confusion and stress always seem to find their way into our lives. Counselors will advise us to put ourselves first for a part of each day. That requires a bit of selfishness to help maintain our sanity. The results make us a better worker, a better parent and overall a better person. There is nothing selfish about that!

Henri Nouwen called it a still place, "This still place is where God can dwell and speak to us. It also is the place from which we can speak in a healing way to all the people we meet in our busy days." We all need to think about that.

**The** Lord said, "Call to me and I will come to you." —Jeremiah 33, verse 3

**Thought for Today:** As our economy changes and adjusts to market conditions, many of our friends and neighbors are undergoing unplanned changes in their lives. Let us pray that God will be present in their lives as they pursue the opportunities presented to them through these changes.

**Prayer for Today:** Heavenly Father, the world around us is confusing, sometimes cruel and always difficult to understand. Please allow us time to step aside from our busy schedules and dwell upon "your will" rather than "our needs." Let us find the peace or stillness to allow "…thy will to be done on earth as it is in heaven."

# A Nervous Breakdown

J.L. Glass has written a humorous article titled *"Five Ways to Have a Nervous Breakdown."* He lists the ways as follows:

**The** fruit of the Spirit is... peace.
—Galatians 5, verse 22

And the peace of God... will guard your hearts and your minds in Christ Jesus.
—Philippians 4, verse 7

1. Try to figure out the answer before the problem arises. "Most of the bridges we cross are never built, because they are unnecessary," Matthew 6, verse 34 says: "Do not worry about tomorrow, for tomorrow will worry about itself."

2. Try to relive the past. As we trust Him for the future, we must trust him with the past, and He can use the most checkered past imaginable for His good. Paul's letter in Romans 8, verse 28, states "And we know that in all things God works for the good of those who love him, who have been called according to his purpose."

3. Try to avoid making decisions. Doing this is like deciding whether to let weeds grow in our garden: while we are deciding, they are growing. Decisions will be made while we are procrastinating. Choice is a man's most godlike characteristic.

4. Demand more of yourself than you can produce. Unrealistic demands result in beating our heads against stone walls. We do not change the walls. We just damage ourselves. Romans 12, verse 3, says "Do not think of yourself more highly than you ought, but rather think of yourself with sober judgment."

5. Believe everything Satan tells you. Jesus described Satan as the "father of lies" (John 8, verse 44). But our Lord declared that his sheep follow Him because they "know his voice"(John 10, verse 4). They have listened to it in His word.

**Thought for Today**: Let us feel the Lord's presence in our daily lives so that we can keep our stress levels low.

**Prayer for Today**: Heavenly Father, we are masters at leaving you out of our lives and building obstacles in our paths. We pray today that you will guide us through the day and that our troubles will be minimal. Amen

# Power

Power—what a word. What a feeling. We come into the world looking for power. We equate power with security and control. We hear about power brokers. Books are written in the leadership arena telling you how to gain power, retain power and use power. The feeling of power can be addictive. It gives us an adrenaline rush.

In relationships, power usually manifests itself as domination. How sad, when a significant other demands submission, partnership is lost. The relationship cannot reach its full potential. Power sometimes negates God's will. It can become a power broker's God.

I have always said that two heads are four times better than either one. My definition of partnership is when two become one in objectives, dreams and goals. In a good relationship, power is not a problem. Power is only a problem when it is misused.

> **You** are awesome, O God, in your sanctuary;
> the God of Israel, whose power is in the skies.
> —Psalms 68, verses 34–35

In relationships (spousal, parent-child and others) sacrifice and caring (love) will generate a better relationship than power and control. Often power and control are masks for insecurity and a low self image. It blocks bonding and growing in a caring relationship.

"Love one another, Just as Christ loved the church and gave himself up for her."
—Ephesians 5, verse 25

**Thought For Today:** In all of our interactions today, let us keep caring, consideration and love at the forefront of our decision making.

**Prayer for Today:** Dear Lord, during this special period of remembrance, let us find time to think through the story of Easter and life ever after. Help us put the trials of everyday life on earth in perspective. Guide us to the inner peace that can be found in the love of Jesus. Amen

# Leadership

In the '60s my engineering manager at a multi-national company ruled the roost by fear. Three or four times each year he would lay off someone and then the next week warn a few that they could be next. The department output would increase for a while. He kept control of all projects, decisions and empowered no one. There was no compassion in the department or the company. Great things did not happen for them and they no longer exist.

Over the years I have observed that successful leaders use a win-win philosophy that requires compassion. It seems that leaders that have great accomplishments have compassion. Paul said it this way:

> Be kind and compassionate to one another, forgiving one another, just as in Christ, God forgave you.
> —Ephesians 4, verse 32

Yes, it is clear that compassion, forgiveness and caring are strong components of success.

> ...**He** who has compassion on them will guide them and lead them beside springs of water.
> —Isaiah 49, verse 10

**Thought for Today:** Today we will all have opportunities to be compassionate. We may be tired, short tempered or busy. However, let us focus on being compassionate.

**Prayer for Today:** Heavenly Father, we are caught up in a busy world. There is too little time and too many things to do. Pressures to make the fast decision, reaction or remark sometimes lead to a lack of compassion. Please, help us concentrate on your place in our lives. Help us be compassionate and forgiving in all of our activities. Amen

# Commitment

"The Parable of the Sower" hits home with this story and again fits into another phase of my life. As a young family of six, recovering from divorce, trying to restart our lives, there were many times when the pursuit of wealth took president over the depth of our spiritual commitment. We certainly made some interesting decisions.

First and foremost, after starting our business over a period of five years, our cash flow increased significantly. It is embarrassing when I compare the percent increase in income when compared with the growth in our church pledge. Beyond financial commitments, my spiritual commitment was often weak regarding the giving of time. We avoided committee assignments, but had time to get to all the kids activities!

One day while waiting for a tennis match with a good friend and dedicated Christian, we were talking about our schedules. Ken made a comment that I was not saving enough time for the Lord. He promised to pray that my business activities would not cause too much harm.

**Still** others, like seed sown among thorns, hear the word; but the worries of this life, the deceitfulness of wealth and the desires for other things come in and choke the word, making it unfruitful.
Others, like seed sown on good soil, hear the word, accept it, and produce a crop—thirty, sixty or even a hundred times what was sown.
—Mark 4, verses 18–20

He even suggested that I could fit in my long training runs (2 hours) on Sunday before church rather than during church.

The best part about life is often looking back and seeing what we have learned. The "I wish I had known that when..." syndrome. We all think about that at times. However, God allows us to learn, grow and forgive. He rewards us in many ways and the return on investment in God's work is life's true reward.

**Thought for Today:** Let us take a look at our calendars. Let us remember that there are 168 hours each week. Ask ourselves the question, "Have I saved enough time for the Lord?"

**Prayer for Today:** Gracious Lord, the world is very busy and tense. Today and in the future we pray thet we may save enough time to keep you involved in our lives. Amen

# Stress

Stress is becoming an American, if not a worldwide, tradition, part of our lifestyle. We often go through our week wound up like a rubber band that has been twisted tighter and tighter. However, we all recognize that the rubber band eventually breaks. When it is wound too tight or stressed too long—it snaps! We are certainly a higher life form than a rubber band; however we also may snap when over stressed.

We all need a way of unwinding during the most stressed of times. Mine is by writing "Good News" to people that I care about. Yours may be different; many exercise, some use meditation, often we chat with a friend or read. There are many ways to release stress. In Paul's writings to the Philippians 4, verses 8 and 9, he suggests that Faith is a tool to help us.

> Finally, brothers, whatever is true, whatever is noble, whatever is right, whatever is pure, whatever is lovely, whatever is admirable— if anything is excellent or

**Do** not be anxious about anything, but in everything, by prayer and petition, with Thanksgiving, present your requests to God.
—Philippians 4, verses 6–9

praiseworthy—think about such things. Whatever you have learned or received or heard from me, or seen in me—put it into practice. And the God of peace will be with you.

**Thought for Today:** Today let us focus selfishly on ourselves. Let's feel the peace and presence of God in our lives. When the "stress monster" wants to control our lives, let's read this passage and let "the peace of God" into our lives. As Christians we deserve peace.

**Prayer for Today:** Heavenly father, the world seems to be a breeding ground for stress. Everywhere we look there is something to worry about; terror, hate, employment troubles, stock market woes—even severe weather. Today we pray that we may keep you and peace in our thoughts, that we have the presence of mind to make wise choices and release our stresses to find tranquility. Amen

# It's In The Spirit

If you are reading this devotional, you probably believe that the Lord is with you. You are blessed. However, often we meet people who are under-achievers, dead-end kids, those who don't bounce back from a negative experience. They have buried potential that was given them at birth that is not being discovered.

In the story of Joshua, he was being advised to take over from Moses and be a leader. He did not think he was capable and had never led before. He was told, he believed and he successfully led because the potential was part of the Spirit. Many of us experience challenges in our lives that we would just as soon not meet.

Recently a friend who works with underprivileged youth when they are released from jail told this story. A client he was working with was having trouble surviving so he stole again so he would be returned to jail and have a roof over his head. That was a step he knew would work and he had the skills to implement it—thus he was successful. The question we face as Christians is how do we transfer

> Then you will know which way to go, since you have never been this way before....
> —Joshua 3, verse 4

our spirit to those who need help? How do we let them find the talent that the Lord gave them?

Another friend has a clinically depressed husband. He faces the same challenge. Depression seems to magnify obstacles and hide opportunities and he fails to see his opportunities. We need to find a way to help people take the tiny steps in life that will release the person or talent that the Lord gave them. This needs to be done through the Spirit.

"Not by might nor by power, but by my Spirit," says the Lord Almighty.
—Zacharias 4, verse 6

**Thought for Today:** Today let us simply help someone take a small step forward; someone at work, at home or someone whom we have not met yet.

**Prayer for Today:** Dear Lord and Father, today we give thanks for having your Spirit within us. We pray that we may share it with someone who is in need. Amen

# Personal Prayer

As we watch the news, read our newspapers and study life around us and throughout the world, we see a lot of stress and confusion. The media present us with more negatives than positives. We might wonder how to overcome these challenges and bring peace to the world.

We need to consider what our contribution to peace will be. Certainly we cannot go out tomorrow and solve the world's problems and create "World Peace." However, each of us can start every day with the goal to be at peace and stay that way. Stay within ourselves through prayer to maintain our own internal peace.

Recently June and I started attending a monthly lunch called Faith at Work. It is basically an interfaith group that has agreed to keep their faith in the workplace. They attempt to make decisions as Jesus would have. Each month there is a speaker with a testimonial proving the concept that the workplace does not have to be mercenary or cut throat. Attendees tend to leave with their internal faith recharged for another month of internal peace through prayer and the ability to serve others through their faith.

> **Let** us therefore make every effort to do what leads to peace and to mutual edification.
> —Romans 14, verse 19

Our contribution to the world can and will start within us. We know that the Lord is with us, we need to let Him in and let others see the results. As Paul stated to the Romans,

> We who are strong ought to bear with the failings of the weak and not to please ourselves.
> Each of us should please his neighbor for his good, to build him up.
> —Romans 15, verses 1 and 2

**Thought for Today**: There is an old expression that suggests aggressive reactions: "When the going gets tough, the tough get going." That is always an option. Today for us let's think about this: When our going gets tough, let's start to pray and be at peace. Let's all demonstrate a better way!

**Prayer for the Day**: Heavenly Father today we pray for gentle solutions to our problems. We pay that when things get tough we may peacefully resolve the issues the way Jesus did. Amen

# Style Change?

The more we change the more we seem to stay the same. People that focus on being as good as they can be, people that help others, people with spirituality seem to live "…without fear of harm." When we lose that focus, negatives start to build in our lives and we start down a slippery slide.

When we do not have any time for God, it is a sign of over commitment, reacting to our "to do" lists rather than planning our day. The concept of putting one's self first for part of each day is the key to maintaining sanity and generating personal growth. We need to take the time to grow every day, to be a good parent, employee, and friend; just be as good as we can be The question is how do we do all that we need to do and meet all of our obligations? The answer is priorities, and including the Lord on the list!

Pat McNamara, a four time Olympian from Minneapolis advised me that if I was going to stay in shape, I had to give fitness a priority part of every day. That is, make it a calendar item and follow Nike's advice, "Just Do It!" OK, then if we want to live better we need to schedule time to listen to the message so we "…will live in safety and be at ease, without fear of harm."

> **For** the waywardness of the simple will kill them, and the complacency of fools will destroy them; but whoever listens to me will live in safety and be at ease, without fear of harm.
> —Proverbs 1, verses 32 and 33

**Thought for Today:** We need to recognize the internal conflict in our lives. The conflict between our over committed "to do" lists and the time required to have personal growth. The concept is simple, we all want to be better in spirit, mind and body, but we do not have the time. Our wants look like needs and our stress builds. Today let's try placing the Lord first for a few minutes a day and try to feel the difference as we go through the day.

**Prayer for Today:** Father, today you are at the top of my list. I look forward to the peace that you will bring. Amen

# Learn To Receive

It is better to give than to receive. Yes, and we all feel better when we are giving than when we are receiving. We all come in contact with persons that we know are really hurting and we ask, "How is it going?" Often the answer is OK, fine, good…etc. That answer raises the antenna on a counselor. Many of us are relieved when we hear it because now we can change the subject and avoid the real issue.

On a Friday in January 1998, I was diagnosed with cancer and made aware that surgery was a good solution. That Sunday, June and I were scheduled to be greeters for a church service. God forgive me but I lied a lot that morning. Most people greet with, "Hi, how are you?" and they did not really want to hear my answer.

The point is that in 1998, we needed to take from the church more than we could give. Oh yes, we gave them financial support, but that is not what I mean. I needed prayers to cover my fear. June needed prayers to cover her tears. The kids and grandkids also needed spiritual support. The support was not for the weekend but for an extended period that lasted most of 1998. The good news was that "…He who began a good work in you

> I thank my God every time I remember you.
> In all my prayers for all of you, I always pray with joy because of your partnership in the gospel from the first day until now, being confident of this, that He who began a good work in you will carry it on to completion…
> —Philippians 1, verses 3–6

will carry it on to completion…" The support was available through our Christian community.

In 1998, the Pickering family was blessed; that was the year we learned to accept the support and prayers from our friends in Christ. We learned to receive the benefits that are available to all, that, unfortunately, some are too proud to receive. We need to remember "In all my prayers for all of you, I always pray with joy." We are welcome and it is OK to take and receive.

**Thought for Today**: Today let us recognize when we need support. Let us stop and pray about it. If there are any real bad moments, let's call a friend in Christ and ask for help. The friend will be grateful. Also, if we have a great day, let's hope that we get a call from someone that could use our support.

**Prayer for Today**: Dear Lord and Father, we offer our prayers for peace and understanding in the world. As a nation, we seem to accept terror and murder on a daily basis in the Mid East. Today we pray somehow for the understanding and that we, in some way, can contribute to the spreading of your love throughout the world. Amen

# Control

Getting through valleys so that we may experience the peaks, the good times, our faith is often tested in subtle ways. We find it easy to take the credit for recovery. After all, we generally "take control" and work our way through problems. That's the human way.

Several years ago upon finishing a program at church, the pastor presented each of us with a pin, Christ's feet. The pin is symbolic of the footprints in the sand. It serves as a reminder that we never walk alone. When in control, we may not be aware and often do not feel God's presence. We tend to think of God as a "Macro" rather than a personal assistant.

When we are in "full control" we are misleading ourselves. There are too many outside factors playing out in life for that to be true. We need to always have the trust that our faith teaches to have. With God as a partner, it is always easier to get through the crises periods. He is always our partner.

> **Trust** in the Lord with all your heart and lean not on your own understanding.
> —Proverbs 3, verse 5

**Thought for Today:** Today let's really control the ball. Keep our problems in our grasp! Yes, we can handle it all. Then after we have finished take out this meditation and think back to how we played out God's will, how He helped us in our many tasks and give Him thanks for the help.

**Prayer for Today:** Dear Lord, Heavenly Father, the world seems out of control. We are having doubt as to what role you are playing out with all the ills that exist. Economic struggles, terrorism, world poverty all seem to dominate our lives. It is hard for us to keep trust and show the love that is needed. We pray for some guidance. Guidance on how to trust you more, how to do your will in tough times and to be a good follower of Christ's teachings. Amen

# Joyful

The Psalmist who wrote this knew what Christianity was all about. We are told to be happy, to enjoy our loves and even to sing it out loud! I am not sure that I can do that every day.

All days are not created equal and some seem downright awful. As I write this today we have not seen the sun in four days and have dealt with drizzle, hoar frost and ice. Bah! Humbug! to a joyful noise! That is what I wrote and it would have been easy to feel that way but this is what June and I did instead.

We went to an early service at our church and took communion with friends. That is our way to start Sunday; in the chapel with our pastor. It was a joyous time. Then June and I had breakfast together and had time to discuss our week's plans that include having a pool party for our Sunday school; great thoughts!

**Shout** for joy to the LORD, all the earth. Worship the LORD with gladness; come before him with joyful songs. Know that the LORD is God. It is he who made us, and we are his; we are his people, the sheep of his pasture.
—Psalm 100, verses 2 and 3

At 11 we returned to church to attend the annual budget meeting and visit with the entire congregation. Our church has enough money, great people and we again had a great visit with friends.

You see, gloomy is a mind set. When you keep the Lord in your life it is easy to make a joyful noise!

**Thought for Today:** When you are feeling down and out— think about the joy of our faith!

**Prayer for Today:** Dear Lord and Father, today we pray that we can keep our focus on the joys of our faith and that we may share those joys with those around us. Amen

# Peaks And Valleys

Life is full of peaks and valleys. It is very human to take credit for the peaks and blame something else for the valleys. It is hard at times to identify with our own "piece of the action" when there is pain. It is often hard to appreciate the lessons learned through the suffering process.

We look to our faith more often when we are in a valley than when we are at a peak. Many people that visit our churches come through crises. Divorce, illness, grief, loneliness, etc. are among the common reasons for a visit. I have personally never greeted someone that told me that they had such a great week that they came to say thanks to God.

However, one of the beauties of our faith is that we recognize God's role in helping get us to the next peak. We recognize God's role in getting us to the final peak. Each peak gives us a reason for a stronger faith, the lessons learned in the valleys gives us the "...perseverance; perseverance,

**Therefore**, since we have been justified through faith, we have peace with God... And we rejoice in the hope of the glory of God. Not only so, but we also rejoice in our sufferings, because we know that suffering produces perseverance; perseverance, character, and hope. And hope does not disappoint us....
—Romans 5, verses 1–4

character, and hope" that carry us throughout our lives.

**Thought for Today:**
Today let us recognize if we are at a peak or in a valley. Let us recognize the lessons we are learning if it is a "valley" and give credit to those things that helped make it a "peak." Either way, let us give thanks to God.

**Prayer for Today:**
Heavenly Father, we are in a confused world. Many people are concerned about their future in tough economic times. There is war, fear, terror that seems to dominate the news. Certainly there are many needing a "peak" to help them out. We pray that through your Son Jesus, that we all may find a peak and a way to share your Love with someone. Amen

# Setting Examples

One of my recurring themes is that we are all ministers of the Gospel. Within our individual congregations we hire ordained ministers to lead and teach us as we move forward on our spiritual journeys. Sometimes we catch ourselves in the Sunday-only mode.

A very dear friend of June's and mine is in spiritual crises. For whatever reason faith has left and bouts of depression have occurred. It is probably not coincidental. For Christians, there is a strong tie between our faith and our inner peace. When our faith is doubtful we take control of things. We forget to "Let go and let God."

**Who** is wise and understanding among you? Let him show it by his good life, by deeds done in the humility that comes from wisdom.
But if you harbor bitter envy and selfish ambition in your hearts, do not boast about it or deny the truth. Such wisdom does not come down from heaven but is earthly, unspiritual, of the devil.
For where you have envy and selfish ambition, there you find disorder and every evil practice.
—James 3, verses 13–16

As Christians, we need to demonstrate our inner peace to others. Show our caring spirits and our love. Not on Sunday but every day in every activity. Our ministry needs to be subtle, persistent and very public. When we function in a very Christian and public way, people in doubt will come to us.

**Thought for Today:**
Today let us demonstrate our inner peace to all we meet. Let us look for opportunity to talk about our tranquility and our faith. Let us offer to share with others.

**Prayer for Today:** Dear Lord, there are many great events that are masked by tragedy. Today we pray that somehow we as Christians may find a way to contribute. That we may have our prayers answered with a lasting miracle. We all need an end to hate and hateful decisions; we pray for world peace. Amen

# Enough Is Enough

The competitive nature of our society has generated a workaholic mentality. In the '60s, we occasionally met someone who worked a 50-hour week and in some families both the wife and husband had full-time jobs but they were not commonplace. It seems today that it is fairly common that people work way too much. We work on the internet every day, we are attached to our cell phones and when we have a break we seem to be overloaded with our recreational commitments.

Tim Hansel wrote the following regarding our present state.

> We are called to be faithful, not frantic. If we are to meet the challenges of today, there must be integrity between our words and our lives and more reliance on the source of our purpose. Unless the LORD builds the house,
> its builders labor in vain.
> Unless the LORD watches over the city, the watchmen stand guard in vain.
> In vain you rise early and stay up late,
> toiling for food to eat—

> **Unless** the LORD builds the house, its builders labor in vain. Unless the LORD watches over the city,
> the watchmen stand guard in vain.
> —Psalm 127, verse 1

for he grants sleep to those he loves.
Most Christianity reveals itself in feverish work, excessive hurry and exhaustion. I believe that the Enemy has done an effective job of convincing us that unless a person is worn to a frazzle, running here and there, he or she cannot possibly be a dedicated, sacrificing, spiritual Christian. Perhaps the seven deadly sins have created another member—Overwork!

We need to remember that our strength lies not in hurried efforts and ceaseless long hours, but in our quietness and confidence. The world says today— Enough is not enough. Christ answers softly—Enough is enough!

**Thought for Today**: Today let us all slow down. If that is a problem, may I suggest that you bookmark this Good News and when you feel overloaded, take a break and read it again or discuss it with a friend.

**Prayer for Today**: Dear Lord today I want to thank you for my many blessings. Today I have realized that I have enough through you. Amen

# Spring

Spring is a wonderful time of the year. Short winter days are replaced with warmer and longer evenings. Spring bulbs emerge from the ground with green sprouts, color returns to the woods, parks and our own yards. It is a time when the wonders of God bring peaceful thoughts to us all.

We also live in a world surrounded by fear. Terrorism, anger, financial problems and many other crises fill our world along with the wonders of spring. I do not know about you, but I ponder the why of it all. Where is our "peace on earth?" Spring shows us how close it is and that God is trying to bring it to us. What is our best way to participate in having a peaceful world?

The message in another hymn, "Let there be peace on earth and let it begin with me" (Jill Jackson Miller and Sy Miller) gives a hint. If each of us does our part, we can influence the world.

**Crown** Him the Lord of peace, whose power a scepter sways from pole to pole, that wars may cease, and all be prayer and praise.
—Mathew Bridges, *Crown Him with Many Crowns*, Methodist Hymnal, number 327, 1851

John F. Kennedy put it like this. "One person can make a difference and every person must try."

**Thought for Today:** Each week we encounter negativity. There are angry drivers, frustrations in the workplace and certainly opportunities to be frustrated in our family lives. We can chose to be anxious or at peace. When given the chance, let us demonstrate our Christian and peaceful side. Let peace begin with each of us.

**Prayer for Today:** Heavenly Father, each day we see negativity around the world. We as people seem to have very little control over it all. We pray that we may lead by the example of Christ; we pray that our living example may contribute to a better world.

# Patriots' Day

Growing up in Boston we celebrated Patriots' Day. That gave me two choices to write about today: Paul Revere's ride or the Boston Marathon. There is a similarity and it is not direction!

The marathon involves over 20,000 participants, one lady and one male will make a six figure pay check and be declared winners. As many as twenty others will receive appearance money and have a good pay day. The majority will receive personal gratification, be the recipient of a great engine for their body from their training and recognition for a great effort. That is all they want. They do it out of the passion that endurance runners have and the feeling of accomplishment.

In 1775 Paul Revere and William Dawes raced out of Boston with a message that the British were moving out. Their message to the people of greater Boston

**Do** you not know that in a race all the runners run, but only one gets the prize? Run in such a way as to get the prize. Everyone who competes in the games goes into strict training. They do it to get a crown that will not last, but we do it to get a crown that will last forever.
—1 Corinthians 9, verses 24 and 25

was the call to arms. Unfortunately, Paul did not get very far because he was picked up in West Cambridge by a British patrol. However he did get the poem named for him; I guess William Dawes did not rhyme as well! They were both on a mission to benefit humanity, both were unselfish and both are American heroes.

Life is not a sprint. It is a marathon. We need to race it and live it with our eye on the ultimate prize that is promised through our faith.

**Thought for Today:** For today let us focus on our race for the prize. Let's take a step closer to perfection.

**Prayer for Today:** Dear Lord, today we pray for the safety and success of the many runners in Boston. May they be blessed with fitness and great memories. Amen

# Infants

This is my confession to you all: I cannot quote a lot of scripture; do not know a lot of biblical history; have never visited the holy land; sometimes skip my Friday bible study to play golf or work out. At best I am an infant in Christ.

In fact, I like that because it gives me plenty of room to grow, a reason to keep trying and even a reason to keep writing. There is always hope in knowing that there is growth ahead when we do the right things. Our lives are spiritual journeys without limits or even an end. That's a great thought.

As a young engineer my mentor used to quote "The more you know, the more you know you don't know." It apparently is an

**Brothers** and sisters, I could not address you as people who live by the Spirit but as people who are still worldly—mere infants in Christ.
—1 Corinthians 3, verse 1

old Confucius quote that I have not confirmed. It is certainly true with our faith. The more we learn the more the mystery and the higher our thirst becomes. That may be the best part of it all!

**Thought for Today**: Today let us recognize the opportunity to grow in the spirit. Let us recognize we are in our infancy and have room for exciting growth!

**Prayer for Today**: Heavenly Father, today we give thanks for your presence in our lives and the peace brought to us through our faith. We will face challenges today as we go forth with the knowledge that you will be with us. Amen

# Capacity To Love

Are we made in His image? Are we the children of God? When we are trudging along through life it is often hard to think of ourselves like either of those. First we are taught to be humble so if I am in God's image or God-like, am I being arrogant? That's a challenge. To be a child of God seems more acceptable to me, at least it cannot be interpreted as me claiming holiness. To me these are conundrums and part of the mystery.

So here is where I *know* we are like *God*. When my first child was born it amazed me how much love I felt in my heart. She, Karen, meant more to me than anything I had ever experienced. It was unbelievably good.

When my wife was pregnant with my second child I was anxious. It was impossible for me to believe that I could feel the same way. My fear was that there would never be enough love in my heart; at least certainly not to the same extreme!

> **See** what great love the Father has lavished on us, that we should be called children of God! And that is what we are!
> —1 John 3, verse 1

Guess what, there was plenty there; and for the third and the fourth child, the first grandchild and through the ninth grandchild. Back to the two questions—the answer is yes. We are told of God's never ending capacity to love and in that sense we have the same capacity.

The word is "Love your neighbor as yourself" and we have the God-given capacity to do it!

**Thought for Today:** Today let us recognize our capacity to love, care and respect everyone we contact and meet.

**Prayer for Today:** Dear Lord, today we have love in our hearts that you have shared with us. Today we pray that everyone can find this love and that we can take a step forward to world peace. Amen

# Our Fortress

Folks, there are certain beliefs that were instilled in me by my dad who was an engineer. His thoughts were reinforced by many of my instructors at engineering school. One of them was that engineers are not writers because we think in numbers and theorems. Everything in an engineer's life is parallel or perpendicular to something! They do not teach us in geometry that the prettiest distance between two points is a curved line!

Today's message is, do not believe that stuff. Good news friend and spiritual mentor of mine, George from Minneapolis, wrote this poem. He is an engineer. Remember the punch line.

**Thought for Today:** God is our rock, our fortress and our love.

**Prayer for Today:** Lord, we give thanks to people like George, the contributions they make to our lives by helping us to remember You. Amen

God is our refuge and
strength, an ever-present
help in trouble.
Therefore we will not fear,
though the earth give way
and the mountains fall into
the heart of the sea,
though its waters roar and
foam and the mountains
quake with their surging.
The LORD Almighty is with
us; the God of Jacob is our
fortress.
—Psalm 46,
verses 1–3 and 7

With the rising sun God starts our day
We check our schedules and are on our way
In our hearts we may feel a twinge or a prod
Be still, and know that I am God!
As we look to those with lives in doubt
Many homes are lost and families shut out
We bring them in with a prayer and a nod
Be still, and know that I am God!
The phony games of life we choose to play
We do not seek to know God's will for our day
Strange voices about Jesus may seem very odd
Be still, and know that I am God!
Now as I kneel down before the cross
Has life passed by leaving me at a loss?
Then Jesus' arms pick me up from the sod
Be still, and know that I am God!
—Psalm Forty-Six
by George Ewing

# Strongholds In Our Lives

Throughout our lives we have issues that dominate our thoughts and distract us from our spiritual selves. They may be either negative issues or even very exciting and positive issues. On the surface they may be very good for us. Distractions that have a strong hold on us, "strongholds," block us from being Godly or spiritual.

In our case, the Pickering family had some very successful years in our 40s and 50s. We led the good life. We actually owned and ran two businesses, traveled and raised four children. Those were also my triathlon years and both June and I kept very fit. (I just looked at some old photos and wondered how we ever looked like that!) There were a few people, including my pastor, who talked with me about possibly being OCD! That could never have been true, making money, having fun, great family trips, etc. and we did go to church. That is the American way! We were victims of a positive stronghold.

Also in those times there were some negatives. In the early '80s there was a

> For though we live in the world, we do not wage war as the world does.
> The weapons we fight with are not the weapons of the world.
> On the contrary, they have divine power to demolish strongholds.
> —2 Corinthians 10, verses 3 and 4

recession that caused a lot of business stress that dominated our thoughts for several years. Then there was a business lawsuit that dominated our lives and thoughts for a year. Another time when there were two kids in college our first business had issues that caused us to hedge our bets and start a second business.

We had both positive and negative events that had a strong hold on our lives and thoughts. Somehow, June and I developed a spiritual focus. We prayed a lot and meditated about the Lord's role in our lives. We made it through spiritual growth and so can you.

**Thought for Today:** Today let's recognize our strongholds and pray for release. We can take a break from them.

**Prayer for Today:** Dear Lord and Father, today is the day you made for us to enjoy. We are often distracted by life and ask your support so that our concentration on the spirit stays at the forefront. Today we pray that we will contribute to doing your will here on earth. Amen

# Strong Defenses

Today is confession time after yesterday's meditation. My message is on how to recognize strongholds; things that have a strong hold on our lives.

Yesterday I wrote that some were positive and some negative. I will mention some of the things that we did that should have been keys that some additional prayer was needed in our lives.

> A. We often spent more money on vacations than we gave to the Church.
> B. We would skip church when I needed a long training run for my next triathlon.
> C. Getting up on Sunday morning and working before church and then skipping church to finish.
> D. Not being active in faith organizations because we were way too busy!

**The** weapons we fight with are not the weapons of the world. On the contrary, they have divine power to demolish strongholds.
—2 Corinthians 10, verse 4

E. Lack of bible study in our lives.

OK, it is positive to stay fit; but maybe I could have run early or after church. Family vacations are expensive but the church needs support or it will not exist. Respect of the Sabbath leads to a more peaceful life; we figured that out relatively early. Being involved in support of the local church and attending a weekly study can keep you at peace and has many rewards.

In our lives, keeping things in perspective and having family and personal priorities leads to inner peace. They will help us keep the spirit in our lives.

**Thought for Today:** Today let's think about our distractions and meditate about them. Let us keep the spirit in all of our activities.

**Prayer for Today:** Dear Lord and Father, we pray for personal peace and that through our tranquility we may contribute to peace around us. Amen

# Idols

It is hard for me to relate to the ancient gods and idols like RA the Sun God; Bacchus the God of Wine and Revelry; Aphrodite Goddess of Beauty and Sexuality; and the lengthy list of others. Living in Minnesota it is understandable to appreciate the warmth of the sun and of a fire. Years ago I certainly appreciated Bacchus' influence on my youthful life and Aphrodite's contributions. Although they were often important influences, they were not God-like.

Growing up in Boston, Ted Williams of the Red Sox and Bill Russell of the Celtics come to mind because they were worshipped as heroes. My dad had a fantasy for the Olympic swimmer Johnny Weissmuller, so my brother Wayne and I became swimmers. As a national populace we tend to put a lot of emphasis on our sports heroes. However, it is wrong when that emphasis approaches worship status.

**Therefore**, fear the Lord and worship Him in sincerity and truth. Get rid of the gods your ancestors worshiped beyond the Euphrates River and in Egypt, and worship the Lord.
—Joshua 24, verse 14

We need to recognize where our real bread is buttered; who will never desert us; who will always be with us. We do not always have sunshine, wine and beauty; we do always have the Lord. We are blessed.

**Thought for Today:** For today we will read and hear about our heroes. The games of summer are approaching, basketball and hockey playoffs are beginning. For today when we hear or read of them, let's take a minute to review our commitment to the Lord and His never ending commitment to us.

**Prayer for Today:** Dear Lord today we give thanks that you are with us; to nurture, support and help us through our every need. We are glad you are listening and helping us every minute today. Amen

# Frozen Chosen

Listening to Beth Moore; recently she talked about evangelism, sharing our faith, and singing praises. Not only during Sunday services but all week long! That is evangelism, an invitational ministry, a welcoming format. In our small Methodist church we are far from being evangelists. The young families are too busy and we in the older generation seem too tired. The actuality of it is we are too conservative. A term that I like is that we are the "frozen chosen."

Twenty years ago we had a gospel group come to our church for what they thought would be a rousing concert. The leader did all he could to get a group of Methodists to stomp their feet and clap their hands. He had limited success. We enjoyed the music but foot stomping was not an apt description!

At a worship team meeting several years ago a group came to complain because people often applauded when our quartet or a soloist finished a piece. They requested that we put a notice in the announcements asking for no such show of pleasure or appreciation. As a team member I stated that if applause was outlawed they would have to deal with me standing upon a pew shouting "Halleluiah—Amen!" Our pastor said "Pass the motion. I want to see that!" I was blessed and the motion failed and we still applaud.

We make decisions every day as to how we will interact with others. So today we will decide whether we will be inviting Christians or members of the frozen chosen

**Thought for Today:** For today let's mention our faith or our church to show someone why we are who we are. Let's take our faith public at least for a day.

**Prayer for Today:** Dear Lord and Father, the world is blooming into spring and your wondrous work surrounds us. There is still strife and tensions that are un-Godly. Today we pray that we may contribute to peace and help relax the tensions around the world. Amen

> **Praise** the LORD.
> How good it is to sing praises to our God,
> how pleasant and fitting to praise him!
> …Sing to the LORD with grateful praise…
> Praise the Lord.
> —Psalm 147, verses 1 and 7

# Happy Landing

Perseverance is life. We need to persevere in many ways and the easiest way is through meditation, prayer, and having the faith that the Lord will bring us through our lives. We all hope for an easy life without illness or discomfort; always having a job; a life partner to share things with; and the list goes on. In other words, we want to be born to live happily ever after!

If we were, we would not build character or learn. As I write this in beautiful Minnesota, we are nearing the end of what has been a record-breaking winter. A year ago there was green grass, no ice and this year we are sitting on 15 inches of dirty snow with two storms scheduled for the next five days.

June, myself and our neighbors will get through it and when spring comes it will be later than usual and appreciated more. It is a good example of why trials are in our lives. They cause growth and appreciation of the good times. In the instance of our Minnesota weather, in

> **Blessed** is the one who perseveres under trial because, having stood the test, that person will receive the crown of life that the Lord has promised to those who love him.
> —James 1, verse 12

1974, our real estate agent talked about our beautiful summers and said they were worth the wait. Praise be to God, we need help this year!

There is a church that I drive by that posts a weekly slogan that describes it very well. I do not know the author but it said something like "Life is not about having a bumpy flight. It is about having a smooth landing!" We need to keep our faith to persevere on our bumpy ride. The best part will be the landing!

**Thought for Today:** Today will be the first day of the rest of our lives. Let us be spiritual and use it well.

**Prayer for Today:** Dear Father, we are experiencing a very bumpy ride. We have concerns about money, pollution, violence, and more. Today we give thanks for having the spirit and will to get through it all so that we may experience the landing.

# Skin Deep

In New England growing up on the north shore of Boston, there was a lot of what my mom called "old money." She used to say that if you were interacting with a member of a family with it, you would never know it. They would not be overdressed or act superior in any way. She was exactly correct, they did not. They spent a fortune on training on how to speak, dress and behave so as not to stand out in a crowd.

My best friend in high school and through my early years represented an old money family and his dad was one of my mentors and role models. Old Bert was always around to give me advice and unknowingly helped me throughout my life. It was Bert that said things like "The harder you work before you are thirty the better your life will be after thirty." "No matter how hard it may be, always be honest and you will win the battle." Bert was always dressed neat rather than gaudy, kept lean and fit. He was a great example.

Bert also was the first person I ever knew that mentioned bible study. He was willing to speak the Lord's word and incorporated

> **So** we do not focus on what is seen, but on what is unseen; for what is seen is temporary, but what is unseen is eternal.
> —2 Corinthians 4, verse 8

it into his life. Bert's beauty went deeper than skin deep. He was also a spiritual man, perhaps the first that I had ever really noticed. He took Sunday School stuff and incorporated it into his personal and business life. His beauty was not only skin deep.

We do worry about how we appear and we need a look that fits and is self-satisfying. We also need to extend our beauty deeper, into our hearts through prayer and meditation. As Christians our beauty is not skin deep.

**Thought for Today**: Today let's look in that mirror and make sure that we meet society's specifications for being neat and trim. Let's dress for what we will do to fit and function. Then, by all means, let us take a few moments to meditate, pray and prepare our souls for a day of true beauty.

**Prayer for Today**: Dear Lord and Father, today we thank you for our wonderful lives and the opportunity to represent you and your ways. We pray that we can contribute to doing your loving will here on earth. Amen

# Endurance

"Endure to the end." I am not sure what that means because to me there is no end! June and I have spent time in twelve step programs and as Stephen Ministers working with people with life issues. Some fight chemical demons, some mental issues and others with social issues. Often we dealt with anger, depression and the "why me" syndrome. Asking the question "What did I do to deserve this?" is of no use to the recovery process. Dealing with the steps of growth to become happy and satisfied citizens is what matters.

We are all here in a very interesting lifetime and do not know where it leads us. That is the wondrous mystery. What we do know is that while we are here on earth, we will leave a mark, a legacy.

We recently attended an eightieth birthday party of a lady in our church. She is an extremely upbeat and positive force in her life, our church, and as matriarch of her family. There were three generations of her family in attendance. The love, closeness and happiness within the family was flowing and glowing for all of us to see. Their love will someday become their memories, her legacy.

> **But** the one who endures to the end will be saved.
> —Matthew 24, verse 13

We Christians are told on Sunday and celebrate on Easter that there is no end; a mystery to others. What is not a mystery is that we will leave our mark in the memories of others; we will leave a positive legacy through our faith spirit and love of Christ.

**Thought for Today**: For today let us go out and live our Christian lives full of enthusiasm and joy. Let us live like there is no end!

**Prayer for Today**: Heavenly Father, today we give thanks for our wondrous lives and the many gifts that you have given us. We especially thank you for the opportunity through Christ to help accomplish your will here on earth through our faith by sharing with others. Amen

# Relationships

Relationships are similar to spirituality in the sense that when they are growing they move toward a goal of perfection. We cannot ever reach perfection in our spirit because we cannot be God. In relationships we also cannot become perfect, but we can approach perfection.

Once at a marriage seminar the instructor was talking about the expectations of a wedding day and the futility of thinking that one spouse could impart change on the other. He pointed out that many marriages fail because "the other" did not adjust! You see, a person changing to fit is seldom accomplished.

Another piece he addressed was who walked into the church and who walked out on a wedding day. His point was that two lovers went in and in marriage different expectations were set. As he stated it, the wife's model for a husband is her dad; the husband's model for a wife is his mother. Wow, if something doesn't change this will never work!

> **My** dear brothers and sisters, take note of this: Everyone should be quick to listen, slow to speak and slow to become angry, because human anger does not produce the righteousness that God desires.
> —James 1, verses 19 and 20

June and I talked about this recently; without change the growth in marriage will not occur; expecting one to change to fit will not work. We concluded that like spirituality, both persons in a relationship need to stay the same but the couple needs to grow together. A good analogy is the two must evolve together into something new, they need to polish their edges and fit together in a new mold.

That sounds simple, let's pray that it is.

**Thought for Today:** Today let us look at our relationship with others; spouses, friends, fellow employees, siblings, and recognize our expectations. Let us understand how we can grow to make them better.

**Prayer for Today:** Dear Lord, we give thanks for your guidance and the chance to grow in our faith. We appreciate that you are with us. Amen

# Pride And Humility

My mom used to use some interesting terms and expressions when describing humanity. One of her favorites was "foolhardy" when someone did something out of line. Another was that "It is better to be silent and be thought a fool that to speak out and remove all doubt." Somehow, when we are proud in the context of today's text, we are not paying attention. When we kid ourselves with false pride, it helps us grow to have an appreciation for the realities of life.

We are often overconfident. It seems that the younger we are the more likely we are to suffer from "cockiness." Somehow that is God's way of teaching us. We constantly have to monitor our pride and confidence. The elders of society have knowledge and experience but are not always correct. Technology and society are changing faster than fifty years ago. Therefore many of the rules of life have changed.

In our spiritual lives, the rules have not and will not change. We need to take

> **Before** his downfall a man's heart is proud, but humility comes before honor.
> —Proverbs 18, verse 12

inventory on our pride and be real. The ethics, love and traditions taught to us by Christ will endure regardless of technology changes and cash flows.

We need to hold up our values to serve the Lord in an ever-changing world.

**Thought for Today**: Every day is the first day of the rest of our lives. The mistakes and experiences of our past are nothing more than learning experiences and enable us to move forward with confidence. Today let us focus on being humble and dealing with the realities of our individual worlds.

**Prayer for Today**: Heavenly Father, today we give thanks for the lessons we have learned and the great loves that we have. Through all that Jesus taught us and what we learned from the past, thank you for putting it before us. Amen

# Joy

Is there joy in our lives? Let us face it, most of us have a lot more joy (positives) than negatives. Our family, friends and associates are sources of great joy. It is spring, the grass is green; the trees are budding with leaves and spring flowers are showing their colors. It is easy to see this kind of joy.

Many people today have a problem seeing the joys in their lives. Several of my good friends have recently lost their jobs and another has a fatal illness. There are always two sides to our lives. When we are down, it is important to remember the Lord and his place in our lives. As Paul said to the Romans (15, verse 13), "May the God of hope fill you with all joy and peace as you trust in him, so that you may overflow with hope by the power of the Holy Spirit."

Yes, in our lives there are physical and emotional joys. Our surroundings and life styles generate them. The real joy, however, comes through our Christian beliefs. It is this belief that gives us the "strength" and "shield" mentioned in Psalm 28, verse 7.

**The** Lord is my strength and my shield. My heart trusts in him and I am helped. My heart leaps for joy and I will give thanks to him in song.
—Psalm 28, verse 7

**Thought for Today:** Let us keep joy at the forefront of our thoughts. When challenged with life, let's use our shield—the Lord.

**Prayer for Today:** Heavenly Father, many of our friends are fighting battles. Illness, unemployment, unwanted career changes and many others. We pray for them to understand your strength and love. We pray that they may find the joy that is only available through trust in you. Amen

# Happiness

Recently, my granddaughter was picked up at 6pm and taken through McDonald's for a Happy Meal on the way to buy a Mother's Day gift for Mom. How many of us rush our way to the drive-through, curse the length of the line and the fact that we would be held up ten minutes waiting for lunch? I certainly have done that.

What is the hustle and bustle all about? The pursuit of "things" and "stuff?" We are all working our hearts out; many have too little time to look at their lives and what really matters. Yes, I realize that it is easier at my age (71, as of this writing) to say slow down and smell the roses, but I pray that you do.

**A** man can do nothing better than to eat and drink and find satisfaction in his work. This too, I see, is from the hand of God, for without him, who can eat or find enjoyment. To the man who pleases him, God gives wisdom, power and happiness, but to the sinner he gives the task of gathering and storing up wealth...
—Ecclesiastes 2, verses 24–26

**Thought for Today**: Today, let us look at our pursuits and find the time to meditate and understand where God fits into the puzzles that are our lives. Let us be sure that our puzzle does not have a piece missing.

**Prayer for Today**: Dear Lord, please help me locate what you want from me today. There are many options in my life: The celebration of a "Hallmark Holiday," the celebration of my Christian Family, a round of golf, opening of fishing and many others. Somehow help me keep you in this puzzle so that there are no pieces missing. With love for you and Jesus. Amen

# Ministers

My pastor says that we are all ministers in some way. Is that true? I believe that it is a fact that most of us want to keep under our hats. Perhaps the term closet minister applies to many of us. We help, we lead by example, we attend services to learn more and we silently minister to those around us. Often, we do not know when we are leading.

> **You** are the light of the world. A city on a hill cannot be hidden. Neither do people light a lamp and put it under a bowl. Instead they put it on its stand, and it gives light to everyone in the house. In the same way, let your light shine before men, that they may see your good deeds and praise your Father in heaven.
> —Matthew 5, verses 14–16

other. My mind crossed over and today I think that couple, without intent, set an example for older couples. They were ministers.

"In the same way, let your light shine before men, that they may see your good deeds...."

**Thought for Today**: Let us be thankful for those around us. Be at peace and demonstrate our passion and love to others. Spring flowers have burst into color; warm weather makes us feel great, so let's utilize our spring spirit to demonstrate our faith.

In any Sunday congregation there are takers and givers. Silent ministries occur in many ways. Twenty-odd years ago, a young single couple was acting in a very special way; holding hands, whispering in each other's ears and an occasional peck on the cheek. My personal thoughts were that they were inappropriate. The pastor announced their pending wedding during that service.

After the service, a good friend of mine mentioned how neat he thought they were and that he wished he and his wife still had that level of enthusiasm for each

**Prayer for Today**: Heavenly Father, you have blessed us with many friends. We are surrounded and can not avoid them. At work, on the streets and at home we are blessed. Today we want to pray for them all and especially pray that they recognize the beauty of Christian friendship. Amen

# Footprints

The overwhelming support that we have as people of faith is certainly wonderful and one of the greatest advantages of Christianity. Often, as an A-type personality, I awake before June and go jogging (now walking!) at sunrise, "...when the dew is still on the roses...." The sound of mourning doves and early robins is the dominant sound rather than traffic or other social activity related noise. Often I find myself humming "In the Garden."

Another time when it comes to mind is before a tough meeting or event. Whether a business meeting, neighborhood meeting or a hospital visit, it is great to know that you are never alone if you let Him join you.

Many of you often see me with a lapel pin that is a pair of feet. They are from "Foot prints in the sand." They are to invite conversation regarding the

I come to the garden alone, while the dew is still on the roses, and the voice I hear falling on my ear,
the son of God discloses.
and he walks with me,
and he talks with me,
and he tells me I am his own, and the joy we share as we tarry there,
none other has ever known.
—C. Austin Miles, *In the Garden*, Methodist Hymnal No. 314

concept of walking with Christ every day. It us always an interesting conversation.

We are blessed.

**Thought for Today**: Let us simply remember that we are never alone. Let us enjoy His presence as we walk through our lives.

**Prayer for Today**: Heavenly Father, we are certainly glad that you are here for support. Often the world around us is confusing and it is difficult to understand your wishes. However, we give thanks for the role that you play in our everyday lives and the help you give you give our friends and families. Amen

# Young At Heart

Throughout our lifetimes, June and I have met people that seem at peace, people that have never quite joined the "rat race" of life, people that had something that we were looking for.

**Be** happy, young person, while you are young, and let your heart give you joy in the days of your youth. Follow the ways of your heart...
—Ecclesiastes 11, verse 9

**Thought for Today:** Today let us avoid the rat race by praying for serenity and doing what we need to obtain peace.

**Prayer for Today:** Dear Lord we give you thanks for the opportunities you have placed before us. Today we pray for serenity and peace in our lives and the opportunity to help the cause of peace in our community. Amen

The interesting fact was that they crossed all socioeconomic boundaries. The common thread always seemed to be their faith. They always believed that things would work out.

The strong message here is that the things that bring peace, serenity and happiness to our lives are found in our spiritual growth and it will be found in yours.

# Faith And Forgiveness

Faith seems to be a constant challenge to us. Yes, sometimes we need to understand where God is in our lives. We can doubt that He is with us; we challenge his input and even knowingly violate His rules and submit to temptation. Does this make us bad people?

The answer is a resounding *no*. As we look back at our lives we often see a trail of mistakes, moments or events that we would like to edit or replay. Surely we know that reliving life is not an option. But, feeling guilty or bad about these things can cause a faith crises or low self image and have a negative effect on our future. This is true at any age.

At a bible study this week we talked about letting go of past indiscretions. Others forgave us long ago and somehow as adults we seem to hold on to past errors.

When we learn to forgive others, we find it easier to accept the forgiveness we receive from God.

**Consider** it pure joy, my brothers, whenever you face trials of many kinds, because you know that the testing of your faith develops perseverance. Perseverance must finish its work so that you may be mature and complete, not lacking anything. If any of you lacks wisdom, he should ask God, who gives generously to all without finding fault, and it will be given to him.
—James 1, verses 2–4

**Thought for Today:**
When we are very busy, it is difficult to feel God's presence in our lives. Today, let us all try to take time to understand and appreciate His contributions.

**Prayer for Today:**
Dear Lord and Father, today we give thanks for the knowledge that we are forgiven through the grace given us through Jesus. We pray that somehow we can find a way to forgive ourselves for our own sins. Amen

# Spring

This is a glorious time of the year. The northern hemisphere goes into the transition to summer. It is a time when the resolutions from a new year are long since successful or forgotten. A time of vacation planning, garden planting and the anticipation of the beauty of the warm season. A time of hope led by the visible evidence of God's presence around us.

This is a time for reflection and review of our dark side. A review of the negative forces in our lives. This is spring and we need to recover the "...hidden promise..." in our personal lives "... that God alone can see." Through our faith and belief, our Lord will share with us the pleasures of life.

> **In** the bulb there is a flower, in the seed an apple tree; in co-coons a hidden promise: butterflies will soon be free!
> In the cold and snow of Winter there's a Spring that waits to be, unrevealed until its season, something God alone can see.
> —Natalie Sleeth, *Hymn of Promise,* Verse 1, 1986

**Thought for Today**: It is spring. Let us take special notice of it's wonders. Smell the flowers and enjoy the showers. Let us share these positive feelings with others and encourage positive feelings around us.

**Prayer for Today**: Heavenly Father we pray for an end to senseless killing and the guidance to understand this violent world that surrounds us. There seems to be a dominant hate factor that is not created by Godly forces. There needs to be more prayer and less negative logic. We pray that the world's religions may see You as one God. We pray that somehow through your divine guidance, killing, hate and violence may come to an end. Amen

# Promise

A recently retired pastor listed this as one of his favorite hymns. It is easy to see why. After all, we put our lives in God's hands, he knows and loves us, and we know that through our faith we have a future.

This second verse talks about the times when life is too quiet—when we need to talk. It talks about the dark times and assures us that there will be light; better times. It mentions the past, that we are not always proud of, will become a bright future through Him. It points out that we do not know or predict what He has in store for us.

A case in point is a friend and "Good News" recipient who called me a few months ago. He had been with his company for 18 years and was undergoing the job stress that many of us experience in today's world. I saw him this week and his comments were that he was now OK. Management, led by another "Good News" recipient,

> **There's** a song in every silence, seeking word and melody; there's a dawn in every darkness, bringing hope to you and me.
> From the past will come the future; what it holds a mystery, unrevealed until its season, something God alone can see.
> —Natalie Sleeth, *Hymn of Promise*, Verse 2, 1986

solved his problems. His comment was that in 18 years, it was the first time that anyone in management told him he was wanted and that they wanted him to be happy. What a concept for a company today!! Ask yourself if God was at work here.

**Thought for Today:** Some days are brighter than others. The symbol of a gray or bright day is an easy one to relate to. Our lives are like that. Through our faith, we understand that there will be brighter days following the dark ones. Let us focus on the bright times.

**Prayer for Today:** Heavenly Father, throughout the world there are many dark areas. The Middle East is in turmoil over social and religious differences. There are epidemics in on the African continent. There are century-old tribal wars on the European peninsula. Today we pray for the understanding that you are with us through dark times and that we can appreciate the light at the end of the tunnel. Amen

# Following the Way

Society does not fit the biblical model that we are taught and often desire. Truth, honesty, integrity, love and many other virtues seem rare at times. Often in our human desire to "fit," we join in and need correction. It is normal to err and join in. It is also forgivable.

In a discussion last week in a business environment, we were discussing several long term successful business men. We were comparing the successful men with some that were sinking fast or already out of business. It seems that the ones that have long term success may have read Paul's message to the Romans. Fairness was their trademark and perpetual growth seemed to be a trait. They were not always right, but always seemed to be growing and striving for excellence.

**Therefore**, I urge you, brothers, in view of God's mercy, to offer your bodies as living sacrifices, holy and pleasing to God—this is your spiritual act of worship. Do not conform any longer to the pattern of this world, but be transformed by the renewing of your mind. Then you will be able to test and approve what God's will is...
Do not think of yourself more highly than you ought, but rather think of yourself with sober judgment, in accordance with the measure of faith God has given you.
—Romans 12, verses 1–4

They earned the respect and trust of those around them. They were not "sharks" but win-win business men. Somehow, they incorporated their Christian beliefs into the tough world of doing business. That is truly doing God's will.

**Thought for Today**: Today we will all have a chance to stand up and be counted. We will have opportunities to demonstrate our faith in circumstances where we would not normally do so. Let us demonstrate that we are considerate and Godly in our daily activities.

**Prayer for Today**: Dear Lord, the world we live in is distracting and volatile. We all have too much to do, too many commitments, and too many fears. Throughout all of this we pray for peace. Peace in our own lives, peace around the world, and an end to hate and prejudice. We pray that we end anger and hate in ourselves and can demonstrate the value of peace to others through our example. Amen

# Letting Go

Recently I was talking to a group of 60ish guys about a pending class reunion. The subject broke down to the many things we did in our youth that we would not consider doing today. The events we talked about were items on our conscience, things we were not proud of doing. They were the acts of youth and part of growing up. Each helped develop the person that we are today. None of the events made us a bad person, however, at the time there were people (neighbors, school authorities, mom or dad, friends, etc.) that did not appreciate our behavior. These indiscretions and memories are perseverance finishing its work "…so that you may be mature and complete, not lacking anything."

At a bible study this week we talked about letting go of past indiscretions. Others forgave us long ago and somehow as adults we seem to hold on to past errors. As we work through our faults, we learn that life goes on. God eventually works his miracles in our lives. When we lack the wisdom he comes through for us.

> **Bear** with each other and forgive whatever grievances you may have against one another. Forgive as the Lord forgave you.
> —Colossians 3, verse 13

**Thought for Today:** When we are very busy, it is difficult to feel God's presence in our lives. Today, let us all try to take time to understand and appreciate His contributions.

**Prayer for Today:** Heavenly Father, we thank you today because we are not what we were. We have sinned along the way and are grateful of the grace and forgiveness we receive through Christ. Amen

# Stewardship 1

Money is a tough subject to grasp in today's life. How do we fit the pursuit of money and a good life into our Christian values. As a church finance chair I need to comment about the pursuit of wealth.

Surely, the competition for wealth is a God-given right and necessity that goes back to the beginning of time. The operating style in which we pursue wealth and what we do with our wealth can be totally compatible with God's will. Working with others, serving others, meeting other's needs generates money and wealth. What we do with that money and wealth makes the difference. Do we pursue wealth in a manner that helps society, or do we take advantage of others to obtain wealth? That is always a gray area that we must have clear in our own minds. If, in your heart, you are competing in this society with the Lord first in your mind, you are on the right track.

> **Honor** the Lord with your wealth, with the first fruits of all your crops; then your barns will be filled to overflowing, your vats will brim over with new wine.
> —Proverbs 3, verses 9–10

**Thought for Today:** As we go through the day, let us ask if we are contributors to society and others. Let's also think about how much of our efforts and time we contribute to God's work.

**Prayer for Today:** Heavenly Father, please help me understand this complex life we live. Within our society it seems that people that give are happy and at peace. The Bible says give it all away and trust in the Lord while our social system seems to demand accruing wealth. I pray that I can understand your place and keep you in the forefront of my heart. Amen

# Stewardship 2

In follow-up to yesterday, I want to mention two examples. First is a fellow I represented for 30 years. He built a company that became the largest of it's kind in the world. He made tens of millions of dollars. In doing so, he created wealth in the families of his employees, jobs for thousands of people around the world and in recent years has gifted millions of dollars to schools for technical education facilities. He has made the Lord smile.

Another example on a grand scale was Charles M. Schultz of Snoopy fame. Throughout his life, he brought pleasure to millions. In his community, he contributed generously, also to the benefit of millions. He used his God-given vision and talent to help the world and was rewarded with his "barns overflowing."

> **Honor** the Lord with your wealth, with the first fruits of all your crops; then your barns will be filled to overflowing, your vats will brim over with new wine.
> —Proverbs 3, verses 9–10

In summary, it is not bad to pursue wealth and it is a necessity. Pursuing wealth by contributing to society and the art of giving back first, rather than last, makes the difference.

**Thought for Today:**
As we go through the day, let us ask if we are contributors to society and others. Let's also think about how much of our efforts and time we contribute to God's work.

**Prayer for Today:** Heavenly Father, please help me understand this complex life we live. Within our society it seems that people that give are happy and at peace. The Bible says give it all away and trust in the Lord while our social system seems to demand accruing wealth. I pray that I can understand your place and keep you in the forefront of my heart. Amen

# Temptations?

Oh yeah, here we go again on being good, not succumbing to temptation. We sure get tired of that don't we? In twelve step programs there is a lot of talk about the goal of spiritual growth rather than spiritual perfection. I guess that means we will never be perfect. I am OK with that.

This proverb goes on and on about being good by mentioning "…guard your heart, your lips, look straight ahead etc." I did not print it all because *we all know that!*

I ask but do not want to know your specific temptations and I have no intent on sharing mine. The bad news is we all have them. The good news is that the Lord is with us. Purity, ethics, commitments and standards begin in our hearts.

> For where your treasure is,
> there your heart will be also.
> —Mathew 6, verse 21

> **Above** all else, guard your heart, for everything you do flows from it.
> —Proverbs 4, verse 23

**Thought for Today:** Each day we need to be the best that we can be. Today we will make choices. Let us make them from our heart— in purity with ethics, commitments and high standards. WWJD!

**Prayer for Today:** Today we give thanks for your presence in our lives and the way that you guide us. Today we pray that we will rise above our temptations and represent your will here on earth. Amen

# Maturity

The piece of twelve step programs that I like best is the part where it is explained that our goal is spiritual growth rather than spiritual perfection. That lets us off the hook regarding being perfect which we cannot attain. It removes a lot of guilt!

Yes we always need to grow in spirit, we need to work on it daily and we need to measure our progress. The question we have is what do we measure ourselves against? Recently I read that I must measure against "…nothing less than the character of Christ."

Hmmm. That is a problem because I cannot attain perfection! That does not diminish the dream of being Christ-like. So what seems to be a conundrum is actually a gift. When we are faced with options and choices we need to ask, What would Jesus Do? Then we need to do it to insure our growth.

> **Until** we all reach unity in the faith and in the knowledge of the Son of God and become mature, attaining to the whole measure of the fullness of Christ.
> —Ephesians 4, verse 13

**Thought for Today:** Today let's do things the way Jesus would by being loving and forgiving in all of our activities.

**Prayer for Today:** Dear Lord we are blessed with your presence, Today we pray for guidance and the ability to be more like Jesus; the ability to do your will. Amen

# Finishing Again

In the spring my thoughts gravitate toward the good old days when my friends and I trained 10–14 hours a week for endurance events. The camaraderie of the group, the support offered by the group when one of us was having a bad day, and the feeling of spirituality in the early mornings as we traveled on our way was priceless. Last year on June's and my 40th anniversary, many of these people came and the warm feelings were instantly present. There was an interesting bond.

As an unranked runner but former elite masters swimmer and Triathlete, there were many times that finishing a running event near the bottom of the pack was more rewarding to me than a swimming or triathlon trophy. A trophy is a nice memento, but over time becomes an unimportant dust collector. As an elite you are supposed to be near the top, but that really is not what it is about.

In the early '80s my friend Billy and I ran a half marathon. He finished a good half hour ahead of me and felt great. I was not ready and thought I was going to die out there. The following year, Billy was again a half hour ahead of me but I met my personal goals and expectations. I fondly remember that day and have that finishing picture on

> **It** is better for you to finish now what you began last year. You were the first, not only to act, but also to be willing to act. On with it then and finish the job.
> —2 Corinthians 8, verses 10–11

my office wall. It reminds me that being at the bottom of the pack is not a bad thing when you are at the top of your game. The goal is personal, to be the best *you* can be. Neither of us won that event or our age group. Both of us were proud winners because we finished. Life is like that—when we finish what we start, we win.

**Thought for Today**: It is spring, a time of renewal. God brings us flowers, green grass and warm temperatures. It is easy to be busy enjoying it all and put a few serious issues on that famous "back burner." Today let us identify what we need to finish; who we need to help; who needs our prayers; who could use a visit. Let us complete the tasks that the Lord has put before us.

**Prayer for Today**: Heavenly Father, we need your guidance on how to use your love to succeed. In our cities, our neighborhoods and the world we pray that we can find a way to contribute so that your love will somehow "finish" the race for peace and security. Amen

# Play Christ's Way

We are faced with decisions every day regarding our relationships with others. Sometimes there is aggressive behavior that needs to be dealt with. In business there is a competition to get to the top; in school, the head of the class; in sports to be number one, etc. It is the way it is.

**Help** us accept each other as Christ accepted us; teach us as sister, brother, each person to embrace; Be present, Lord, among us, and bring us to believe we are ourselves accepted and meant to love and live."
—Fred Kaan, *Help Us Accept Each Other,* UMC Hymnal, number 560, 1974

When growing up I was taught that winning is not everything, it was how you played the game that mattered. In the '70s I attended a business management seminar sponsored by Green Bay coach Vince Lombardi. The emphasis was on detail, being service oriented, and planning ahead. Of course, every day his famous quote was stated quite clearly. "Winning isn't everything, it's the only thing."

Over the years the operating principals that were learned at that seminar have made my life very successful. However, that last quote bothered me then and now. Often I have seen people climb over others in an attempt to get ahead. In almost every case they fail either financially or personally. People that play by the old rule always do better.

To play by the old rule takes faith in yourself and God as well as a love and caring for people. Good News recipients are a varied lot from all walks of life and socioeconomic backgrounds. Two are very successful Christian CEOs and how their companies behave matters to them. Christian ethics take great faith. No matter where or who we are, fairness and love of others is the real key to success.

Then how do we deal with the aggressive ones? …the inconsiderate neighbor? …the cut-throat business man? …the ones that bend rules? John quotes Jesus in chapter 15, verse 17, "This is my command, Love each other." We need to pray for and love our competitors in life.

**Thought for Today:** Let us practice unconditional love in our lives. If confronted with opportunistic or aggressive behavior, let us find a way to get through the situation in a positive and loving way.

**Prayer for Today:** Dear Lord, let me reach out to people. Help me understand them and care about them. We pray that through our faith in your ways we can improve our selves and our surrounding world. Amen

# The Navigator

Often when we wake up in the morning we do not have a plan. Sometimes we are energized and happy, other times we are stressed and depressed. Many times we need to adjust our thoughts to the spiritual side of the balance. We need to open the windows to our mind and allow God's fresh breeze to liberate us when we are down. This morning I am waiting for the breeze.

When waiting for the breeze, there seems to be a need. In my case that need is often met with strong coffee, sugar and perhaps some Ibuprofen. That is not the best solution. It has a physical and temporary lift, but the need is better met spiritually.

This morning the need was met through prayer. The breeze that arrived came through Isaiah 58, verse 11. Sometimes we forget what we need. We forget that God is with us; we leave Him in the back seat rather than use Him as navigator for the day.

> **The** LORD will guide you always; he will satisfy your needs in a sun-scorched land and will strengthen your frame. You will be like a well-watered garden, like a spring whose waters never fail.
> —Isaiah 58, verse 11

As navigator He will take us to places that we would not have gone on our own.

**Thought for Today**: Today there will be stress, problematic decisions and times of anguish. We need to focus and remember that "God is with us" and we need to let Him lead. We need to pray over the tough decisions and focus on following His will.

**Prayer for Today**: Heavenly Father, we pray for your guidance. We need to understand our immediate world and area of control and also understand the happenings around the global World. Neither seems very well organized today. We pray that we can find a way to contribute through You to help your will prevail in tough situations. Amen

# Impact Play

The Fellowship of Christian Athletes sends out a daily meditation that tends to be sports based. It often comes from a member and is relative to an event that I watched. I thoroughly enjoy hearing from them as they share their glory with the Lord. Two of my favorite members played or grew up here in Minnesota, former Viking Chris Carter and pro golfer Tom Lehman. In fact Tom and Gerhard Langer used to lead bible studies when they were on the PGA tour together. Faith is something that seems to be swept under the rug in sports.

Yesterday I received this passage in what they call "Impact Play." I like the name because the function of a daily reading is to have an effect on your life, an impact. Psalm 84 did that yesterday—I still feel guilty!

As I was reading my email, there was an urgent request for someone to usher at two special services this week. I had just replied that I did not care to participate.

> **Better** is one day in your courts than a thousand elsewhere; I would rather be a doorkeeper in the house of my God than dwell in the tents of the wicked.
> —Psalm 84, verse 10

The next email was the "Impact Play" with the wording "…I would rather be a doorkeeper in the house of my God than dwell in the tents of the wicked." Oops, does that mean that I should change my mind? Is there a message here somewhere?

I can't find it to refer to today, but I seem to remember Tom Lehman saying that when he keeps the Lord in his life, good things seem to happen. He also said that it was hard to do when lining up a fourth putt! My belief is that by starting the day with a meditation, it puts the Lord closer to the forefront of your mind and makes the day better. He is with us either way but more visible when we are paying attention.

**Thought for Today:** Let's simply pay attention to the Lord's involvement in our life today!

**Prayer for Today:** Dear Lord and Father, today we give thanks for the wonderful lives that you give us. We pray for peace, friendship and the ability to contribute to your will here on earth. Amen

# Run For the Prize

Since the late 1980s we have been involved in two running races. It is something that June and I have done because we feel that we are contributing to society in some way. We also enjoy it because of the many people that we have met and get to support or are involved with. The race the last Saturday in April this year was no different. The winners of the money were two professionals from Ethiopia. They were special people with a special gift, they run *fast*. The story of the race is not about them.

**Do** you not know that in a race all the runners run, but only one gets the prize? Run in such a way as to get the prize. Everyone who competes in the games goes into strict training.
They do it to get a crown that will not last; but we do it to get a crown that will last forever.
Therefore I do not run like a man running aimlessly; I do not fight like a man beating the air.
No, I beat my body and make it my slave so that after I have preached to others, I myself will not be disqualified for the prize.
—1 Corinthians, verses 24–28

Each year the race announcer announces as many finishers as possible as they approach the finish line. It gives people a positive feeling to hear their name. Last year the announcer announced the name of a lady from church. When I caught up to say hello, she was with her husband. They had spent the morning walking and jogging with 4,000 others. She describes the time spent training with her husband as almost spiritual because they are alone together with a single common goal, without distractions!

This year a friend and Good News recipient, Don, came with his son. A parent and child running a race together for the first time is a very special event. Don told me afterward how proud Andrew was after the race. I could tell from the tone in Don's voice that the pride was not all Andrew's.

The professionals also can generate some interesting stories. This year a skinny little guy from Iowa, Nick, came to run against the field of Kenyon, Ethiopian and Romanian pros. He had just decided that he would try to become a professional runner. His friends from a local college and his parents drove five hours from Iowa to see him run and to support him. None of us on staff had very high hopes for Nick; the competition looked awesome. To the surprise of most of us, Nick passed the second place Kenyon on a bridge ramp a mile from the finish and chased the leader across the line. His mom and dad were the proudest people in the crowd.

**Thought for Today:** Today we will be running through our lives. The normal schedule will keep us busy. Many of us will fall short of the goal. Many of us will accomplish our goal. All of us will be winners if we follow the rules. Let us compete in our lives as models of winners, as people of faith.

**Prayer for Today:** Heavenly Father, today life will again be flying by. Things move very fast in today's world. It is easy to forget principles when under pressure. We pray for the guidance and judgment to follow your will in our daily activities. We pray that we lead by example and make those around us glad we were with them. Amen

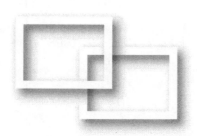

# Looking Forward

Keeping your eye on the prize, the good life and focusing on the positive events and memories is life's biggest challenge. A long term marriage, career or presence in any group (specifically a church family) is in my mind, the toughest challenge placed before us by the Lord. However, to do what He asks is to stick it out, focus on the positive experiences and learn from the negatives.

Recently three close families that are friends of mine have experienced marital stress after over twenty years. There are always marriage dissolutions in the paper after long standing relationships; often empty nesters. In any long term relationship, it is easy to remember bad times and save them as resentments and when we reach a certain level of resentments; we forget to "… press on toward the goal to win the prize...."

**Not** that I have already obtained all this, or have already been made perfect, but I press on to take hold of that for which Christ Jesus took hold of me. Brothers, I do not consider myself yet to have taken hold of it. But one thing I do: Forgetting what is behind and straining toward what is ahead, I press on toward the goal to win the prize for which God has called me…
—Philippians 3, verses 12–14

I want to share with you that two of the above families actually split up for a while. They went to work and struggled with their relationships, worked on their resentments and over six to twelve months have reunited and are rediscovering their relationships. Observing this process is a blessing for me because when they refocus on the positive memories and look toward the prize, they grow closer and more grateful of each other—that is love.

**Thought for Today**: Today let us become more open in our relationships—with our significant others, family and friends. Let us look at our resentments, possibly share them and resolve them so that we may "… press on toward the goal to win the prize... for which God has called me…."

**Prayer for Today**: Dear Lord, today we pray for courage, the courage to be open and honest in our daily lives and our relationships. We pray that we may become closer so that we may press on toward the prize together. Amen

# Talking Faith

When Paul wrote Second Timothy he was concerned about the welfare of the church during a time of persecution. He was asking Timothy to guard the gospel. So what does that have to do with us in 2012 Christianity? Christianity is a part of the world's society. What is there to guard?

Well, how about guarding our own faith against the "Godless chatter" that surrounds us daily. We read it, hear it and sometimes participate in it. There are many examples of this in an election year. The candidates' negative campaigning with partial truths, facts taken out of context and drilling into their opponents' pasts certainly apply. We need to put their chatter in perspective and pray about it all.

In our personal lives it is also easy to become wrapped up in ungodly thoughts and chatter. Years ago I attended a very spiritual breakfast meeting every Friday. Over time it became a political talk time dealing with issues way out of our control. That is very natural.

> **Keep** reminding them of these things. Warn them before God against quarreling about words; it is of no value, and only ruins those who listen. Do your best to present yourself to God as one approved, a workman who does not need to be ashamed and who correctly handles the word of truth. Avoid godless chatter, because those who indulge in it will become more and more ungodly.
> —2 Timothy 2, verses 14–16

My daughter recently dropped out of a bible study that she had attended for several years. In her eyes it had evolved into a social support group rather than a study group. It did not fit for her any more. The group and she had grown in different directions. That is also very natural.

Those examples do not mean that those groups evolved into godless chatter. It simply demonstrates that the term is totally relative to each individual. It demonstrates the need for each of us to listen to others; to pay attention; to speak out and demonstrate our faith and thoughts. We need to work our faith into our daily lives and conversations.

**Thought for Today:** Today we will hear some Godless chatter. Let us recognize it, correct it when we can and keep it in perspective. Pray for those who promote and participate in it.

**Prayer for Today:** Heavenly Father, we give thanks to you for all the things that are reborn in the spring. Flowers, leaves, green grass all make us appreciate your world. We pray for the opportunity to enjoy and love each other. Amen

# Can't Get Away

There are unfortunate people around us that do not believe. They go through life assuming full control of their surroundings and do not need any help or support. My recently deceased brother was one of the unfortunates.

He was not churched and was uncomfortable discussing the possibility of spirituality with us. We differed in the way we felt but still loved and respected each other. He could not understand why June and I would go to church on a nice Sunday morning when we could be at the lake. That was the way it was.

In the last year, an interesting change occurred. He started counting his many blessings and recognized the role that God had played in his life. He talked about people and events and the role the Lord had played throughout his life. He developed a spirituality that surprised both June and me. Often he would give thanks and talked about the great memories given him by God. In the end, June and I observed that the Lord was with him.

> **The** Lord Almighty is with us; the God of Jacob is our fortress.
> —Psalm 46, verse 7

As believers, we understand that God is our sidekick, our supporter, our fortress. This was the first time June and I have observed that even the non believers cannot get away. God is with all of us, always.

**Thought for Today:** Today let us share our beliefs with someone who needs us; someone who may not believe. We may find they welcome us and the Lord into their lives.

**Prayer for Today:** Dear Lord and Father, we give you thanks for being with us always. We pray for those that do not believe so that they may find your gifts and love. Amen

# Respect

One characteristic that we all seem to want is respect. We earn respect through our interactions with other people. It is earned both with words and actions. Saying good things without commitment and follow-through does not earn it. Great actions with coarse words, sarcasm and hurtful methods also will not earn respect.

From my youth I remember two of my family's favorite expressions: "If you don't have something good to say, then say nothing," (don't be negative) and "It is better to be silent and be thought a fool rather than speak and remove all doubt." Most of us have violated these rules more than once!

We are all born with God's blessings and a high level of respect. If we are not satisfied with the respect we have in our present lives, we need to recognize that we have not earned it yet. The good news is that we can turn it around by living our lives the way our faith has taught us.

> **The** lips of the wise spread knowledge; not so the lips of fools.
> —Proverbs 15, verse 7

**Thought for Today:** Today let's focus on earning respect through our words. Let us search out the good things to say, avoid any put downs and remember that our faith teaches praise and love. Let us sing the praises of the Lord in our daily lives.

**Prayer for Today:** Heavenly Father, we are living in a confusing world. Hate seems to run rampant and integrity seems to be on the wane. We are confused by it all. We pray for some understanding and a way to contribute to a solution. We pray for a way to help. Amen

# Communication 1

There are several proverbs regarding communication. Many who have learned the style of the good book are sought out by others who connect with them. People want shared knowledge and praise.

When we are asked, it is great to share our knowledge. The operative word is "asked." People who respect our knowledge and experience will benefit when we share. Two heads are generally better than one when working together. We always want to remember to contribute as well as to ask when we need support.

> He who rebukes a person will in the end gain more favor than he who has a flattering tongue.
> —Proverbs 28, verse 23

Umpires and referees are trained to "Call them as you see them." We humans often want to cushion any criticism and often avoid the issue and hope it will go away. Loving and sensitive criticism is a great help to others and, as an aside, a great relationship builder. When we avoid we do not help and we need to help and contribute.

> **Plans** fail for lack of council, but with many advisors, they succeed.
> —Proverbs 15, verse 22

**Thought for Today:** Today let's be more than honest. What do I mean by that? Let's focus on being "open and honest." Expose ourselves in our communications with people we are with so they will know us better and become closer to us.

**Prayer for Today:** Dear Lord, today we pray for those that are manipulative and opportunistic in their communication style; that they may become open, honest and learn how to communicate according to the book of Proverbs. Amen

# Communication 2—Lighten Up

Today we follow up on communication. In our world of high stress and over-commitment it is important to lighten up, keep a sense of humor.

> **All** the days of the oppressed are wretched, but the cheerful heart has a continual feast.
> —Proverbs 15, verse 15

This is not to say that we laugh at the expense of others. Rather we have an obligation to look at the more humorous side of life.

> A man finds joy in giving an apt reply and how good is a timely word!
> —Proverbs 15, verse 23

> An anxious heart weighs a man down, but a kind word cheers him up.
> —Proverbs 12, verse 25

Somehow when we grew up, many of us looked at religion as "God-fearing" and the Bible as a set of rules. With that in mind, how do we interpret these passages? We are clearly being told to relax, keep it light and enjoy while demonstrating to others how to do the same.

In life we need to deal with the negative forces. Today we are dealing with increasing costs of basic living. Our society is in a state of change. Our attitudes and actions as Christians need to be clear. We need to deal with the issues as best we can and demonstrate to the world that we can change and stay happy along the way through Christ Jesus.

**Thought for Today:** Let us all be happy—not by being busy but by taking time to smell the spring flowers. Let us demonstrate to those around us that as Christians we have something that keeps us at peace in times of stress.

**Prayer for Today:** Dear Lord and Father, our world has some issues. There are floods, tornadoes and financial issues that seem to dominate the news. Today we pray for those areas and people around the world that are affected by natural disasters and give thanks to those people who have the ability and opportunity to help. We pray that we can help to bring normalcy back to the lives of the victims. Amen

# Perfect Will

In other Good News we have discussed the whole person: spirit, mind and body. In Paul's message to the Romans there is an emphasis on the mind. If you are reading this you probably don't need it.

When growing up in the late '40s and '50s, we would spend a lot of time reading. There were whole groups of us, kids, reading and trading books. Yes, sometimes comic books, but also everything from Uncle Wiggly to Sherlock Holmes. As we grew older the books changed to National Geographic and Mickey Spillane. It was a period of intellectual and physical growth.

Personally, in the '60s my reading habit was broken and I went years without reading a book. The ability to imagine myself in a story, to fantasize about being the great Sherlock Holmes, Huck Finn or Superman passed me by. Surely my intellectual growth was stagnant or at least slowed down. I fit the pattern of the new television world, visual rather than intellectual.

> **Do** not conform any longer to the pattern of this world, but be transformed by the renewing of your mind. Then you will be able to test and approve what God's will is—his good, pleasing and perfect will.
> —Romans 12, verse 2

A career change to sales saved me from being stagnant. Engineers need to work on their skills to become salesmen. The best source of information was reading books. So after a fifteen year drought, my reading habit was initiated out of necessity. Reading again became part of my life and it spread to both growth and recreational works. I feel blessed by this today.

**Thought for Today**: Let us ask, What may we choose to do differently to "...be transformed by the renewing" of our minds. Let us take the time to renew our commitment to intellectual growth.

**Prayer for Today**: Dear Lord and Heavenly Father, we pray for guidance regarding love and peace. We are a nation and world community out of control. We as Christians pray for our leaders and the leaders of the world to find a solution. We pray they do your will, follow your path and resolve our problems through love, peace and understanding. Amen

# Respect And Love

Love and respect are the two things that abound in our faith. If we could spread this around the world we could save a fortune on armaments. Unfortunately, jealousy, hate, and disrespect tend to fester all around us also. Maybe we just have to learn to live with it.

The founding fathers set us up as a democracy; a free nation of free people. They also said "In God we trust" and then set up a clear separation between the government and religion. We want to be free and we Christians want our God, our friends and peace on earth. It is a conundrum!

Our role is stated clearly by Paul's message in Thessalonica: Our role is to grow in the Spirit and with that will come love. The result of spiritual growth is that love and respect blossom and jealousies, hate and disrespect fade away.

> **May** the Lord make your love increase and overflow for each other and for everyone else, just as ours does for you.
> —1 Thessalonians 3, verse 12

**Thought for Today:** Today we will interact with people. Many we will choose to see and are glad. That is the easy piece. We will also have to interact with someone we would rather avoid. No matter what the reason, let us show our Christian love and respect for them.

**Prayer for Today:** Dear Lord, today we give thanks for our friends, family and acquaintances; the people that bring pleasure and peace to our lives. Today we pray that we can also bring pleasure and peace to everyone through our love and respect. Amen

# New Beginnings

Today is the first day of the rest of your life; believe in it. We have a great chance every day to start over. Yesterday is past, tomorrow is in the future and today is a gift from God. It is up to us how we are going to use it; carry around our old baggage or go out and harvest new joys. It is our choice.

To use a golf analogy, life is like match play, hole by hole versus day by day. A bad golf hole in match play does not cost you the match, it counts as one of eighteen! In life, a bad day is painful and certainly not wanted and may contribute to a bad week. However, it can be a bottom and life can be all uphill from there, or not. We can turn bad into good.

One of the benefits I get out of writing these is the phone calls and emails from readers. A year ago my mobile rang and it was a non recorded number. I was way too busy to answer a call from someone I did not know and was going to let it ring through. The old softie in me answered after four rings and it was from an old friend and Good News buddy. She was

> **Therefore**, if anyone is in Christ, he is a new creation; the old has gone, the new has come!
> —2 Corinthians 5, verse 17

having a really bad day and had gone to the Spirit of Hope UMC website looking for relief. She found my messages and the first one she opened applied to her issue. She made my day by calling to say thanks for being there.

If you are reading this today you are on the right track and giving yourself the opportunity for a better day. Meditation and prayer will jump start your day and open the window to the light of our faith.

**Thought for Today:** Today let us start a new beginning and reach out and help another do the same.

**Prayer for Today:** Heavenly Father, we give you thanks for our many blessings and especially for a new day. Today we pray that we capture the joys of life that you lead us to and that we may help someone else also find them. Amen

# Honor Them

Celebrate Memorial Day, pray for all who served; who went before us and all those that we love.

For several years my son-in-law Rick played in the 451st Fort Snelling Army band. We went to a lot of parades and concerts and had a lot of fun. At each concert they traditionally played the military anthems of the Coast Guard, Army, Marines and Navy while the veterans in the crowd stood and saluted. Each time my eyes teared up with emotion as I thought of what these people had done for all of us.

There are places in the world where my writing these messages would be prohibited and criminal. Here, that is not the case. What makes America great is our freedom of speech, the ability to express ourselves and to hear from the other side. Abraham Lincoln said it like this:

> I am nothing but truth is everything.
> I know I am right because I know that liberty is right, for Christ teaches it, and Christ is God.

**Here** is a trustworthy saying: If we died with him, we will also live with him; …Keep reminding God's people of these things.
—2 Timothy 2, verses 10 and 14

**Thought for Today:** Today let us remember all who have gone before us and be thankful.

**Prayer for Today:** Dear Lord and Father, today we give thanks to all of those who have gone before us; those who have contributed to our lives today. First all of those who fought in our military that contributed to our freedom; second to our family ancestors who built our traditions and lifestyle; and last to Jesus who gave us grace. Amen

# Spiritual Growth

Several years ago June and I made a decision that our families would not remember us as angry old people. We decided that based on our time spent interacting with elderly people as Stephen ministers. Recently I have been involved with two such people and have concluded that somehow being happy has everything to do with spiritual growth. Let me share a story with you from a recent Saturday.

My friend and I were volunteering at a race in a very cold rain and many volunteers were complaining. My friend stated that as bad as it was he was dreading his next appointment even worse. Trust me, we had been out in the rain for four hours serving over 8000 participants and worse seemed impossible!

He was going to his parents place to do a few odd jobs that his dad could or should not risk doing any more. He said that somehow dad would get angry, be disagreeable and be dissatisfied. He could not understand why. In my usual big mouth way I asked him about his dad's spirituality. The answer was that Mom and Dad go to church every Sunday!

> I gave you milk, not solid food,
> for you were not yet ready for it.
> Indeed, you are still not ready.
> —1 Corinthians 3, verses 2

This lead to my favorite discussion: religious versus spirituality! You see, there are a lot of people who attend church every week that do not experience spiritual growth. In a recent discussion it was said that too many religious people just never get to know the Holy Spirit! I believe that the people who are edgy, angry or uncomfortable fit that description.

In summary, the Lord wants us to be happy, cheerful and appreciative. He has given us the tools and we need to use them every day. The tool we have is faith and the Holy Spirit. We need to keep them in mind and in our hearts to be happy!

**Thought for Today:** Today let us drink our milk but demonstrate with our happiness and spirit that we are ready for the Lord's solid food.

**Prayer for Today:** Dear Lord, today we pray for all who are experiencing anxiety and anger. We pray that they may find peace and tranquility through the Holy Spirit. Amen

# Desire

Paul sounds a lot like my mom sounded during high school. During the teen years listening was not my strong suit. How could a ranked athlete and honor student be a bad guy? In my mind my record justified my behaviors and the price paid was ten years that, today, I refer to as my dark period. Those years were the times I spent learning how life really was a two way street as opposed to a one way street that I owned.

Faith somehow stayed with me and praying was often present when the darkness was dominant. God was with me in spite of my behaviors. He was always there and I would reach out to him just as Popeye would grab for his spinach. And, just like Popeye's spinach, He always came through for me. He will also come through for you.

> **Flee** the evil desires of youth, and pursue righteousness, faith, love and peace...
> —2 Timothy 2, verse 22

**Thought for Today**: Today will not be perfect so keep your prayer close by and ask for support!

**Prayer for Today**: Dear Lord, today we thank you for the goodness in our lives and the hope and love that tomorrow will surely bring. Amen

# Peace Through Faith

Forgiveness is the way of Christian life. It is not always an easy path. We Christians are challenged throughout our lives with anger and resentment. Sometimes we grow vindictive and just want to get even. Wow, what a curse. Is it possible to find peace through revenge? Absolutely not!

Several years ago our business life was saturated with lawyers, claims and counter claims, arbitration and mediation. It demonstrates a serious challenge that we Christians need to deal with. How do we find peace when someone has done us wrong? How do we keep God at the forefront of our lives when our livelihood is being attacked?

The answer is in good Christian friends, mentors, readings and prayer.

> ...**The** Lord's servant must not quarrel; instead, he must be kind, able to teach and not resentful.
> —2 Timothy, verse 23 and 24

**Thought for Today:** This week we are asked to wear red to our church because the bright color will help us focus. Throughout our lives "focusing on the positive" always seems to be a challenge. Let us all focus on the great things that we have and deal promptly with the negatives so that we may enjoy life to its fullest.

**Prayer for Today:** Heavenly Father, our lives are full of the challenges that are placed before us. Sometimes these challenges create fear and hurts that are difficult to deal with and easy to hang on to. Friendships and relationships become challenged. Please help us keep the many great and positive gifts you have given us at the forefront of our thoughts and give us the power and wisdom to deal swiftly and honestly with the challenges. Amen

# Perseverance

The key word today is perseverance. Somehow in our lives we search for serenity or peace. Where does it hide, or do we hide it on ourselves? Certainly we all go through phases when we are not at peace. Careers get in the way, illness occurs and the general business of our lifestyle disturbs tranquility.

When we are not at peace, which is in control? About three years ago, my daughter gave me a daily meditation book. Two years ago I gave up reading the morning newspaper and replaced it with reading a meditation. It helped me have a better day. I no longer knew the baseball scores, how Tiger did or, better yet, how many negative things occurred in the world the day before. Meditating gave me a level of peace at the start of the day.

So where does perseverance fit in? Well, peace is illusive and hard to grasp, or even to define. The search may be everlasting. Paul's message to the Romans

> **Therefore** since you have been justified through faith, we have peace with God... we rejoice in the hope of the glory of God. Not only so, but we also rejoice in our sufferings. Suffering produces perseverance; perseverance brings character; and character brings hope. And hope does not disappoint us.
> —Romans 5, verses 1–5

is fairly clear. Throughout the ups, downs and general activity of our lives, we must be persistent in our faith and keep God in our lives. Through the grace of God, we will find the hope, peace and tranquility we desire.

**Thought for Today**: Today let us review our long standing frustrations. The demanding boss, the developing teenager, the morning commute, whatever is in our lives. Let us pray for God's guidance on how we should help Him deal with the frustration. If He is involved, we will be less frustrated.

**Prayer for Today**: Dear Lord, I give thanks for the many blessings that are present in my life: The good friends, the lifestyle, the rain and flowers. There still are many issues that need attention. I pray for your guidance so that as I work through the issues, you are with me and somehow I am doing your work. Amen

# Forgiveness

When we truly believe, we will be at peace. Not because we have been perfect, but because we will know that we are forgiven through our faith. That is a powerful and moving statement. There are many moments in our lives that we have erred and perhaps are not proud of that memory.

There are many twelve step programs and clinics full of people that have never let go of these memories. They are searching for peace. It will find them when they "...turn their will and their lives over to the care of God...." That is an interesting thought.

In our lives, we also have an obligation to turn these memories over to God, i.e., the expression: "Let go and let God." How do we accomplish that? Perhaps through the forgiving of those who have harmed us.

Colossians 3, verse 13, says "Bear with each other and forgive whatever grievances you may have against one

> **Blessed** are they whose transgressions are forgiven, whose sins are covered. Blessed is the man whose sin the Lord will never count against him.
> —Romans 4, verse 7

another. Forgive as the Lord forgave you." When we learn to forgive others, we find it easier to accept the forgiveness we receive from God.

**Thought for Today:** Today, let us focus on the many positive things we accomplish, the people we help and the positive memories that we all appreciate. When a negative or remorseful memory comes to the forefront, let us stop a moment, pray and remember that God is forgiving.

**Prayer for Today:** Dear Lord, thank you for the opportunity to find grace and live in peace. Today, please help me focus on the positive things in my life and help me see the good in others. Amen

# Love and Hospitality

There are almost as many ways to find joy and peace as there are people. It can be found anywhere at any time. It is something that we all measure in our own way. As Christians we have the tools and knowledge to reach out and find it.

However, often we let our every day tasks and challenges disturb our peace. This past week it seemed that the traffic situation was a threat to many people's tranquility. The construction season combined with heavy rains slowed things down to a crawl. Frustration seemed to replace grace on the highways.

A Good News friend wrote a book called Finding Grace. In regards to traffic his comments were "...leave early, take the pretty route and listen to good music." He was right on.

> **'Twas** grace that taught my heart to fear, and grace my fears relieved; How precious did that grace appear, the hour I first believed!
>
> Yea, when this flesh and heart shall fail, and mortal life shall cease; I shall possess, within the veil, a life of joy and peace.
> —John Newton, *Amazing Grace,* verses 2 and 5, 1779

As Christians when we find our tranquility threatened, we need to use our tool kit; prayer, meditation and even a chat with a friend. They all will work. God did not put us here to be frustrated. Experience grace as He wants you to.

**Thought for Today**: Let us all keep grace at the forefront of our daily prayers. Let us expect the daily challenges and be ready with our tool kit. Let's experience grace and joy every day.

**Prayer for Today**: Heavenly Father, we recognize that your joy and tranquility are always available and you are always with us. We need you to help us daily. We pray that we may keep You on our minds and in our thoughts as we work through the challenges of our Christian lives. Amen

# Acceptance

One of my favorite topics is that love leads to peace. However, to love requires acceptance of others. The verses are slightly chopped out of context, but their message is clear. I spoke at a funeral last weekend and the above describes the way the deceased had lived his life and some of the reasons he was loved by his friends.

We all have some associates who are not easy to get along with. Some are opportunistic, angry, selfish, etc. Is the best way to deal with them confrontation? …or by explaining to them the errors of their ways? That usually fails or makes the problem worse.

I suggest the golden rule: Do unto others as you would have others do unto you. Treat others well and, when the relationship is difficult, pray for them and the relationship. When all else fails, read Paul's message to the Romans.

**Thought for Today**: Let us focus on our troubled relationships and how we may recognize our role in them and how to improve them.

> **Accept** him whose faith is weak without passing judgment.
> —Romans 14, verse 1
>
> …let us stop passing judgment on one another. Instead, make up our minds not to put an obstacle in our brother's way.
> —Romans 14, verse 13
>
> Let us make every effort to do what leads to peace and to mutual edification.
> —Romans 14, verse 19

**Prayer for Today**: Dear Lord, please help me understand and accept others. Help me understand those who do not practice the principles taught by Jesus in their daily lives. Help me accept them and help me live my life in a loving and caring way. Amen

# Forgiveness

This week in our neighborhood we watched as a family fell apart. There were court orders, police escorts and all the ungodly things that go with a broken home. The respect, love and spirituality had left the relationship. It was very sad.

Since it is Sunday, let me confess that we in our family did not always go to church. (Sunday was a long training run and then clean the pool.) Also, there were many times when the kids were small, that church on Sunday was our only "quiet time." Not a very good reason for being there. Somehow, however, within our family unit there was always a trust and a spiritual presence that held us together.

Consider this analogy. If your car battery was dead this morning, you could put it on a charger and be able to get going. However, if your alternator was weak, your car would quit running in a few hours. Many of us use Sunday's service as our time to charge our spiritual batteries. This is a good thing to do.

> I urge Euodia and I urge Syntyche to live in harmony in the Lord.
> —Philippians 4, verse 20

Families and individuals with strong spirituality tend to survive. They grow while meeting life's challenges, developing deeper friendships, and learning the value of love. Somehow we all need to carry Sunday's charge throughout the week. I pray that Good News helps.

> And I pray that Christ will make his home in your hearts through faith. I pray that you have your roots and foundation in love.
> —Ephesians 3, verse 17

**Thought for Today**: Somehow we need to be sure that the weekly calendar does not overwhelm our spirituality. We cannot be too busy to love each other. We all know that is a formula for tragedy. Today and always let us focus on positive interaction with our friends and families.

**Prayer for Today**: Dear Lord and Father, our lives are full of distractions. Children's activities, work projects, and many other issues get in the way of peace and love. Somehow, we just don't have time. Today we pray for the presence of mind to focus on your love and include it in our daily lives. Amen

# Good Name

In the '60s when I desired to change careers from engineering to sales I had several interviews that changed my life.

On my very first one, I did not have a clue what I was doing and was sliding into a deep hole fast. The fellow conducting the interview let me know quickly and for whatever reason gave me a lecture on selling myself and dressing for success. He pointed out that the most important product that I would ever have to sell would be myself and how important it was to make sure the product was of high quality. Frankly, that was in 1964 and my next sales interview was in 1972. He scared me to death.

In 1972 a gentleman named Warren started my second sales interview with a question, "What have you ever sold?" That question would have sent me packing in 1964 but not this time. I talked about selling myself to my company to get my job, selling management on budgets and projects, and that I believed everyone was a salesman every day whether they knew it or not. The job was mine and it has been all uphill ever since.

> **A** good name is more desirable than great riches.
> —Proverbs 22, verse 1

During the time from 1964 through 1972, I did a lot of product development; there were college courses, business books, church and, of course, mentoring by my partner, June. You see, that first interviewer was put in my life to advise me that the Lord gave me two ears to listen and understand.

In a recent *Winner's Minute,* televangelist Mac Hammond stated that we are all "Brand Managers." He stated that George Washington said that one of the most precious things this side of the grave is a good reputation.

**Thought for Today:** Today let us consider what we are selling in every situation Let us make sure that we are the best possible brand. Also, we will be interacting with a lot of people that may not be as good as they can be. Let's be sure that they hear the message so that they may benefit from our experience.

**Prayer for Today:** Dear Father, today we will be working with younger, less experienced folks. We pray that we may influence them in a positive Christian way. Amen

# Listening To Criticism

People do not criticize just for fun or to be mean. They generally have a concern or have been hurt in some way. Often negativity is misdirected and unearned. Sometimes we have earned it. It always seems to hurt.

These verbal wounds are an opportunity to display our faith, our patience and understanding. Our gut reaction to criticism is to ignore the hurt and go towards anger. However, when we are criticized, we need to understand the other point of view, the reason why. Then we will learn and be better persons.

> **Wounds** from a friend can be trusted, but an enemy multiplies kisses.
> —Proverbs 27, verse 6

**Thought for Today:** Today we will be criticized and will have the opportunity to react. Let us react as Christians. Instead of becoming angry or defensive, let us try to emulate Jesus. Listen and pray about it. Learn from the experience.

**Prayer for Today:** Dear Lord and Father, today we pray for the simple things. We pray for our families, our friends and ourselves, we pray that we can understand the world and your master plan and that somehow we may contribute to the peace and good will toward others. Amen

# Smile!

This is being written in the food court at Midway Airport in Chicago at 8am after a 6am flight. There are smiling faces all around; even the TSA security people seem upbeat today. The smiles are almost infectious. It is not the normal scene that I observe in airports.

It seems that most of the people here today read Paul's advice to the Romans and are being zealous and hospitable. It is infectious. I was not looking forward to this trip because there is a lot of work lying ahead at Mom's in Massachusetts helping reorganize the house after my brother's passing.

I awoke in a pensive mood and have dealt with smiling happy people for two hours. First the TSA security people were in good spirits, then a flight attendant greeted me with an exceptional smile, a guy helped me with my carry on when I almost dropped it, the flight out is on time and I had a first class upgrade. It also helps that I am writing Good News and having an omelet between flights!

**Never** be lacking in zeal, but keep your spiritual fervor, serving the Lord. Be joyful in hope, patient in affliction, faithful in prayer.
Share with God's people who are in need.
Practice hospitality.
—Romans 12, verse 11

Today I had forgotten my own rules about the start of a new day. Up at four, fly at six, stop in Chicago, and then on to a stressful week! My funky start has been turned around by others. Somehow, the spirit and joy of those around me has affected my mood. It is like I can feel the spirituality around me.

**Thought for Today:** Today let us give thanks to those around us that support our lives: even those who do not realize the effect that they have on us. Let's follow Paul's advice: "Share with God's people who are in need" and "Practice hospitality."

**Prayer for Today:** Dear Lord, today I simply give thanks for those around me that have lifted my spirits. Amen

# Walk With the Lord

Wow, we are sure all busy. Often when saying "Hi, how are you?" the reply is "busy" and a review of their calendar follows. It seems that when Paul wrote this passage, he was advising an active life style.

Even many retirees comment that they do not know when they ever had time to work. At the moment, my first attempt at retirement does not seem to be a slow down in activity. The weeks seem to pass by faster.

There are many blessings in being involved. As "qualified" retirees, June and I often reminisce about frantic past lifestyle. Many of the times that seemed the craziest and most out of control have generated the fondest memories: The Blessings.

Paul goes on to say in verses 17 and 18, "Always giving thanks to God the Father for everything, in the name of our Lord Jesus Christ."

**But** everything exposed by the light becomes visible, for it is light that makes everything visible. This is why it is said: "Wake up, O sleeper, rise from the dead, and Christ will shine on you."

Be very careful, then, how you live; not as unwise but as wise, making the most of every opportunity...
—Ephesians 5, verses 3–17

**Thought for Today:** Yes we are busy. It seems that being busy is a good thing. As we move through our schedules this week, let us take the time to thank God for the opportunity to be involved or busy. Let us stop and appreciate and feel good about our contributions.

**Prayer for Today:** Heavenly father, we live in a world of hate and fear. We pray that somehow it will all end, but it seems that it is just beginning. We pray for some sort of love attack to break out. Somehow for the world to recognize the advantages of Godly love. Amen

# Correcting

Our faith teaches us to be open and honest with everyone. That is a tall order when it comes to correcting someone. There always seems to be a fear of the negative or the possible confrontation. It is always easier in the short term to be silent.

Proverbs 28, verse 23, tells it like it is. We will earn more respect and have a better relationship if we express our concerns promptly and honestly. In all of our relationships, the ideal situation is when everyone's feelings are shared. There are justifications for holding back. Fear of disturbing our families or risking our careers is the most common. However, over time, appropriately sharing our feelings always works out better than keeping quiet.

Proverbs 25, verse 11, tells us that "A word aptly spoken is like apples of gold in settings of silver." We need to express ourselves and share those feelings under all conditions.

> **He** who rebukes a man will in the end gain more favor than he who has a flattering tongue.
> —Proverbs 28, verse 23

**Thought for Today:** Today we will be tempted to avoid issues. We need to recognize those feelings and think about them. We need to find a way to deal with the issues that reflect the way our faith teaches us, by being open and honest.

**Prayer for Today:** Heavenly Father, you teach us to be open and honest with everyone. It seems very unreasonable and at times impossible. Today we pray that we can deal with all of the problems that come our way in an open and honest way. We pray that we may do this in good faith. Amen

# Positive Focus

Many of us today are challenged with issues. Some have lost jobs, some have divorced, others have significant others who are terminally ill; anger, fear and resentments are fostered in this way. How do we deal with the issues without destroying the peace in our life?

Obviously challenges that threaten our livelihood and families are difficult. Some are hard decisions but get dealt with quickly; others seem unsolvable and could drag on forever. The quickies are best dealt with on the spot and then go away. The long term issues need other techniques and the best are through our faith.

Several years ago there was a serious issue that involved discrimination within our church. Unfortunately I was in the middle of it and there was no obvious solution and prayer did not work for me. So I went with plan B, when prayer does not work, pray again—but the second time was with my spiritual mentor. It eventually worked out the way the Lord wanted it.

> **Whoever** of you loves life and desires to see many good days, keep your tongue from evil and your lips from speaking lies. Turn from evil and do good; seek peace and pursue it.
> —Psalm 34, verses 12–14

I like to say that when the going gets tough the tough start praying! Sometimes that is the only solution.

**Thought for Today:** Today let's recognize the tough spots or bumps and pray for a win-win solution.

**Prayer for Today:** Heavenly Father we give thanks today for the ability to insert You into our life's problems through prayer. Amen

# Perfect Peace

Peace is a direct result of faith and trust. When situations are not what we would like we often focus on the bad results that may occur. When we do that we may bring the negative result upon ourselves. We were not steadfast!

In life we need to keep our eye on the sky, look upward and outward for the positive results. We need to be steadfast and positive. With a positive outlook and a strong faith we will get the most positive results. This outlook can lead us to perfect peace.

> **You** will keep in perfect Peace those whose minds are steadfast, because they have trust in you.
> —Isaiah 26, verse 3

**Thought for Today:** Today let us all be positive in the face of all challenges. Let's snatch peace from the grasp of negativity.

**Prayer for Today:** Dear Lord, today we give thanks for the opportunity to have peace in our lives. We pray that we may focus on doing your will and that through your steadfast love we will have peace and contribute to the peace of others. Amen

# Tough Love

Serving others has more to do with following God's will and sharing God's word than it does with being a caregiver or a soft touch. Often he is referring to what therapists call "tough love."

It often means saying no or advising people of a direction that they would rather not go. That is real love and not an easy thing to do. Each time we follow through with the tough decision, somehow we experience spiritual growth. The results are usually very positive. We take a step up the ladder of success.

> **For** even the Son of Man did not come to be served, but to serve and to give his life as a ransom for many.
> —Mark 10, verse 45

**Thought for Today:** Today let us look forward to the tough decisions rather than shying away from them. When they need to be made, let us think about the question, "What would Jesus do?" Decisions made with love and faith are the correct ones.

**Prayer for Today:** Dear Lord, we often have to advise friends, colleagues and family to do things they would rather not do. Today we pray for the ability to recognize what is correct and the strength to do the right thing as we walk the walk. Amen

# Live the Life

Spiritual growth is an important part of living a peaceful and rewarding life. Defining it is sometimes difficult. It is more than reading a passage, it is living the life. It is climbing the Christian ladder of success, not running around preaching a passage. It is demonstrating the lifestyle. In the above passage Mark mentions greatness and to be great, one must be at peace. This peace can be found by walking the walk; Serving others as a lifestyle.

TV Evangelist Mac Hammond defined serving others as "...meeting another person's needs when they do not believe you are serving them."

> ...**whoever** wants to become great among you must be your servant, and whoever wants to be first must be slave of all.
> —Mark 10, verses 43 and 44

**Thought for Today**: Today let's reach out and help someone in need. Let's serve their every need.

**Prayer for Today**: Heavenly Father, today we feel the need to help. We pray that we recognize those in need whom you have placed before us. We thank you for the opportunity to serve. Amen

# The Valley

Recovery from surgery is a tough mental and physical battle that frequently ends in the deepening of spirituality. Healing physically is something we all are used to; our bumps and bruises over the years, minor cuts, all go away in time. It is easy not to recognize the miracle of God with the minor problems.

> **Even** though I walk through the valley of the shadow of death, I fear no evil, for you are with me.
> —Psalm 23, verse 4

However, when a big one comes, it is equally easy to ask, "Where are you God?" or, "Why are you doing this to me?" It is easy to lose sight of what matters when facing a life-threatening event. Often, we are caught up in the analysis of the doctor's skills and the various treatment options and where is the best place to go for help. Yes, let's get technical and analytical to make darn sure that the doctor can take care of us. Let's make sure we go to a hospital with the latest equipment. But somehow, let's not forget God in the process.

In 1998 when I had cancer, my impatience and outright fear chased me into the hospital in only three weeks, no analysis or wait and see. Just my typical impulsive, "Just do it" (thanks Nike). As many of you know, somehow, I threw it over to *Him* with reckless abandon.

That brings to mind the last line of the Psalm 23, "Surely goodness and love will follow, all the days of my life, and I will dwell in the house of the Lord forever."

The Lord and physicians came through for me and my family. We all need to remember Him during times of fear and illness.

**Thought for Today:** Let us focus on the unfortunates around us that are ill and keep the 23rd Psalm in mind. Let us see if we can contribute to helping in some way.

**Prayer for Today:** Dear Lord, many of our friends have health issues. Some are minor, some serious and some fatal. We pray that we may find a way to assist, help and calm their fears as they walk through their valley. May we help by following your guidance through prayer. Amen

# Talkers!

Growing up in Boston there were often what we called "talkers" on Boston common. They virtually stood on milk crates (soap boxes!) and discussed political issues and their religious beliefs. As a teenager I considered them nut cases because from my perspective no one in their right mind would do that. Apparently not even Moses!

Lately I have coined the term "closet ministry"—we are there when we are needed and we all do some great work. Be proud of that because God is with us in that effort. Most of us prefer to do God's work quietly and on our own terms. We have the belief to do that.

Tomorrow we will talk a bit about doing more!

> **Moses** said to the LORD, "O Lord, I have never been eloquent, neither in the past nor since you have spoken to your servant. I am slow of speech and tongue.
> —Exodus 4, verse 10

**Thought for Today:** Today let us continue our "closet ministries." Helping others, praying for the sick, the underprivileged, serving the shelters, etc. We do that well.

**Prayer for Today:** Dear Lord and father, life is good for us. We have food, shelter and love around us. We give you thanks for our abundance. Today we pray for the opportunity to show our appreciation to others. We pray for the opportunity to share our faith and the opportunity to represent you in our daily lives. Amen

# Trust Versus Belief

More on our closet ministries!

Is that what God really wants? Should we speak out more? Be Evangelical?

The answer to that is a definite *yes!*

God's answer to Moses was simply "I will be with you." We hesitate to talk the talk in public. After all, the human resources department at work has a policy against it. We would make someone uncomfortable in the workplace. Sometimes we need to show trust and say what needs to be said. We need to go beyond our belief system and trust that God wants us to speak out.

**The** LORD said to him, "Who gave man his mouth? Who makes him deaf or mute? Who gives him sight or makes him blind? Is it not I, the LORD? Now go; I will help you speak and will teach you what to say." But Moses said, "O Lord, please send someone else to do it." —Exodus 4. verses 12 and 13

**Thought for Today:** Today let us continue our closet ministries as we look for the occasion when God would want us to share our faith. Let us recognize that opportunity and speak out! Let's take the risk and be Talkers.

**Prayer for Today:** Dear Lord and Father, we pray for the opportunity to share our faith and the opportunity to represent you in our daily lives. Amen

# God Is With Us

Like Moses, we are not always enthusiastic about what God wants. We are a humble lot, conservative and considerate of others' views and feelings. Almost to a fault. We are humble before God.

However, in our lives we are often asked to perform tasks that require an assertive posture. Many of us are leaders in the community, at work and at church. We are often leaders that require strength while still being humble. That is a great leader.

God's response to Moses was "...I will be with you." and he will be with us always.

When you are feeling hesitant and inferior, God says, "I will be with you."

When you are wondering if you can make it another day with the job stress, He says, "I will be with you."

When you're faced with a tough decision and wondering what to do, He says, "I will be with you."

When you are experiencing great joy, God is with you.

You may be a bit reluctant, as was Moses, but we need to remember that as we go through life, God is with us always.

> **Now** Moses was a very humble man, more humble than anyone else on the face of the earth.
> —Numbers 12, verse 3

**Thought for Today:** Today we need to remember that we are not alone. Through our faith we have help meeting our obligations. Let us take control of situations in a humble manner and allow ourselves to be led through the tasks ahead.

**Prayer for Today:** Dear Lord and Father, we thank you for being with us. We are often confused in a world of activity. Often when things go well, we feel that we controlled the situation. We pray that we can recognize your involvement in our everyday lives and have the forethought to give you thanks through our actions and prayers. Amen

# Finding Others

As we move through life we meet all kinds of people. Some we warm up to; some we don't. We often cannot quite explain why, but most often it is that their behavior and operating style fit our comfort zone.

Recently I was experiencing a technical problem at work that was very perplexing and disturbing to me and my customer. There seemed to be no real good explanation and I was considered an "expert." So, I called in a guy I have known and liked for 15 years. He was not only an expert but a specialist; a person that for whatever reason fit technically and personally; a person that would help even if there were no financial gain. A person that fit.

After discussing the technical issue, we talked about our work schedules. He, as a small business owner, starts the week with a prayer breakfast with his whole company. To do this, he needs to be on the road at 5 am and drive two hours. He is not only a dedicated business man but a dedicated believer. He is a "good fit" because he "...does what the Lord requires..."

> **He** has showed you,
> O man, what is good.
> And what does the LORD require of you?
> To act justly and to love mercy and to walk humbly with your God.
> —Micah 6, verse 8

**Thought for Today:** Today let us have a look around at our associates. Not the ones we meet on Sunday morning at church, but all of the others. The store clerk, barber, hair dresser or whoever—the ones we are really comfortable with; the ones that fit. Often, they will "fit" because of their beliefs and Christian practices.

**Prayer for Today:** Heavenly Father, today we pray that somehow we find understanding through prayer and your word. We pray that somehow we solve problems rather than create them. Amen

# Chemical Dependency

As a twelve step support person for years, I recently received a call from a business associate who I knew had a serious issue. I was tired, grumpy and not in the mood to listen to his problems.

He talked for an hour and I could not get a word in edgewise. It was a long hour and I did not say much. A few times I got to make suggestions and point him in a few directions but like most of these calls, the guy was not quite ready to listen.

It was getting late so we prayed together before we said good bye and he said "Thanks for listening. You've helped me so much. I can't believe that I hesitated to call you."

At times we need another set of ears to hear our problems. Sometimes the listener may be a friend. But we also have another wiser, more faithful listener—God. In Psalm 28, David cries out for help. Like David, when we express our feelings to God, we always find a patient and willing listener. At the end of the Psalm, David is able to express abiding trust and confidence in God. We can too.

**Blessed** be the Lord, for he has heard the sound of my pleadings.
—Psalm 28, verse 6

**Thought for Today:** God is willing to listen and to help you.

**Prayer for Today:** Let us pray for those people that suffer from the self inflicted, cunning, baffling and powerful disease, chemical dependency. Let us pray for them and their loved ones that they may find the honesty, openness and spirituality to straighten out their lives and recover.

# Life Goals

In our democratic society we are encouraged to compete in the workplace and elsewhere. In the '50s there was the term "Keeping up with the Joneses." In the '90s that seemed to become "Leave the Joneses behind." The two car family of the '60s became the two home, four cars and a boat family of the new millennium. It is easy to understand why attendance and giving in church declined; no one has any time or money left!

This is not meant to be a stewardship message asking for more. It is meant as a caution and designed to provoke thought. One of my blessings was being raised in a household with two cars and two homes. When we moved to Minnesota, the land of 10,000 lakes and 10 million lake homes, we said no way. You see, I grew up maintaining two homes with my dad and did not want to ever do that again!

In confession, June and I did have too much stuff and too many things. We downsized five years ago and have not finished yet!

> **Watch** out! Be on your guard against all kinds of greed; life does not consist in the abundance of possessions.
> —Luke 12, verse 15

Jesus is clear in his message as reported by Luke. Life is about spiritual growth, love within the community, helping others, being comfortable in your own skin, etc. Happiness has nothing to do with stuff or things.

**Thought for Today**: Today let us think about what we need to get through the day and contemplate what we want. Let's try to understand the differences.

**Prayer for Today**: Heavenly Father, today we are blessed and live in a great society. We ask forgiveness for our participation in the blatant consumption encouraged in our world. We pray that as we move forward we experience the blessing of learning what our real needs are and experience the true abundance of your love. Amen

# Lighter Life

Yesterday may have seemed like a stern message regarding our society, so on a lighter note I do not believe that the Lord is wasteful, but wants us to be ecologically sound, not waste our resources. So with my tongue in cheek let us consider the benefit of having many things.

June and her many friends all do crafts and have rooms dedicated to their hobby, craft rooms. These rooms have years of unfinished projects; cross stitch kits, quilt squares waiting to be finished, skeins of yarn and spools of thread awaiting the needle—even an unfinished braided rug! Quite often when they are together one will comment that they know the Lord will not take them until they have finished their last project!

Men are not much different. The fisherman has a tackle box full of jigs and lures; he cannot be taken until the last lure is lost or the last fish caught! The gardener and landscaper can never be done until every crop has been harvested and every tree and shrub matured! The hunter has his many guns and the game is never ending—certainly his job will never end. We are safe guys.

> **For** life is more than food, and the body more than clothes. Who of you by worrying can add a single hour to your life?
> —Luke 12, verses 23 and 25

We know the above is levity and I am not serious. Our reality is that when doing a craft, fishing, hunting or gardening we are quiet and at peace. We are blessed by the Lord through our many activities. Using our stuff contributes to our peace and compliments our spirituality. We must always be careful and remember that it is love and the holy spirit that will bring the everlasting peace.

**Thought for Today:** Today let us remember our faith and commitments with joy. It is OK to have fun and laugh.

**Prayer for Today:** Lord hear our prayer for the good life; one of joy, love and abundance. We pray for these for all throughout the world. Amen

# Lean on Me!

Sometimes rejoice and celebrate are hard words to implement. At the moment spring floods abound. Here in Minnesota, we have had nine inches of rain and in some locations even more. My triathlon training and golf game are in the tank because of a shoulder injury. One of my spiritual advisors challenged me on doing my meditations often enough! With all that stated negativity, I choose to listen to Paul!

This morning I walked a golf course "marking" for my grandson Chris' foursome in a junior league. June and I just finished an after dinner walk under a clear blue sky at 75 degrees F. (I need to specify scale because of my Euro-readers!) This afternoon I bumped into a friend and Good News buddy at the outdoor pool and she is doing well after losing her husband three years ago.

Also, I talked with Mom today and at age 94 she was having a great day. She had a problem and I suggested a great idea. She was already working that specific solution and we had a great laugh. She was ahead of me 71 years ago and she still is! If you live to be 94, you want her life and spirit.

> **Rejoice** in the Lord always. I will say it again: Rejoice!
> —Philippians 4, verse 4

Erma Bombeck wrote a book entitled "If Life is a Bowl of Cherries, What Am I doing in the Pits?" We need to focus on the good stuff and listen to Paul.

*Rejoice in the Lord!*

**Thought for Today:** Today it will be too hot outside, the air conditioning inside will be too cool, the sun too bright and there may be a thunderstorm. It just will not matter so rejoice in the Lord and enjoy it. It is a present from the Lord.

**Prayer for Today:** Dear Lord and Father, there are many things wrong in our world: wars, revolution, both national and local money issues. Today we give thanks for what we have and the ability to seek peace through you. We pray for the strength and guidance to find a way to contribute to a world wide solution. We pray that we may help find peace amongst the peoples of the world. Amen

# Listen

Today while driving to the trail to do my morning walk there were a father and son in the car behind me. The son was wearing a head set and probably listening to his iPod. The dad was on his phone. That is something that we see a lot in our society today; together but separated by technology.

My folks and I rode together a lot and they would not turn on the radio. It was our time to talk. Often I felt like I was getting grilled but once in while it was my turn to ask and question. I especially liked to grill my mom when we were heading to school. She was a teacher and I learned a lot. My dad was a talker and it was my time to listen and learn. I can't say how much and about what, but we sure talked.

I could see in my mirror that there was no conversation between the boy and his dad. They were in different worlds. I felt sad and wanted to scream at them, This is your alone time. Use it! I guess they communicate at a different time. Let's hope so!

> **Listen**, my sons, to a father's instruction; pay attention and gain understanding.
> —Proverbs 4, verse 1

**Thought for Today:** Today let us be communicators with those around us. Let us share our love and faith as well as some hints on life.

**Prayer for Today:** Today we pray for future generations. We pray that the technology that makes their lives simpler does not block their understanding of Jesus and his grace. Amen

# Anxiety and Faith

Stress is becoming an American, if not a world wide, tradition, part of our life style. We often go through our week wound up like a rubber band that has been twisted tighter and tighter. However, we all recognize that the rubber band eventually breaks. When it is wound too tight or stressed too long, it snaps! We are certainly a higher life form than a rubber band, however we are similar when stressed.

We have a way of unwinding during the most stressed of times. Mine is by writing Good News to people that I love. Yours may be different, exercise, meditation, a chat with a friend, reading. There are many ways to release stress. In Paul's writings in Philippians 4, verses 8 and 9, he suggests that Faith is a tool to help us:

"Finally, brothers, whatever is true, whatever is noble, whatever is right, whatever is pure, whatever is lovely, whatever is admirable—if anything is excellent or praiseworthy—think about such things.

"Whatever you have learned or received or heard from me, or seen in me—put it into practice. And the God of peace will be with you."

> **Do** not be anxious about anything, but in everything, by prayer and petition, with thanksgiving, present your requests to God.
> —Philippians 4, verse 6

**Thought for Today**: Today let us focus selfishly on ourselves. Let's feel the peace and presence of God in our lives. When the "stress monster" wants to control our lives, let's read this passage and let "the peace of God" into our lives. As Christians we deserve peace.

**Prayer for Today**: Heavenly Father, the world seems to be a breeding ground for stress. Everywhere we look there is something to worry about: terror, hate, employment troubles, stock market woes—even severe weather. We pray that we may keep You and peace in our thoughts, that we have the presence of mind to make wise choices and release our stresses to find tranquility. Amen

# The Answer

We certainly do not feel filled with the spirit every day (or at least I don't!). Quite often when I sit down to write these messages there seems to be a writer's block. To me that says that my spirit may need more coffee or, better perhaps, a prayer. Often it is both.

With our busy schedules today it is easy to jump out of bed and get into our daily activities without thinking about our spirit. I guess that is normal but it may not lead to a peaceful lifestyle. It is the way we achieve our material objectives.

We are however given grace through our faith and we cannot escape it. The message is clear that when we feel empty or down and out, the solution is through the Spirit that lives in us. All we need to do is slow down and let it take over.

> **You**, however, are not in the realm of the flesh but are in the realm of the Spirit, if indeed the Spirit of God lives in you.
> —Romans 8, verse 9

**Thought for Today:** Today when we feel stressed and overloaded let's remember Paul's words above. Let's take a break!

**Prayer for Today:** Dear Lord and Father, we often cannot feel the spirit that we know is within us. Today we pray that when we are too busy and too stressed out that we will remember You are the answer. Amen

# Tough Times

All days are not created equal. Often there are negative forces in our competitive society that seem overwhelming. There are career issues; most people don't awaken every day with enthusiasm to go to work.

Financial issues always need to be dealt with and seem to recreate themselves monthly, weekly or quarterly. The calendar always seems too crowded. All together it is easy to wonder where God is in all of this. Is someone working against us?

Early Christians had it a lot tougher than we do. In David's case the majority of the crowds wanted him dead. That was also the case for Paul and Silas almost everywhere they went. "But other Jews were jealous; so they rounded up some bad characters from the marketplace, formed a mob and started a riot in the city." —Acts 17, verse 5. Being an early Christian required a strong faith dedication and I personally think they had to be able to run fast and far!

> **Contend**, LORD, with those who contend with me; fight against those who fight against me.
> Take up shield and armor; arise and come to my aid.
> —Psalm 35, verses 1 and 2

The early Christians turned things around through their belief system. We can also do that. We do it with prayer and meditation; God is always with us and available to help.

**Thought for Today:** Today let us start out without fear, stress and conflict. If somehow it finds us, interrupts us, let's deal with it in a Godly way.

**Prayer for Today:** Dear Lord and Father, today we give thanks for your presence in our lives; for the opportunity you give us when we speak to you. We give thanks for the peace you bring us. Amen

# Turn Around

In basic physics we are taught that perpetual motion does not and cannot exist. Something in motion will eventually stop due to outside forces unless we apply energy to it to keep it moving. If you don't believe it, take your foot off the gas! For non-technical people reading this, a good summary statement is that there is no free lunch.

Yesterday we read about the resistance felt by early Christians. The majority did not believe or support them and they had some long days. Of course, many were martyred like Paul and Peter. We will have stressful days, negative days. Yesterday's message was entitled "Tough Times" because at some level we encounter it daily.

We need to understand that somehow negativity is an opportunity for growth. When we resolve it, we will feel better.

> **May** those who delight in my vindication shout for joy and gladness; may they always say, "The LORD be exalted, who delights in the well-being of his servant." My tongue will proclaim your righteousness, your praises all day long.
> —Psalm 35, verses 27 and 28

Through dedication and prayer and a bit of effort, we can always turn things around.

We can apply physics to our lives, our congregations, our careers. We need to apply our skills and efforts to keep the ball rolling in a positive way. There is no free lunch and no penalty for success. As stated above "The LORD be exalted, who delights in the well-being of his servant."

We are asked to turn negativity around through our strength and faith.

**Thought for Today**: Today we will have an opportunity to turn over a negative force, to improve our lives. Today let's make it happen through our strength, efforts and prayers.

**Prayer for Today**: Dear Lord and Father, today we pray for the opportunity to help others. We pray that we may do your work by contributing to someone else's growth. Amen

# Sheep

None of us really likes to think of ourselves as sheep. After all, they live in flocks, huddle together against all weather, feed on pasture grasses, etc. The shepherd keeps his watch on them daily and has dogs to round up the ones that get lost. We are a higher level than that and in control of our own destiny.

Sheep do not have a hierarchy like so many animals. Maybe we should look at ourselves as wolves. They have a definite pecking order, a family system; they help each other hunt and kill. That is sounding a little bit more human! The point to understand is that yes we are a higher life form; yes, we control ourselves through the power of logic and yes we are led by our beliefs.

Just today my daughter called me regarding a 95 year old lady that we both love. This lady is having issues with being old and probably having an end of life experience in the not too distant future. This lady also does not have a faith or belief in God. By not believing in a higher power (God), she *de facto* appointed herself in control, and when nearing the end, that is scary!

> **Know** that the LORD is God. It is he who made us, and we are his; we are his people, the sheep of his pasture.
> —Psalm 100, verse 3

Something wonderful was needed to create this world and society that we live in. My preference is to believe in God and the blessing and grace given to us through Jesus. These are Abe Lincoln's comments on it. "The purposes of the Almighty are perfect, and must prevail, though we erring mortals may fail to accurately perceive them in advance."

**Thought for Today**: Today let me follow my Shepherd and do his will.

**Prayer for Today**: Dear Lord, today we will be making decisions regarding life, children, business and anything else that comes along. Today we pray for your guidance your will be accomplished through our work. Amen

# Tim's story

Tim, a very good Christian and friend, is someone that I have known over ten years. He trains for marathons, works in the same industry, loves music and shares many of the same ideals that I do. I like the guy and he had a tough spring. This is his story.

**In** the same way, we can see and understand only a little about God now, as if we were peering at his reflection in a poor mirror; but someday we are going to see him in his completeness, face to face.
—1 Corinthians 13, verse 12

He was dying and did not know why! And yes he did ask God, "Why?"

Well, he had some major surgery and spent 13 days in the hospital recovering. He had been close to death. During this process, somehow Tim realized that his future was not in control of the medical community, but that God was with him and in control. What a blessing and what a great result. The Lord is with all of us!

Training for marathons is often a matter of working through ever-increasing pain thresholds. Everyone experiences them in their own way and in many different ways. Tim used to experience pain in the lower stomach or colon area. I used to think he ate incorrectly. This year the pain grew unbearable, so Tim started searching for the reason. He did not have much success and in February at a major business meeting, he became very ill.

Finally, a doctor identified a blockage in his colon and prescribed surgery. However, there were several more tests and some misdiagnoses over several weeks. Tim lost weight and became very weak. He was, as he described, "in a black tunnel with no light at the end."

**Thought for Today:** Let us focus on the unfortunates around us that are ill and keep the 23rd Psalm and Paul's message to the Corinthians in mind. Let us see if we can contribute to helping in some way.

**Prayer for Today:** Dear Lord, many of our friends have health issues. Some are minor, some serious and some fatal. We pray that we may find a way to assist, help and calm their fears. Let us help them understand that you are with them through it all.

May we help by following your guidance through prayer? Amen

# Commitment

One of the ways to be successful in life is to keep all of your commitments. If you say it, make sure you do it; even after having second thoughts. Become known as one hundred percent reliable. It is probably impossible to be 100% but the closer you are the more you will benefit.

I have a friend who coached youth soccer and had never played. He told the league that he was unqualified but would be available if they could not find someone else. They called and he managed a team and with the help of two assistants that could teach skills they worked things out. He managed the team rather than coached and the kids had fun. This same guy also managed a youth hockey team and could not skate. You see, the people with the skills did not (or could not) make the time commitment.

In the business world one of my jobs was training people new to sales. A trainee working with me heard the word commitment a lot. Fortunately in sales, most of the

> **Whatever** your lips utter you must be sure to do…
> —Deuteronomy 23, verse 23

competition lacked the passion or desire to be fully committed. If you were the one that got back to the customer first, if the customer trusted you would be prompt, if your information was reliable, you would get the first call and the most orders. It was a simple task and the most important.

I took a liberty with the passage with the word "do." I wanted it to be generic. It goes on to say, "…sure to do, because you made your vow freely to the LORD your God with your own mouth." At some time in your life if you read these messages, you made a commitment to God. These messages are an opportunity to review that commitment and recharge your batteries; a way to keep committed and stay on track in a world of distractions.

**Thought for Today:** Today let us all renew our commitment to the Lord and our church.

**Prayer for Today:** Dear Lord, we have not always been faithful. There are distractions in our world that we let lead us elsewhere. Today we pray for forgiveness and make a new commitment to do your will. Amen

# Independence Day

Independence is what makes America great and our many freedoms make this a great place to live. Our constitution is based on our ability to self govern. Below is what James Madison, our fourth president, had to say about our system.

"We have staked the whole of all our political Institutions upon the capacity of mankind for Self-Government, the capacity of each and all of us to govern ourselves, to control ourselves, to sustain ourselves according to the Ten Commandments of God."

Pray about where we were then and where we are now.

**It** is for freedom that Christ has set us free. Stand firm, then, and do not let yourselves be burdened again by a yoke of slavery.
—Galatians 5, verse 1

**Thought for Today:** Today let's celebrate our independence by obeying the Lord's commandments.

**Prayer for Today:** Dear Lord and Father, our country celebrates its independence. Our freedoms are based on your laws and our abilities to obey them. Today we pray for spiritual growth, honesty, integrity and ethics. Amen

# Stand Free

You that know me probably have heard my definition of retirement. It is having four days a week without a calendar commitment and to have a long to do list with the opportunity to choose. For me, that is the definition of freedom and the way Christ would want us to live. Unfortunately, there are few careers that offer that kind of flexibility and most families today have two careers working to clutter up their calendars.

The economy of 2008 and the financial status of the American family does not seem to allow freedom in that way. It is very easy to get caught up in the pursuit of becoming an average family or an average Joe. It takes a certain amount of control to take a deep breath and step out of line to seek peace. The "yoke of slavery" has become habitual and many feel uncomfortable when they have free time. We need to evaluate that, each on our own terms.

> **It** is for freedom that Christ has set us free. Stand firm, then, and do not let yourselves be burdened again by a yoke of slavery.
> —Galatians 5, verse 1

We can experience our own freedom through meditation and prayer. It takes but a few minutes to unwind when we focus on being at peace. My old standard of balance, the YMCA triangle of Spirit, Mind and Body is a model we need to keep in our lives. We need to stop, look and listen to Christ to keep peace in our lives so that we can be the best we can be for our families and society.

**Thought for Today**: Our calendars are full, the financial pressures are mounting and our family activities have us running about. Today let's do that self evaluation of our personal "yoke of slavery." Let us determine what is necessary and what is not; also what are our true needs and separate them from wants. Let's accept the guidance from Christ and take one step closer to being free.

**Prayer for Today**: Dear Lord and Father, today we are confused and challenged by financial issues that seem out of control. We pray to you for the guidance and will to seek relief through your spirit. We pray for light at the end of our tunnel. Amen

# Belief

When we pray we generate a certain amount of doubt in our minds. Often we are testing God to do something we cannot believe in. As we get older some of us pray to be younger or to be able to do the things we did 20 years ago. Those prayers largely go unanswered. Our pastor talks about praying for the terminally ill. He prays that they will find peace with the Lord. He also prays for the family and their future.

Recently on our prayer chain we prayed that a person would receive a liver transplant. That is a Catch-22 because someone has to die for that to happen.

> **Therefore** I tell you, whatever you ask for in prayer, believe that you have received it, and it will be yours.
> —Mark 11, verse 24

What a conundrum. We were not praying for a death, we were praying that if someone died that they could make the ultimate gift, the gift of life. That is still something to consider!

It seems that Mark is correct though when he says "believe that you have received it...." A strong belief seems to improve the success rate through prayer.

**Thought for Today:** For today let us keep it simple and enjoy the day!

**Prayer for Today:** Heavenly Father, today we pray a simple prayer. Today is the day that you made for us and today we thank you for that and the opportunity to enjoy it. Amen

# Subconscious Landmarks

God wanted the Israelites to make landmarks for the future children of Israel. He also wants us to have "landmarks" in our lives. Often when we are about our daily activities, something happens that triggers a distant but fond memory. These memories are landmarks in our lives; landmarks that we have that remind us of the value and pleasure of living.

**So** Joshua called together the twelve men he had appointed from the Israelites, one from each tribe, and said to them, "Go over before the ark of the LORD your God into the middle of the Jordan. Each of you is to take up a stone on his shoulder, according to the number of the tribes of the Israelites, to serve as a sign among you... These stones are to be a memorial to the people of Israel forever.
—Joshua 4, verses 4–8

Throughout our lives we are blessed with many positive landmarks. We celebrate certain ones: birthdays, anniversaries, Holidays, etc, but many of the fondest landmarks are much simpler; often very personal. These are the ones that bring meaning to life.

**Thought for Today**: Today, let us think back and try to remember what brought us to this point in our lives. Let us focus on the "landmark" events that shaped us to be what we are. Let us understand God's role in the meaning of these events and how he shaped and developed us in many simple ways.

Over Memorial Day weekend, my thoughts transgressed to a very early celebration back in my home town in Massachusetts. It was just after World War II and emotions were very high as there were many soldiers to be honored. But something simpler than that affected me as a six year old. At a parade, I heard my first marching band, up close from a curbside seat during the parade. Led by the older kids in the neighborhood, we all jumped up and marched alongside the big base drum. My heart was beating out of my chest with excitement. In fact I can feel it as I write. An experience that had slipped into my subconscious, a landmark saved for me.

**Prayer for Today**: Heavenly Father, as a nation, we just celebrated independence, our many privileges and especially our religious freedoms. We give thanks for all of them. We pray that around the world, people can learn to appreciate their own faith, the love that goes along with it, and appreciation of the faith of others. Amen

# Follow Your Heart

Each and every day we need to make decisions to get through the day. Sometimes we know we are wrong when we make them. In my case today they often involve skipping an exercise session, eating an extra cookie, putting off something until tomorrow that would be better done today. During the '60s, what I call my dark period, the decisions that I made daily were certainly interesting and created a life of darkness. I was not listening to my heart (conscience) and ended up divorced and chemically dependent. My focus during those years had a lot to do with "self."

Somehow we get punished when we focus too much on self interests; good ones or bad ones. Part of my focus as a young married adult was education; another was earning enough money to survive; a third was my golf game. In summary, I attended Northeastern University two or three evenings a week, worked full time, had a part time job at the YMCA teaching fitness and coaching, maintained a 7 handicap and maybe had a few too many beers. My family life was a distant fourth priority. My focus was all on self.

> **Above** all else, guard your heart, for everything you do flows from it.
> —Proverbs 4, verse 23

Dr. Joyce Meyer says, "You cannot be selfish and happy. The two never go together." My life from the late '50s through the mid '60s confirmed that in my mind. Somehow through my church, the twelve step programs and my new-found attention to family, there was a conversion. I am blessed.

My message today is simple: if you are not as happy as you would like to be (are any of us?) the solution lies in spiritual growth; both personal and within our family and friends; or being true to your heart!

**Thought for Today:** For today let us stop when we are feeling stressed or unhappy. Try to feel what it is all about. Chances are it will be a conflict between doing what your heart says rather than what your calendar says. Then let us try to be more true to our hearts.

**Prayer for Today:** Dear Lord, today we give thanks for the many blessings that you have given us. We especially are blessed by friends, family and those around us. Amen

# Forgive And Love

We all hear, read and believe that we are forgiven. We all have, in our histories, reasons to be forgiven. We all have memories of being forgiven. I pray that all readers find the previous statements true and ask that we think about the many times in our lives when we were down and out, possibly guilt ridden. Being within a family or social structure growing together in a spiritual way so that faults are forgiven creates great landmarks in our lives.

Children often misbehave, fight over toys, sneak a treat before dinner; the simple things. We almost always forgive them after a consequence. That is a great example of our love. As teens, some of the behaviors are often more extreme, but we again forgive the behavior and show our love.

When we were growing up, we often had disagreements with our siblings, friends and neighbors. Most of the time, we forgave each other and grew from the experience. That's just life. However, each and every time we forgave someone or were forgiven ourselves, we created a landmark in our lives.

Forgiveness and love are what creates family and social landmarks in our lives. They create the memories that make us

> **Praise** the LORD, O my soul, and forget not all his benefits—who forgives all your sins and heals all your diseases, who redeems your life from the pit and crowns you with love and compassion, who satisfies your desires with good things so that your youth is renewed like the eagle's.
> —Psalm 103, verses 2–5

what we are. To be a positive and happy person it is important to be aware of the many times that God's will has generated forgiveness in our lives and be grateful. We have all experienced His grace through these landmark events.

**Thought for Today:** We all realize that God forgives us for our sins. We also pass forgiveness to others who have wronged us. Through the act of forgiving others, we receive the reward of "good feelings" and a growing relationship. Let us focus on being tolerant and forgiving of others' unique qualities and behaviors.

**Prayer for Today:** Dear Loving God, often we find ourselves offended by the behaviors of others. We have noisy neighbors, careless drivers, inconsiderate fellow employees and many other factors in our lives. Sometimes it is difficult to be a good Christian when dealing with irritants. We pray that we can behave as Christ would behave when tested by our society. We pray that we may display tolerance and love for all. Amen

# Mile Markers

Numbering our days is a great thought; we often catalog them in our minds and many are hidden in our subconscious. Each day of our life is a present and special in some way. Each has a memory, some fade but the great ones stay forever.

The major ones do not take rocket science to remember. I am an elder and remember where I was for each of the following; Pearl Harbor (27 months old!); when JFK was shot; the twin tower assault; Ted Williams last at bat (a home run at age 41!).

The unconscious ones are often more fun when they can be jarred to the front. Recently an old friend from 1955 and I reconnected and reviewed our memories together; high school football experiences, school days, former teachers and of course cheerleaders. He brought back so many memories that one evening while on-line he called me. We talked for two hours.

> **Teach** us to number our days, that we may gain a heart of wisdom.
> —Psalm 40, verse 12

The Lord has been good to us, we are not wealthy, but we are rich; rich in memories, full of love and happiness and wisdom. The numbering of our days has paid off in a worthy life.

**Thought for Today:** Today we will create a memory. Whether it is a major or minor event remains to be seen. Either way let us recognize its contribution to whom we will be.

**Prayer for Today:** Dear Lord and Father, we thank you for all the great memories and blessing you have bestowed upon us. Today we pray that we serve your will here on earth as we go through our day. Amen

# Real freedom

In our society today we find too many ways to become slaves. Along with our careers we take on the church projects, the youth sports, charity events, etc. Then we become aware that we have little time left for meditation and rest. In today's world we tend to create our own brand of slavery. All in the name of lifestyle?

Often our pastors ask us to put down the morning paper, turn off the TV news and pick up the daily meditation book. Start the day with meditation and love! I think at some time we have all tried it and then backed off. That's how Good News was started. My will power kept going back to the news and sports!

Certainly we are better people and have a better life when we keep our faith at the forefront. When we recharge our spiritual batteries. When we are charged with faith, large problems seem to have less impact, it is easier to show others we care and tranquility comes to the

**It** is for freedom that Christ has set us free. Stand firm, then, and do not let yourselves be burdened again by a yoke of slavery. You who are trying to be justified by law have been alienated from Christ; you have fallen away from grace. But by faith we eagerly await through the Spirit the righteousness for which we hope. For in Christ Jesus neither circumcision nor uncircumcision has any value. The only thing that counts is faith expressing itself through love.
—Galatians 5, verses 1, and 4–6

surface. As Paul said above, "The only thing that counts is faith expressing itself through love." Let's take the advice of my favorite philosopher, NIKE, and "Just Do It."

**Thought for Today**: Let us keep meditation at the forefront today. Yes, we are too busy and need to get to the lake home, mow the lawn, the kids have three games, etc. But no one says we need to be formal in our thoughts regarding our faith. Take a mini-break a day; at a stop light, in the parking lot—a few minutes of charging the batteries goes a long way.

**Prayer for Today**: Heavenly Father, we have become calendar slaves. Our lifestyles—and fear of losing our lifestyle—has dominated our lifestyle. Today we pray that we can trust in you and recognize that your grace is what we need. Amen

# Let Go And Let God

What do you do when a problem seems unsolvable? You must let God show you that there is a solution. If you are uncertain about the future or having difficulty releasing the past, do not be troubled. God is with you now. Let go and let God guide you in this present moment.

Let go of worries or concerns about how you think something should be done and let God guide you to the best way to do it. Do not become overwhelmed by the number of tasks before you. Let God's spirit lead you step-by-step to a new life of fulfillment.

As you let go and let God take charge of your life, you will realize that seeming obstacles can be opportunities in disguise. God will never fail you.

> **I** will never fail you nor forsake you.
> —Hebrews 13, verse 5

**Thought for Today**: Let go of the stress and tasks that seem insurmountable and out of our control. Let us do what we can and pray about the rest.

**Prayer for Today**: Dear Lord, today we give thanks for your presence in our lives and our future. We have confidence that by letting go and turning things over to you, and by living by your laws, grace will be ours. Amen

# Ethical Business Wins

In business and life, aggressive and opportunistic behavior is fairly common. Our economies are generally cash driven, sales is often "let the buyer beware." In our more modern economy it seems that service has become a lesser part of the equation.

Often in my younger days as a salesman, my youthful enthusiasm, lack of confidence and immediate financial needs generated behaviors that may have not been as professional as they were later in my career. I was trained to use all the tools of the opportunistic salesman. Win the negotiation. In the long term they do not work. In fact, over the 30 years of

**This** is the confidence we have in approaching God: that if we ask anything according to his will, he hears us. And if we know that he hears us —whatever we ask—we know that we have what we asked of him.
—1 John 4, verse 14

sales, my experience has proven, without a doubt, that open and honest sales and business men out-perform the sharks and slippery every time. Good ethics and Godly behaviors generate good rewards. The term "win-win" should be in the bible but I couldn't find the right passage.

**Thought for Today**: Today let's focus on being open and honest in all of our dealings.

**Prayer for Today**: Father we thank you for our Christian ethics. When we do business or play a game using your rules, life is good. Amen

# Doing God's Will

We are a society of checks and balances and our scale seems to be tipped on the negative or "evil" side. Keep the faith as we proceed; I believe that God plays a role here and we will tip the scale back to more Godly behaviors.

I can remember an early TV personality, Arthur Godfrey, who had Lipton Tea as a sponsor for several years. He touted the great flavor, the best way to make it and praised it highly. Then he changed sponsors and commented on how glad he was to have a great American cup of coffee! He lost half of his audience because he admitted his deception. In the '50s that was considered lying! His show was cancelled when his contract was not renewed. Somehow, actors who never used or checked out a product have become the norm and accepted.

In my mind, faith and values need to be practiced in advertising and business. Sales

**We** know that we have what we asked of him. We know that anyone born of God does not continue to sin; the one who was born of God keeps him safe, and the evil one cannot harm him.
—1 John 4, verses 16 and 17

and marketing are services to the customer; integrity is "don't cook the books;" buying is "get a fair deal;" everybody can win, but only when there is confidence and a Godly presence.

**Thought for Today**: Let us ask a simple question as we go about our day; let us ask where is God in all of this?

**Prayer for Today**: Heavenly Father, we seem to be in a downward spiral. There is fraud, scandal, anger and war in abundance. Evil seems to abound and there seems to be no end to it. Please help us focus and demonstrate that your ways are the correct ways. Help us maintain the confidence and maturity to overcome the evil around us. Amen

# Safety

Peace is something that all of the world's religions teach and somehow we humans manage to mess it up. In our Christian sense if we could ask the old question "What would Jesus do?" we would not go to war. Hymns like Onward, Christian Soldiers and The Battle Hymn of the Republic would not have been written. That is the reality of our world.

Last evening I was talking to a courier who has given up travelling to several cities because they were too dangerous. There was drug activity and a lack of control exhibited. The company he worked for initiated a policy that for every unsafe city you give up you had to yield a safe city. Yeah, fat chance that you can find a safe city! You see there are more couriers than cities and it is a dangerous job.

The fact of life is, peace is something that needs to be from within because bad things happen to good people everywhere, down the street, in the home, as well as when travelling. We need to bring our faith and our prayers with us.

> **Peace** I leave with you; my peace I give you. I do not give to you as the world gives. Do not let your hearts be troubled and do not be afraid.
> —John 14, verse 27

As believers we need to contribute to the other side of the balance sheet. There are three important contributions we are taught to make daily. First we need to pray for our enemies, the bad guys; crooks, burglars, terrorists and the whole lot. Pray that they can find a better way through the Lord. Second we need to pray for our safety and happiness. We need to run our lives confidently and without fear. Third we need to give thanks for the opportunities given us to contribute.

We live in a world of differences. We need to live and set the example for others and ask WWJD!

**Thought for Today**: For today let us exercise the freedom afforded to us through Christ. Let us not be critical of others and demonstrate our love as we do our daily activities.

**Prayer for Today**: Heavenly Father, today we simply pray for a lasting peace.

# Letting Go

With God's help, we can release the past and live in the now. By accepting God's presence in our life, we are able to release the past rather than reliving it. Holding on to hurtful memories takes us down roads that lead nowhere. With God's help we can choose new directions and turn from a nowhere destination to live in the here and now.

There is a piece of all of us that seems to need to live in the negative past. Divorced people can hold resentments for years; accident victims often recant the other driver; people frequently hold grudges against their managers in the workplace; and it goes on. It is easy to do, but in the scope of Christianity, it does not fit.

Forgiveness is what leads to peace and happiness.

Today is a new day in which we can discard the baggage of old habits that limit us. We can start anew with God and through divine guidance, take control of our lives. We need to be receptive to all the goodness that God has to offer.

> **So** if anyone is in Christ, there is a new creation: everything old has passed away...
> —2 Corinthians 5, verse 17

One of June's and my favorite slogans is "Today is the first day of the rest of our lives."

**Thought for Today:** Today let us think about what wears us down. When it is a historical issue, let us deal with it. If you can make an adjustment to the situation, do it. If you can switch to something positive, do it. If you cannot resolve the negativity, pray about it.

**Prayer for Today:** Dear Lord and Father, we need you in our lives more than ever. There are so many negative issues it is often difficult to focus on your goodness. We give thanks for the many blessings that you bring to our lives; the great friends that we need, the world that surrounds us with beauty, and our families that bless our lives. We thank you as our creator for our many blessings. Amen

# Why Judge?

Since 1977 I have been involved in twelve step programs that emphasize spiritual growth. When people walk in the door they usually have lost touch with their spiritual side. In fact, they often never had one. Those of us that offer help usually have problems getting them to the second step, "Come to believe that a power greater than ourselves can restore us to sanity."

Often referring to God at this point in their lives will scare them away so the term "higher power" is often accepted as a starting point. It always bothers me when I hear that term because God was never an issue in my life. However, when a person is hurting and in need it is a good start that opens the door to God and generally works.

The active people who sponsor and work with new members in need cannot pass judgment in any way. Paul's message to the Romans is the key and the start of helping people sort out their lives.

> **Accept** him whose faith is weak without passing judgment.
> —Romans 14, verse 1

**Thought for Today:** Today we will interface with people who do not think the way we do. Let's practice acceptance of our differences without being judgmental.

**Prayer for Today:** Dear Lord, please help me understand and accept others. Help me understand those who do not practice the principles taught by Jesus in their daily lives. Help me accept them and help me live my life in a loving and caring way. Amen

# Differences

Growing up in the '40s and '50s my family was very strict on who was acceptable and who was not; prejudicial to the max. I have come to believe that those types of things that existed were from the fear of competition within our society. Fear that the Italian and Irish immigrants would become equals to the old time New Englanders; the Blacks, Catholics, and the list went on.

There was a definite trend to block the social development of certain sections of the society. It was near the end of the era when help-wanted signage on some factories stated, "Irish need not apply." It was a sad time.

The good news is that I was blessed being a YMCA brat growing up and they were leaders in treating people as equals. I mixed with all factions and never saw any difference so it was hard for me to buy into my family's ideas. At one point I was actually advised by my grandmother that my Italian friends were not welcome at her house.

> ...**let** us stop passing judgment on one another. Instead, make up our mind not to put any obstacle in our brother's way.
> —Romans 14, verse 13

**Thought for Today:** Today we will interact with people of all kinds. Let us recognize them as equals and recognize the blessing of our differences.

**Prayer for Today:** Dear Lord and Father, somehow America, home of the free, still harbors prejudices within our society. Today we pray that we can learn to accept others as Saint Paul suggested. Amen

# Consequences

Do I sound like I am beating on the same drum? That is because it is an important drum to beat; not for those we call "Them" but for us.

The term "network" became popular in the '80s. It generally referred to business relationships and started out as a business terminology.

The internet has created a more informal system of business and social networks. In a social network people are called friends and I like that. Today I reviewed my Friends list of over 200 people to see how many my grandparents would exclude and it would eliminate around half my friends. That is half the opportunities to learn, enjoy, assist and help. It would be sad!

My point is that these exclusionary attitudes harm the person, the "We" far more that the "Them." When we exclude we are the losers! Paul closed with the term "…mutual edification." And we lose that when we exclude.

> **Let** us make every effort to do what leads to peace and to mutual edification.
> —Romans 14, verse 19

**Thought for Today**: Today let's extend our Christian love to everyone we meet and not exclude anyone!

**Prayer for Today**: Heavenly Father, we give thanks for the Grace of Jesus and the forgiveness of our faith. We have not been perfect in our treatment of others. Today I pray for the gift of love and that I may accept and love everyone. Amen

# At Peace

Perfect Peace. Is that something we dream about? It is not in my case. Most of my dreams seem to be about troubles, potential troubles and past experiences. I often wonder what negative and scary dreams mean. Am I being punished? Is my faith weak? Are there unwholesome thoughts imbedded in my subconscious? Or simply was it too darn much sugar in that hot fudge sundae I ate after dinner! It could be all of the above.

It seems that I have come close to mastering peace in my awake hours. On the golf course, the water ball and the fourth putt don't seem important any more. The red lights and traffic jams do not even seem to bother me when I am driving. When I am awake, my focus on positive feelings and having a great day are at the forefront. Life is good, darn good.

**You** will keep in perfect peace those whose minds are steadfast, because they trust in you.
—Isaiah 26, verse 30

Recently in the comics there was a cartoon regarding the patience that we develop as we grow older. It mentioned how things that bothered us in our youth don't seem as important as they once were. I like to think we seniors have matured and have put things in perspective. The punch line in the cartoon was "maybe we just don't give a darn anymore." I assure you that is not the case.

One of Webster's definitions of "steadfast" is "extremely steady and loyal." The prophet Isaiah is telling us that a strong faith rewards us with peace in our hearts. If you are reading this, I suspect that you are blessed with and have a strong faith and are at peace.

**Thought for Today**: Today let's be steadfast and positive in our search for peace.

**Prayer for Today**: Dear Lord, today we pray for a positive attitude as we deal with our activities. We pray that we may contribute to the peace of those around us in your name. Amen

# Being Humble

Is there a meek person in your life? What do you think of the person who is humble, at work, in the family or at church? Would you like to avoid him? We tend to equate humble with being a wimp! In the case of Moses, he was not passive. He took on an Egyptian overseer, stood up to Pharaoh and hiked the desert for forty years. It is hard to see him as a wimp.

Humble doesn't mean what we think. It is being humble before God. It is a choice. Deliberately harnessing your strength and tempering it to use in a controlled way. Humble is not weak. It is believing and obeying God when you don't particularly want to; when it is not the path of least resistance.

Moses was not always enthusiastic about what God wanted. He did not feel capable when God called him to lead the people out of bondage. He didn't exactly say, "right on." It was more like, "Me, you have got to be kidding. Try someone else." (see Exodus 4, verses 10–13).

> **Now** Moses was a very humble man, more humble than anyone else on the face of the earth.
> —Numbers 12, verse 3

God's response, "I will be with you."

When you are feeling hesitant and inferior, God says, "I will be with you."

When you are wondering if you can make it another day with the job stress, he says, "I will be with you."

When you're faced with a tough decision and wondering what to do, he says, "I will be with you."

Like Moses, you may be a bit reluctant. But he obeyed God. Moses believed him, did what he said and said what he was told. We can too, when we humble ourselves.

**Thought for Today:** Let's be humble before the Lord today!

**Prayer for Today:** Dear Lord, today we pray that we can do your will in our everyday actions. We pray for the guidance and humility to accomplish that. Amen

# Sabbath

Rest. God is saying that once a week we need to take a break. He is saying there is more to life than work. He is also urging us to follow his pattern: "For in six days the Lord made the heavens and the earth, the sea and all that is in them, but he rested on the seventh day. Therefore the Lord blessed the Sabbath day and made it holy."
—Exodus 20, verse 11

We need rest physically. There is rhythm to the seventh day of rest that is a good balance of work and rest. In the early '90s my seven-day-a-week running buddie, Bill, advised me that he would no longer do long runs on Sunday. We both stopped Sunday runs and our overall running improved. Many people put themselves out trying their own plan.

Spiritually we need this time to refocus our lives. God wants us to spend one day looking to him and thanking him for being liberated. The Sabbath is a great day to recharge our spirit and rest our bodies. Listen to what the Lord said to

> **Remember** the Sabbath day by keeping it holy. Six days you shall labor and do all your work, but the seventh day is a Sabbath to the Lord your God. On it you shall not do any work...
> —Exodus 20, verses 8–10

Isaiah: "If you keep your feet from breaking the Sabbath and from doing as you please on my holy day, then you will find your joy in the Lord."

In America, most Sunday blue laws requiring stores to close are gone. That enables us to carry on and totally skip the day of rest. Some of us work, some spend the entire day playing. There are youth sports. How are you using it? Who comes first? It is a day to serve, worship, rejoice and rest. Take a look at how you use the Sabbath.

**Thought for Today:** Take some time to meditate and pray for rest and peace in our lives.

**Prayer for Today:** Let's pray for those people who just can't take time to rest and meditate. May they somehow grow to find joy in the Lord.

# The Good Times

There are always good times and bad times and they are relative terms. At a recent Bible study the question was asked if anyone in the room ever had really bad financial times. We all thought our answer was yes. Well, after a brief discussion we changed our minds.

> **Then** Jesus told his disciples... that they should always pray and not give up.
> —Luke 18, verse 1

In one case a fellow had been divorced and certainly had some cash flow issues, feelings of loneliness and despair. However he kept a job, a relationship with his children and remarried and stayed that way for over 40 years.

Several others were raised on farms and lived in small communities in the midwest and certainly experienced the highs and lows of farm life. In two cases the towns where they grew up are now ghost towns. After the corporate farms bought out the family tract there was no town left—communities gone forever. However, none had ever gone a day without food or a family presence.

I guess we were all very blessed.

In today's world there are something like ten million people out of work. I have friends who have gone from being executives to jobs well below their past positions; from six figure careers to hourly rated jobs. They feel slighted by society but recognize that they are blessed to have something.

There are several good news recipients that are upside down with their debts, some losing their homes and their lifelong equity. Their story is all too common in our new world economy. A lot of people's dreams have crashed down and we fear for future generations.

In this environment the Christian church seems to grow. In troubled times the Lord is more visible than in good times as people reach out for His and our support. We need to be there for everyone who comes.

The Lord said, "Call to me and I will come to you." —Jeremiah 33, verse 3

**Thought for Today:** Today let's focus on being there for others. Not just those who seek us, let's be approachable by all.

**Prayer for Today:** Heavenly Father, today we had three square meals, tonight we will have a warm bed. Today we have your grace. Thank you. Amen

# New Beginnings

Often I awaken before sunrise and feel the need to share some Good News. Frankly, it has not happened enough this year but today I am blessed and this afternoon the good Lord will bless me with a nap!

Times are certainly challenging as yesterday's Good News "Inventory" pointed out. There were several of our Good News buddies with challenges or a heavy heart.

If you are reading this you are one that knows there is hope and that you will be a winner in the end.

Psalm 118 is one of my favorites because in my mind it says it all. This year the news has not been very good and it is often scary or depressing to read the paper or watch the news. My recommendation is don't start the day that way. Start the day with a meditation, coffee with a friend (spouse?) or with some exercise. There may be other options, but those are mine. It will change your outlook.

> **Give** thanks to the LORD, for he is good; his love endures forever.
> —Psalm 118, verse 1
>
> In my anguish I cried to the LORD, and he answered by setting me free.
> —Psalm 118, verse 5

People of faith experience a heightened spirituality. New beginnings are a great experience. At our early service Sunday (it has a discussion time) my friend George asked, "What if we let Jesus come into our life every morning?" What would life be like?

Certainly it would be a new beginning.

Blessings to all of you for, without you, I probably would not be here writing.

This is the day the LORD has made; let us rejoice and be glad in it.
—Psalm 118, verse 24

**Thought for Today**: "This is the day..." so let's go out and share it with someone. If possible share it with someone with a heavy heart or fighting a negative battle.

**Prayer for Today**: Today we give thanks for our abundant lives. We pray that you will place someone in need in our path so that we may help them. Amen

# One God?

At a meeting recently I expressed my belief that there is one God worshiped around the world in many different ways. Several people in the conversation jumped on me and advised me of all the reasons I was wrong. It was one of those uncomfortable moments because we were not going to agree.

As many of you know I have been involved with twelve step programs for over thirty years. In that time the mix of people attending has evolved to reflect the mix of people in our society today. In almost any meeting, Hispanic, East Indian and Asian have been added to what used to be a dominant WASP and Afro American mix. The program works for all of them.

The real question is how and why? The reason is simple. Although there is a great mix of beliefs, everyone has to recognize that they need a "higher power" to help them out. Twelve step programs always start out with that "higher power"

> **I** am the good shepherd; I know my sheep and my sheep know me—just as the Father knows me and I know the Father—and I lay down my life for the sheep. I have other sheep that are not of this sheep pen. I must bring them also. They too will listen to my voice, and there shall be one flock and one shepherd.
> —John 10, verses 14–16

terminology because it works. In today's world of un-churched and varied beliefs AA and other twelve step programs have not lost their effectiveness. They still serve individuals by creating recovery through spiritual growth.

**Thought for Today**: For today let's set two goals: First, let us find a personal way to have some spiritual growth; increase our personal faith. Second, let us contribute to another person's spirit and faith; be ecumenical!

**Prayer for Today**: Dear Lord and Father, today we need your help and support. We are weak, tired and too busy. Today we ask for a vision of your will and the ability to help through prayer. Please Lord, make my day!

# Our Grace

My friend Michael is the master of simplification and understatement. He has a great life, gives to more causes that I even know of and is one that is always joyful. His style is simple; he has accepted grace given to us through Jesus.

He often makes me a bit jealous because when I am confused by the facts of life, he will often ask me where grace fits in. Recently I was bemoaning all the lost jobs in America, the state of business and the markets; none of which I have significant control over. Michael pointed that out and asked, "Bob, you are so blessed why wreck your day on that stuff? Do what you can but the best thing you could probably do is be happy!"

He was correct. My light was not shining at that moment. My contributions were going to be negative for that day.

**May** our Lord Jesus Christ himself and God our Father, who loved us and by his grace gave us eternal encouragement and good hope, encourage your hearts and strengthen you in every good deed and word.
—2 Thessalonians 2, verses 16 and 17

However with the oversimplification on accepting grace, life will always be good. When we are not in a good place we need to remember that; we need to use our grace to power the lamp inside us as lights of the world.

**Thought for Today**: This is the day the lord has made, rejoice and be glad in it. Accept our grace which is God given and enjoy!

**Prayer for Today**: Dear Heavenly Father, we here on earth are blessed with your grace. We pray that we can keep that thought in perspective as we work through the confusion of our society. Amen

# Always Be Joyful

Again I am writing at sunrise. It is cool, clear and the view from our new balcony is beautiful and serene. I have no difficulty being joyful and praying. This is a great moment, but.

This month has been a challenge in our world! We have had only seven days without rain; here in Minnesota there are several towns that have lost roughly a thousand homes and buildings in tornadoes; there were several deaths; there is unwanted oil in the gulf; and the list goes on. But today is the first day of the rest of our lives and we need to rejoice in it.

Out of adversity comes greatness. Today there are hundreds of beautiful people volunteering to help in the cities that lost buildings to the weather. Last Sunday here was an inspiring church service amongst the ruins of a country church. How emotional is that? I heard a TV weather man commenting on a much simpler blessing, he had washed his car yesterday without sweating as much as he did on the hot humid days.

> **Always** be joyful. Keep on praying. No matter what happens, always be thankful, for this is God's will for you who belong to Jesus Christ.
> —1 Thessalonians 5, verses 15–16

The summary is that life is not always great and it is sometimes difficult to "always be joyful" but we can always "keep on praying." Now I do not necessarily believe that the Lord helps me with my golf game but Bob Jr and I will play a very tough course on Friday. The challenge I will have personally will be to "always be thankful" when I am lining up a fourth putt!

Bless you all.

**Thought for Today**: Let's find a way to enjoy life in spite of the challenges. Let us recognize that challenges will make us stronger and that the Lord will see us through.

**Prayer for Today**: Dear Lord, today we thank you for the joy in our lives and the ability to sustain it in hard times through prayer. Amen

# Marriage 40th

On July 28th, 2008, June and I celebrated our 40th wedding anniversary. We were married on her 30th birthday. She has been a blessing to me and I often refer to her as being the light at the end of my tunnel. She helped escort me from my dark period of the '60s into something better—that seems to be still growing. Forty years is a long time and it was not all romance and happy times. There was alcohol treatment, recovery, career moves and stress, the challenges of raising four children and just living with Bob who does not always make sense!

I often discuss the many wonderful benefits of a good marriage: the great mutual support, the care when illness arrives, the mutual celebrations of the many events that occur. Yes, marriage is truly a great institution when things are well and blessed by God.

> **A** wife of noble character who can find? She is worth far more than rubies. Her husband has full confidence in her and lacks nothing of value.
> —Proverbs 31, verses 10 and 11

**Thought for Today:**
Today let's keep it simple and enjoy our significant other and those others around us.

**Prayer for Today:**
Heavenly Father, today we give thanks for the people that you have placed close to us in our lives. We pray that as this day progresses, we can share our love with friends, family and others who we meet. Amen

# Marriage Again

Many times it has been stated that marriage is the world's toughest job. Let me quote from *The Mystery of Marriage* by Mike Mason.

> Marriage, even under the best of circumstances, is a crisis; one of the major crises of life. It is a dangerous thing not to be aware of this. Whether it turns out to be a healthy, challenging and constructive crisis or a disastrous nightmare depends largely upon how willing the partners are to be changed, how malleable they are.

"Crisis" seems a bit extreme to me, but certainly marriage is a great opportunity for the fulfillment of life and it certainly is not without its "opportunities" for either success or failure. A marriage blessed by God, one in which the partners have allowed God's love to grow in their relationship is one of the world's greatest

> **A** wife of noble character who can find? She is worth far more than rubies. Her husband has full confidence in her and lacks nothing of value.
> —Proverbs 31, verses 10 and 11

experiences.

June and I have been blessed.

**Thought for Today**: We are facing many distractions in our daily lives: work, busy schedules, terrorism, war, and financial issues are some. Let us look at our primary relationships. Let us focus introspectively, up close. Let us understand that when things are fine in our relationships, the outside problems seem less intense. Basically, let's focus on our loves.

**Prayer for Today**: Heavenly Father, today we give thanks for the people that you have placed close to us in our lives. We pray that as this day progresses, we can share our love with friends, family and others who we meet. Amen

# Whose Macro?

Please do not take this as a political piece but I am feeling a lot like my life is out of control. Not the daily issues but in computer terms it seems my macro is not what I would like. I guess I am looking for the land of milk and honey, the golden years or to live happily ever after. We are trained to look for that in all those books our moms read to us when we were growing up.

Well, another old time expression is "life begins at 40." It may not seem like that as you approach that milestone but at 70 or 90 looking back it will feel that way. It is all a matter of perspective. Believe it or not, ages 40 through 60 are most often the best years of our lives; enjoy them.

**Now**, O LORD my God, you have made your servant king in place of my father David. But I am only a little child and do not know how to carry out my duties. Your servant is here among the people you have chosen, a great people, too numerous to count or number. So give your servant a discerning heart to govern your people and to distinguish between right and wrong. For who is able to govern this great people of yours?
—1 Kings 3, verses 7–10

**Thought for Today**: We need to focus on our daily lives for survival, there is no truer fact. With that said, today let's do what we need to do to survive but keep Paul's letters and the word of our Lord in our daily lives. It will fit in if we let it.

**Prayer for Today**: Dear Lord, today we pray for our world and country. We pray that we can find a way back to Jesus' word and Paul's macro. Amen

# Macro Issues

My macro issues are with what I call the new world economy and what I see happening in the world. I feel quite helpless. It seems that whomever I talk to feels the same way. We all want to end war, be at peace, reduce taxes and live happily ever after. That is the challenge.

The solution to my issue is that I need to focus on the correct macro; the spirit of our Christian Faith as opposed to the Government macro. The politicians around the world certainly have changed things with the new world economy and making war over WMDs. They have not impacted the words of the Lord—the real macro was written by Paul.

**The** fruit of the Spirit is love, joy, peace, patience, kindness, goodness, faithfulness, gentleness and self-control. Against such things there is no law ….Since we live by the Spirit, let us keep in step with the Spirit. Let us not become conceited, provoking and envying each other.
—Galatians 5, verses 22 and 24

**Thought for Today:** Today let's focus on the message and do what we know how.

**Prayer for Today:** Dear Lord, today we pray for our world and country. We pray that we can find a way back to Jesus' word and Paul's macro. Amen

# Vacation Time

Grand events are wonderful. June and I just returned from a two week vacation that was an extended grand event. The first weekend was spent with family in New Hampshire; we then visited friends from the class of 1957 in Maine, then on to lunch with a whole group of classmates from 1957 and followed that up with a visit with my 94 year old mom and 87 year old aunt.

There was a lot of reminiscing and memories discussed. It is always great to hear them and share in the laughter of the good times. Certainly all of us had both good times and bad to talk about but for whatever reason the focus was on the joys and pleasures of the past and there were smiles all around. Good times were the focus.

I am sure that there was anxiety amongst us. Some had experienced cancer scares, some lost loved ones and certainly with the age group from 70 to 94 we are battling the aging process at some level. Overall, anxieties were cast away, joy and love abounded.

> **Humble** yourselves...
> under God's mighty hand, that he may lift you up in due time.
> Cast all your anxiety on him
> because he cares for you.
> —1 Peter 5, verses 6 and 7

There were a lot of great moments, laughter and hugs. Moments like this are a gift from God and we need to focus on them.

**Thought for Today:** Today let us focus on casting away our angst and turning our lives over to the Lord. Let us especially focus on the older generation. Let us reach out to them with love and share the good times.

**Prayer for Today:** Heavenly Father, we pray for ourselves, our friends and loved ones. Many are ill and experiencing fear, uncertainty, loneliness or hurt. Many need you in their lives and have not found you. We pray that we may help be the conduit that strengthens their faith and eases their anxieties. We pray for a way to do your will in this way. Amen

# Forever

In Saugus, Massachusetts, in the '40s and '50s each school day started with saluting the flag, Psalm 100 and Psalm 23 followed by the Lord's Prayer. It was a great reminder of who we were and what America was and represented. I have to believe that hearing them repeated so often was the best training for life they could have passed on to us.

The overall theme of Psalm 100 is joy through faith. Rather than say a lot about that, I will ask you to do a simple comparison in your mind. Today think about those around you who do not seem to be joyful, those who seem angry, those having trouble with stress, etc. Identify those people and pray for them.

**Enter** his gates with thanksgiving and his courts with praise; give thanks to him and praise his name. For the LORD is good and his love endures forever; his faithfulness continues through all generations.
—Psalm 100, verses 4 and 5

**Thought for Today:** Today let us stay focused on being joyful Christians.

**Prayer for Today:** Dear Lord, today we give thanks for the grace guaranteed us by Jesus when he died on the cross. We give thanks for his grace and the joyous lives that we lead. Amen

# Giving Back

Every day as people and Christians, we are giving. In the '60s the expression was "giving off vibes" (That probably came from the Beach Boy's *"Good Vibrations"*). What we give has an overwhelming effect on our lives, our social environment and those around us. Whether we are in the work place, the family arena, or driving alone down the street, we are participating and giving to those around us.

Let's take a look at the place where being positive is the easiest; in the family, where love is the strongest. Certainly, within each of our families, we have always been positive, loving and "real cool." If you say that, you better take a reality check and be sure your other family members see it the same. Most of us do not meet that standard.

> **Treat** others as you want them to treat you… Never criticize or condemn or it will all come back to you…If you give you will get. Your gift will return to you in full and overflowing measure, pressed down, shaken together to make room for more and running over. Whatever measure you use to give, large or small, will be used to measure what is given back to you.
> —Luke 6, verses 31, 37–38

Sometimes we are tired, sometimes the career is not working well, sometimes we anger when we should stop and meditate. Perfection is our goal, perhaps not our reality. When we are down, it is important to remember that we are the children of God, and we have His support in both the good and testing times. He wants us to work with Him to bring peace and good while sharing His love with others. Sharing His love instead of "our frustrations" with others is a lofty goal.

**Thought for Today:** Today when we feel stressed out, let us focus on not bringing it home. Let us remember that it is OK to ask the family for support during stressful times, but unfair and destructive to pass our stresses on to them.

**Prayer for Today:** Heavenly Father, through your love, we are truly blessed. We stand before you covered with your love. Today we pray that during tough times, we can reach out to you and feel and share that love. Amen.

# Priorities

When reading about Paul's work for the Lord, his accomplishments leave me in awe. There are times when it is hard to understand how it all happened. Today's letter gives us a hint that his life had similarities to ours. He was not without stress, he had to set priorities. Today's verse can be paraphrased as "I am too busy right now to…, I will get to you later." In today's society that is really said way too often. Here are some questions for us that are over fifty:

> Did you carry a calendar when you were twelve?
>
> Were there sports, scouts or other activities on Wednesday or Sunday evening?
>
> Did anyone wear an iPod at the dinner table or in a group?

When June and I raised our children, Wednesday and Sunday night were reserved for church and the kids did not carry calendars. My grandchildren not only carry calendars and Personal Digital Assistants full of to-do lists, they need them. It is great training for the future, teaching them to make

> **After** I go through Macedonia, I will come to you—for I will be going through Macedonia. Perhaps I will stay with you a while, or even spend the winter, so that you can help me on my journey, wherever I go. I do not want to see you now and make only a passing visit; I hope to spend some time with you, if the Lord permits.
> —1 Corinthians 16, verses 5–7

choices, setting priorities. High school kids take college classes, college students are helping in the high schools, and there are internships that need to be fitted in. Things have changed.

When reading Bible stories, it is always great to recognize that the issues then are different from now, but then they are also very similar. Disciples were expected to support the church and spread the word. Paul recognized his responsibilities and set his priorities for the Lord.

We have similar responsibilities and need to keep our discipleship high on our priority list.

**Thought for Today:** Tomorrow let's wake up and think about where we can work for God. How can we be a good disciple? He will present opportunities if we are willing and alert.

**Prayer for Today:** Dear Lord and Father, we live in the land of plenty. We often forget you in our daily and busy lives. We give you thanks for your gifts. We also pray that we recognize the opportunities to do your work and that we can help others in your name. Amen

# We

Two are better than one because they have a good return for their work.

When I write I try to avoid using the same words over and over. The next two days the word "we" is used 14 times. It is a good word.

Those of you who have known me a while have heard me say that "Two people working together can do four times as much as the best of two could do alone." It is something that I learned from experience—all the way back to my teens. It just always seemed that way to me and I always had a partner or best friend.

In my early years it was a cousin who lived next door. We were inseparable; we fished, canoed, played ball and had our first jobs together. When we fished, they would seem to follow my lure and bite on his! I always got to take the photo. Playing ball, he pitched and I caught, we played every day and became very good at it. It would be hard to do that alone.

> **If** one falls down, his friend can help him up. But pity the man who falls and has no one to help him up!
> —Ecclesiastes 4, verse 10

When we took a job at Howard Johnson's as counter men (at 16?) we walked back and forth to work together and dealt with the public side by side.

We started on July 4th, 1956—the busiest night of the year. Walking home at 2 am, the police stopped and gave us a ride. That was the only reason we were ever in a squad car. They picked us up a lot and I think they looked for us.

We were a team and accomplished and learned more together than we could have alone.

**Thought for Today:** Today let's remember partners we had when we were young and learning; think about their contributions.

**Prayer for Today:** Heavenly Father, today we give thanks for our life partners you sent us; those who have helped us grow and become who we are. Amen

# We Again

A great example of teamwork can be a spousal or significant other relationship. June married me when I was a single parent—that took courage. She saw something that she wanted and it may have been the challenge. Well, she got it! She married a single parent with two small girls on her thirtieth birthday. In three short years she went from carefree and single to a mother of four. We worked hard together to figure out how to survive. We still do work as a team and are proud of our successes. Things did not always work well but we are proud of the efforts we put in even when things failed. It has been a good ride.

Getting back to my cousin, we went separate ways for 50 years and in 2009 June and I reacquainted ourselves with him at several family functions. He is married to a fine lady whose name is June! We have established a new relationship and recently visited him at his cottage in New Hampshire. Guess what? He needed to move 6 yards of sand and we are still a pretty good team.

> **If** one falls down, his friend can help him up. But pity the man who falls and has no one to help him up!
> —Ecclesiastes 4, verse 10

**Thought for Today:** Today let us think about our life partners and give thanks to the Lord for them. There are times in our lives when we do not have a partner and other times when it is hard to identify one. We must remember our ultimate partner who is with us always and will never let us down. That partner is God.

**Prayer for Today:** Dear Lord, we give thanks to all who have helped us in our lives; those who we know and those who we do not know. We also recognize your contribution to our lives and give an extra *thank you* for that. We pray that we can do your will by helping others as others have helped us. Amen

# Winning

Who in our lives are the winners? Some say the one with the most toys wins. That is a materialistic one liner that gives me goose bumps. However, in our society today, we pursue "things" instead of happiness and peace. So who are the real winners and how do they win?

God placed us here to be his stewards with our first priority to be sharing the gifts we received from Him with others. That seems to be a very tall order. However, we always feel great when we have reached out and helped a friend or stranger. In fact, is that not when we feel the best?

God gives us resources in many different forms. We have money that we earn and knowledge that we have learned. We graciously share these things with our families and children and that makes us feel good. Many people also reach out beyond their own family units and share. There are many ways to share and sow the seeds that God has given us to plant, and we are real winners when we reach out and share our gifts.

**Praise** be to the God and Father of our Lord Jesus Christ, the Father of compassion and the God of all comfort, who comforts us in all our troubles, so that we can comfort those in any trouble with the comfort we ourselves have received from God.
—2 Corinthians 1, verses 3–4

**Thought for Today:** Let us look for an opportunity to help someone; perhaps someone who is sick, someone hurting or someone lonely. If we fail in finding someone, let's share some extra with our Church. Sharing a bit of our resources will make us feel better.

**Prayer for Today:** Heavenly Father, we are living in a troubled world. Suicide bombings, road rage, families in strife and many other incidences confuse people. Today we pray for an opportunity to help and share with someone, an opportunity to demonstrate your Grace through our actions. Amen

# Importance

A job can provide great satisfaction. As Christians we have to be on our guard not to be tempted to live for our career instead of God. Our relationship with the Lord and the people around us will far outlast our careers.

Luke 12, verse 15 speaks to us about greed and our attitude toward possessions: "Take care! Be on guard against all kinds of greed; for one's life does not consist in the abundance of possessions." Christ tells us to remember what is important as we approach our work and the people we encounter each day.

At some point in our lives, we will no longer have a job. That does not mean we will not have a career. There will be service to humanity, family, friends and the Lord. It is not that life style is not important because it is. However, without good health and a strong faith, life style can be very empty and unrewarding.

> I saw that there is nothing better than that all should enjoy their work, for that is their lot; who can bring them to see what will be after them?
> —Ecclesiastes 3, verse 22

**Thought for Today:** Today let us make every part of our lives an arena for deepening our faithfulness to God, and our fellow man.

**Prayer for Today:** Dear Lord and Father, please help me have a healthy attitude toward my daily activities and relationships. Please show me how to put money and possessions aside and the people around me up front. Amen

# Joy and Peace

We Christians often seem celebration conscious. Easter, Christmas, Pentecost, Rally Day, etc., all seem to be great celebrations that hold our church families together. In our private lives, we always seem to be looking for a reason to celebrate. There are birthdays, anniversaries and many holidays that trigger family gatherings and create great memories.

The most significant of all of our celebrations is the celebration of one's life at a memorial service. The end of life experience brings grief and sadness. It is often a time of depression for close loved ones. The memorial service is one of joy, hope and the power of the holy spirit; a time when the faults, idiosyncrasies and character defects that we all have are forgotten. It is a time to remember the many blessings that a person received in their lifetime and the blessings that they have given to those around them.

> **May** the God of hope fill you with all joy and peace as you trust in him, so that you may overflow with hope by the power of the Holy Spirit.
> —Romans 15, verse 13

Throughout our lives there is always someone who is experiencing or expecting end of life events in their families. We all need to pray for them. We need to pray that the Lord will help them celebrate the lives of their loved ones and that they find the joy and peace as they move forward in their grief.

**Thought for Today:** This is the day that the Lord has made, let us rejoice! We will experience ups and downs but with the hope of God in our hearts, the downs can be short, the ups can be high; it can be a day of joy. It is our choice.

**Prayer for Today:** Dear Lord and Father, we live amongst the wonders of your creation. We have four seasons, mountains, oceans and the grandeur of creation. Today we thank you for it all and the wonderful lives that we live through you. Amen

# Values

Several years ago we attended the birthday party of a business man and mentor of mine. The attendees covered all areas of life and all age groups. There was a *Roast* and the underlying theme of nearly every speaker had very little to do with money. The recipient was certainly focused on money during business hours, that's just business. He was, however, gracious and generous with his outside activities.

The general discussions involved how many young people he helped along with their careers. Among the guests were former interns, people from help organizations that specialized in helping people who had lost their jobs and representatives from schools where he had helped out with programs and placements. Outside of business, he demonstrated a tireless generosity.

There is room in business for strong Christian values. We need to be profitable to survive and that requires good financial practices. However, we

> **I** saw that there is nothing better than that all should enjoy their work, for that is their lot; who can bring them to see what will be after them?
> —Ecclesiastes 3, verse 22

owe it to ourselves to keep Christian values in all areas of our lives and make every attempt to create win-win situations. Jesus' words in Luke 12 ,verse 15 speak to us about greed. "Take care! Be on guard against all kinds of greed; for one's life does not consist in the abundance of possessions." Christ tells us to remember what is important as we approach our work and the people we encounter each day. We need to share and demonstrate our values every day.

**Thought for Today**: As Christians we need to keep our principals in focus. We need to keep our positive attitudes and demonstrate them in our daily lives.

**Prayer for Today**: Dear Lord, today we thank you for the principles and ethics we have learned at Jesus knee. Today we pray that we may keep them in focus and apply them in all situations. Amen

# Helping Others

Last year a friend called after a twenty year lapse. June would say he was "down on his uppers." (I think that is English for on the rocks!). He was broke, getting divorced, having a "nobody likes me, everybody hates me, I'm going to eat some worms..." kind of day. In fact he was suicidal.

For whatever reason these kinds of calls are never convenient. They often trigger the question in my mind, "Why me, Lord?" The first conversation lasted around an hour and finished with me refusing to visit him (a good rule to follow) but to call him back. I also committed to pray for him if he would pray with me.

We often need another set of ears to hear our problems. Sometimes the listener may be a friend. But we also have another wiser, more faithful listener— God.

In Psalm 28, David cries out for help. Like David, when we express our feelings to God, we always find a patient and willing listener. At the end of the Psalm, David is able to express abiding trust and confidence in God.

We can too.

My friend has been calling for over a year now and is doing a lot better.

> **Blessed** be the Lord, for he has heard the sound of my pleadings.
> —Psalm 28, verse 6

**Thought for Today:** Today let us take that call. Let us pray that someone asks for our help and that we may contribute to their success or recovery.

**Prayer for Today:** Dear Lord, we ask you to hear our prayers and pleadings. We pray for the faith to let go of our stresses and have faith in your solutions rather than our own. Amen

# Rewards Of Faith

We live a long time and quite often the road is bumpy. The statistics on our world economy indicate that we are either entering or already in some economic decline. Economic difficulties always hurt the lower third of the income range first and hardest. This time with the decline in real estate values, the layoffs occurring in middle income jobs, and the drops in the equity markets, difficulties are reaching far beyond the bottom third. Globally, decisions are being made and priorities are changing. The world is being challenged.

My thoughts are not about policy, elections or the economy. They are about prayer and priorities. First, we all need to pray for the lower third of our socioeconomic world. Not just in the USA but worldwide. Food here is expensive, but in many nations it is scarce and unaffordable. There will be more people starving around the world next year than this year. We need to pray for those that are suffering and starving.

One of the ways to measure impact here is looking at charities and nonprofit organizations that require donations from the public. Right now, food shelf inventories are at an all time low, churches in our neighborhood have closed because of a lack of funding and many charities are making special appeals for extra. That says something about us—we are tight and holding back.

> **Yet** you are enthroned as the Holy One; you are the praise of Israel. In you, our fathers put their trust; they trusted and you delivered them. They cried to you and were saved; in you they trusted and were not disappointed.
> —Psalm 22, verses 3–5

OK. Where is this going! When times get tough we need to stick with our faith and beliefs as followers of Christ. We need to pray for our neighbors and those less fortunate. We need to give more of ourselves and our resources and follow the basic principles of our faith. We need to remember that the Lord is with us and demonstrate our faith. The Psalmist states that we will not be disappointed—we need to believe. It is now that we all need to gather our resources to help. We need to believe that the Lord will be there for us and we need to be there for Him.

> I am the LORD your God, who brought you up out of Egypt. Open wide your mouth and I will fill it.
> —Psalm 71, verse 14

**Thought for Today:** Let's think about trusting the Lord to be there when we need Him. There are some that need help and some that can help. Let us all do what we can in the name of the Lord. Let's trust and show our faith.

**Prayer for Today:** Father, today we pray for those who are having trouble feeding themselves. We pray for the resources to assist, not only where we live but around the world. Amen

# The Lord's Will

In life and business there are temptations. Opportunities to take more than we know we deserve. In many parts of the world, that is thought of as the American way. The relentless pursuit of things or money. After all, that is what makes our economy run.

A classic example is the negotiations between young athletes and the team that drafted them. Often, these people are grappling over extra millions and the relationship and respect between those involved is permanently damaged.

Recently, Harvey McKay, one of my favorite business authors, wrote about this subject. He pointed out that good negotiations were not opportunistic, but "win-win." The temptation to go for it all leads to ultimate failure because the team spirit is damaged.

> **Be** very careful, then, how you live—not as unwise but as wise, making the most of every opportunity, because the days are evil. Therefore do not be foolish, but understand what the Lord's will is.
> —Ephesians 5, verse 14

Harvey is a business man, tennis player, marathon runner and author. In all of his endeavors, he is a winner and has that burning desire for excellence. Harvey built his life around playing by the rules and constructing a win-win lifestyle. I do not know Harvey well enough to know his spirituality, but from a casual observation, he does God's work very well.

**Thought for Today:** Let us search out the temptations in our lives. Let us recognize them for what they are and follow good Christian ethics in our decisions. Everyone can win.

**Prayer for Today:** Heavenly Father, our World seems to be full of ungodly events. Kidnappings, suicide bombers, illness and many others cause us to focus on the negative. Today, please help us maintain our focus on the good things in our lives and give us the will to spread goodness in our confused world. Amen

# Straight To Our Hearts

When driving in the UK where the roads are windy and twisty, occasionally we come to a long straight road that goes on for miles. My wife, a Brit, explained to me that those are ancient Roman roads laid out 2000 years ago. I found that impressive.

In ancient times leaders built roads in the desert for their armies to move. They are long and straight and efficient so they could move quickly. The valleys are filled by pushing the tops of the hills. They facilitated the need. In New England where I grew up there are very few straight roads. They paved the cow paths and horse trails which tended to follow the river beds. It is tough for strangers to find their way.

The message today is that we need to be sure of our road to the Lord; that it needs to be straight. There needs to be a

> **In** the wilderness prepare the way for the LORD; make straight in the desert a highway for our God.
> —Isaiah 40, verse 3

straight connection between God and our hearts. We need to allow the simplest two-way travel possible in our complex world; straight to our hearts.

**Thought for Today**: Today let's think about where our road takes us; where are we going. Perhaps we can take a few bends out and travel straight.

**Prayer for Today**: Heavenly Father, we live in a complex world and are surrounded by too much activity and are over committed. Today we thank you for being with us and pray that we may keep our hearts open to you and stay on a straight and holy path. Amen

# Acceptance And Happiness

We are often happiest when surrounded by family. These are people we love and often demonstrate that love in very demonstrative ways. On a recent vacation we attended a family reunion of around 30 people from age 2 to 90. It was a wonderful experience, full of hugs and compliments. Grace and love were everywhere.

**Let** your acceptance change us, so that we may be moved in living situations to do the truth in love; to practice your acceptance, until we know by heart the table of forgiveness and laughter's healing heart.
—Fred Kaan, *Help Us Accept Each Other,* verse 3, Methodist Hymnal, number 560, 1974

It is socially acceptable to be more reserved when in public. Being reserved in our behavior, however, does not mean that we need to feel uncomfortable. We do not need to lose sight of ourselves and our caring nature. We can be caring, considerate and demonstrate God's will when in a crowd. When we do, we will have a better time and be happier, less stressed people.

At other times we were in crowded tourist areas and were uptight, not as openly caring. The situation became somewhat competitive; lines for service, competing for the best view of the fireworks, the best seat on the beach, etc. During these times I suggest the difference is a choice that we made, a choice to feel different, a choice to be stressed out. We made ourselves uncomfortable.

**Thought for Today:** We all will make choices this today. We will choose to be angry, stressed or frustrated by others' actions and social situations. We have an alternate choice as Christians. We have the choice of prayer and meditation. We have the option to turn the stressful issues over to God and be happier. Let us focus on being a happier person through prayer.

**Prayer for Today:** Heavenly Father, we have often failed to use your tools. We know better but in our daily lives we forget your lessons. Today we pray that we may use meditation and prayer when we become stressed, fearful or angry. We pray that we can use your tool kit to improve our lives and the lives of those surrounding us. Amen

# God's Code Of Ethics

A classic error of human ways is that we tend to hear what we want to hear. This often leads to a miscommunication and an expectation that will not be met. Disappointment occurs. Often there is a disagreement after the fact. In business this even happens with written contracts because people do not read the same meaning into the words. Lawyers get rich on this stuff.

In a profit-driven economy the focus often becomes dollars and return on investment. Thus a win-lose mentality can develop. That is not how God planned the world. Experience shows that consideration of others creates a win-win in our society always and works best.

In our own lives we need to have a clear conscience. "... My (our) steps have held to your paths; my (our) feet have not

**A** prayer of David:

Hear, O LORD, my righteous plea; listen to my cry. Give ear to my prayer—it does not rise from deceitful lips.
May my vindication come from you; may your eyes see what is right.
... My steps have held to your paths; my feet have not slipped.
—Psalm 17, verses 1–2 and 5

slipped." We need to meet God's code of ethics in all of our dealings to sleep at night. Every day it is important to keep that in mind; important to keep God in our "operating style." People that follow those principles are the real winners in life.

**Thought for Today:** Tomorrow will be a great day. We will be cooperative rather that competitive. We will save the competition for the card game, the sport, etc. When working or in our dealings with others we will be cooperative and seek a win-win situations in our lives.

**Prayer for Today:** Heavenly Father, we pray for a good life. We pray that we may contribute to the goodness in the lives of others. We are often confused by the negativity and violence in our society and feel incapable of helping. Today we pray that we can see a way to contribute more of ourselves; a way to share your love with others. Lord, please help us contribute so that your will may be done here on earth. Amen

# Pleasant Temptations

In the words of Dr. Norman Vincent Peale, "Temptation is the urge to do or say something wrong, something contrary to the will of God and the law of Christ. Temptation often comes in pleasant and seductive form and the mind always attempts to rationalize it to make it seem right." That certainly hits home for us. We face it every day.

Throughout our lives we are given the opportunity to chose, the correct path or the wrong path. The opportunistic path from the Godly path. None of us has always chosen the right path, the path that follows the law of Christ. We have all crossed that line and felt the remorse, the guilt or the doubt that follows. Yes, admit it, you just are not quite perfect.

It is common for us to hold on to the memories that we have of the times when we slipped and took temptation. Often this sorrowful thinking leads to a bad self image or a subconscious guilt that effects our lives. Working with others for the last 25 years, June and I have seen people turn their lives around by accepting the concept of "spiritual growth" and making amends to those that they have harmed.

We are not perfect, but when we are growing spiritually, we feel good about ourselves and turn down the temptations

> **Blessed** is the man that endures temptation, for when he is tried, he shall receive the crown of life, which the Lord has promised to those that love Him.
> —James 1, verse 12

that confront us in our daily lives. The secret of success is spiritual growth through prayer and daily meditation.

**Thought for Today:** In our personal lives there are many temptations: ways to cheat, subtle dishonesty, procrastination, lust, etc. We all have the opportunity to break the law of Christ. Let us be conscious of these opportunities. Let us note our wise decisions and give thanks for the spirituality and maturity that gets us through the day.

**Prayer for Today:** Heavenly Father, our world is a very confusing place. Religious wars and terrorism abound. Neighbors use their version of God to discriminate against others. Within our society, there are many opportunities for us to help. We pray that we will recognize that part of our lives. We pray that we may find opportunity to help bring peace and love. We pray for the time to counteract the fear and hate in our world. Amen

# Speak the Word

In business and in life in general, few of us flaunt our Christian beliefs. Few of us are willing to stand on a corner or go to a podium and speak the word. Rarely do we speak out that our goals are to follow Jesus' Laws. In business today, the human resource rules generally state that religion is a taboo subject in the office. We certainly would not want to make a person of a different faith "uncomfortable in their work place." In fact, out of over two hundred Good News subscribers, very few go through a company firewall and some companies reject anything with a referral to God in the text.

Several years ago, I started wearing a gold lapel pin that is two feet. As a runner, I am often asked if they represent a prize or a race. However, more often, I am asked if they are from "Footprints in the Sand." These questions lead to a discussion of faith

**You** are the light of the world. A city on a hill cannot be hidden. Neither do people light a lamp and put it under a bowl. Instead they put it on its stand, and it gives light to everyone in the house. In the same way, let your light shine before men, that they may see your good deeds and praise your Father in heaven.
—Matthew 5, verses 14–16

and I have made many fine acquaintances this way. Why, because we do not stand on a soap box, but we want to share our faith and need to open the door to the discussion.

The feet in my lapel are my light for everyone to see. Yes, even as a salesman, I am reluctant to stand on the corner and speak the word until I have screened the audience. We Christians are an interesting group.

**Thought for Today:** Today let us all be aware that we are the light. Yes, people see what we do and copy our example. We can choose to have a positive or negative influence on our surroundings. Let all of us recognize our position and be a positive force following the laws of Christ.

**Prayer for Today:** Dear Lord, today we pray for the opportunity to share our faith with a friend; someone who needs to hear the story! Amen

# Do It

One of my Pickeringisms is that there are two types of people in the world; givers and takers. That is certainly a gross oversimplification I use to describe humanity. It came from my sales and business training and has overflowed into my teachings on living. In business I was taught to watch for those who would want to win at any cost; those who would think they were climbing a corporate ladder rather than building a pyramid of support. On a ladder you step on the rungs as you climb and often the ladder breaks. In the pyramid you build a base wide and tall as you move forward and up. I like that.

In Christian life there are also givers and takers. We are all people in need and the level of that need is relative. Often our needs vary from year to year, decade to decade. When June and I were raising four children we were active in our Christian family. However, we often needed love and support from our peers. I feel there were times when we took a

**Never** tire of doing what is right.
—1 Thessalonians 3, verse 130

bit more than we gave; emotionally and financially.

Today we are in what I think of as the elder mode; we have more time and the children's educations have been paid. Today we give more than we take. That gives us a much warmer and more rewarding feeling.

Both being a taker and a giver in the Christian sense is OK. You see, if there were not people in need, there would not be anyone to give to and that would be a conundrum.

Paul's message says never tire of doing what is right; my experience is that when you are doing what is right you will not get tired! OOPS- is that Pickeringism? Bless you all for being my friends.

**Thought for Today**: Today let us live as good Christians. If we need support let us accept it without guilt and recognize that we have made the giver feel good. If we are givers, let us give freely where there is need.

**Prayer for Today**: Dear Lord, today we pray for those in need. Whether the need is great or small, physical or emotional, we pray that we recognize it and give them support in your name. Amen

# One Loving God

I believe that somehow there is one God and we all will love Him.

This week June and I hosted a group of people that shared a common bond. A group that we had hosted regularly during the '80s but had not assembled in over ten years. It is a truly mixed group, economically, religiously and socially. You see, the bond is physical fitness and it crosses all lines. There were opportunities for the differences to show through, but none were apparent.

This is a group that helped June and I start a charity event in the late '80s and many had not seen each other in ten years. Since then, there were many stories. One fellow brought his adopted son: he was Jewish, his son was black. Another was fighting Parkinson's disease and could not join us for a short jog but was glad to be with us. A 73 year old was complaining about how slowly he runs now. (I hope I can stand up at his age!) Another brought his college age son to join us.

> **And** so we know and rely on the love God has for us. God is love. Whoever lives in love lives in God, and God in him. In this way, love is made complete among us so that we will have confidence on the day of judgment, because in this world we are like him.
> —1 John 4, verses 16–17

The mix of people crossed most social and economic boundaries. The common social bond was fitness, but somehow, in His way, I sense that God was contributing to a great mix of people. These were people that helped a charity, these were all people of God.

The Gospel 1 John 4, verse 17 states "Whoever lives in love lives in God, and God in him." It does not specify any qualification other than a Love of God.

**Thought for Today:** Love is a world leader. When it exists, people are happy and successful. When love is not present, everyone suffers. Today, let us search for opportunities to convert our anxious moments into positive events through caring and love. Let us recognize resentments, jealousies and other negative forces. Let's bury them with God's love.

**Prayer for Today:** Heavenly Father, we are trying to live our lives showing love and compassion by following Jesus laws. We get confused by the hate in the world and in the neighborhoods around us and we get caught wondering what it is all about. Today we pray for some understanding of it and the ability to affect negative forces with our loving and caring ways. Amen

# Birthday Special

Each year on my birthday, I give thanks to something that I learned in my youth as a YMCA brat. The symbol for the Y is a triangle, each side has a meaning, "spirit, mind and body." Each year I give thanks for my role as a father, son and my place in society. But let's talk a bit about what it takes to be in a good place with ourselves. It is selfishness. Yes, being selfish in pursuit of a healthy self: mentally, physically and spiritually.

In each of our lives, we must fit into some basic places in society: a family, a workplace and a social setting. We fit best when the three sides of our personal triangle are in a healthy balance. That is to say we focus on each a little every day so that we minimize life's problems.

In all areas of our lives, it is important to demonstrate the forgiveness and love that comes from a strong spirituality. We need to be physically fit enough to deal with the long days without being fatigued and run down. Also, we need to be mentally sharp enough to make the decisions that are expected of us. That is a lot to ask of mortals and not an easy task. So be a bit selfish, take care of

> **Always** be joyful. Keep on praying. No matter what happens, always be thankful, for this is God's will for you who belong to Jesus Christ.
> —1 Thessalonians 5, verses 15–16

yourself so that you may be all that God wants you to be and be capable of doing God's work when the opportunity presents itself to you. Take care of yourself so that you can be all that your family needs you to be. Remember the logo of the YMCA, spirit, mind and body. Keep totally fit and enjoy life!

**Birthday Thought**: Today is the day the Lord has made, a day for me to enjoy. Friends will recognize it, family will celebrate it and I will enjoy it. It is a blessing that we all have and a great day to give thanks to the Lord for all of our many blessings.

**Birthday Prayer**: Heavenly Father, today is a very special day, the day that you brought me into your service. Throughout this day, I give thanks for all the opportunities that you have given to me; the opportunity to have a healthy relationship with family and friends. Today I will often hear the words "happy birthday."

To those words I say, "Thanks be to God." Amen

# Birthday Celebration

From the early 1980s through the late '90s we hosted Pick's birthday run and cookout. The guests were truly a diverse group, economically, religiously and socially. The bond of physical fitness crossed all lines. (We also had the desire for good food and a party!) There were opportunities for the differences to show through, but none were apparent. This is the group that helped June, my wife, and me start a charity event in 1989 that had 12,000 plus attendees on Thanksgiving 20 years later.

If you are a relative or friend of mine you probably have received special attention on your birthday. June dreads what I may do next. She does not like surprises and we have had a few. Other friends have been taken on mystery rides, special lunches, walks etc. You see, everyday each of us is special but one day a year we are "extra special." Two days ago I used the following passage from John,

> **Now** may the God of peace make you holy in every way, and may your whole spirit and soul and body be kept blameless...
> —1 Thessalonians 5, verse 23

"Whoever lives in love lives in God, and God in him." (1 John 4, verse 16) The Bible does not say not to love yourself. On this one special day, love yourself as Christ loved you. You have earned it.

**Thought for Today**: Love is a world leader. When it exists, people are happy and successful.

When love is not present, everyone suffers. Let us search for opportunities to convert our anxious moments into positive events. Let us recognize resentments, jealousies and other negative forces and cast them aside with a loving heart.

**Prayer for Today**: Dear Lord, today we give thanks for friends. We find them everywhere we look; all colors, shapes, sizes, nationalities and faiths. Through your love we cannot see the differences. We are blessed. Amen

# Helping Hands 1

It is another early Saturday morning and I am guilt ridden because the world events over the last few years have not affected me as much as they have several of my close friends. I do not think that makes sense, but that is where my feelings are. I guess we need prayers for the people of the world.

Several of our Good News friends are in financial stress and are losing their homes; three recent widows are making adjustments in their lives; two elderly couples have given up their homes and moved to assisted living; many of us are worried about our children and grandchildren's future. The aforementioned list is only partial because I am not aware of everyone's problems and fears. But what does Paul ask the Corinthians? "…who comforts us in all our troubles?"

> **Praise** be to the God and Father of our Lord Jesus Christ, the Father of compassion and the God of all comfort, who comforts us in all our troubles, so that we can comfort those in any trouble with the comfort we ourselves have received from God.
> —2 Corinthians 1, verses 3–7

Let's face it, all days are not created equal; or are months, quarters or years. However the constant in our lives is God. He is always with us to assist in new beginnings.

**Thought for Today**: Each day we make a choice to look forward or look back. Today let us recognize the new opportunities presented to us and be thankful as we work through them.

**Prayer for Today**: Dear Lord, today is a new beginning. We thank you for all that you have let us have and welcome your help as we face the new challenges that will come before us. Amen

# Helping Hands 2

Following from yesterday, one of the widows, who I do not know very well. is closing on the sale of her house. On one hand she is sad selling the home she and her husband shared; on the other side she is excited about a new home closer to her children and grandchildren. As a new beginning, how positive is that!

A second widow had difficulty finding the spiritual support that fit her needs when her husband died three years ago. She shared with me that she is focusing on helping others work through their grief and feeling good about herself. God is with her as she helps others.

In another instance a very good friend went through the loss of a family home and bankruptcy. She and her family have regrouped and started to rebuild their lives. They have put together a new

**For** just as the sufferings of Christ flow over into our lives, so also through Christ our comfort overflows. If we are distressed, it is for your comfort and salvation; if we are comforted, it is for your comfort, which produces in you patient endurance of the same sufferings we suffer. And our hope for you is firm, because we know that just as you share in our sufferings, so also you share in our comfort.
—2 Corinthians 1, verses 5–7

beginning and a life plan that will work. They have their eye on the sky and welcome God is their helper.

In every instance, our Good News friends are experiencing opportunities for new beginnings and the Lord is with them to help. We all are in that mode each day when the sun rises. Every day we will be challenged and every day we have a helper. That helper is God.

**Thought for Today:** Today is the first day of the rest of our lives. Let's move forward and enjoy it!

**Prayer for Today:** Dear Lord, today we thank you or your support; for being with us during good and bad times. Today we look forward to our new beginnings. Amen

# Peace

It is the time of year when ministry teams in Christian churches make a lot of phone calls and home visits. In August and September, our Pastor Ed calls everyone in the church directory and invites them to the fall programs. With the help of a ministry team there will be home meetings, visits in coffee shops around the city and often just messages on answering machines saying that we care. It is a time of invitation, a time to lead people back to the Rock, the Rock of stability and peace.

For families, school is about to start, the fall activities are about to begin, the summer slowdown and vacations are over. We empty nesters are looking at the leaves starting to turn and thinking about the winter season, warm weather travels and the holidays. For the most part, the human race is kicking into high gear—back to being too busy. In many cases it means not being at peace.

> **Who** is God besides the Lord? And who is the Rock except our God?
> —2 Samuel 22, verse 32

In the next few months many of us will find ourselves in busy and challenging situations, we need to be reminded not to leave the Rock, our Lord, behind as we move forward into these exciting times. We need to keep Him in our lives to maintain our tranquility and keep us on an even keel. It is a time to accept the invitations from our ministry teams and keep the Lord in our everyday lives.

**Thought for Today:** Let's take a look at our calendars and schedule a few minutes with our Lord; a few minutes for meditation; a few minutes to give thanks and a few minutes for ourselves. Let's do this so that we will be at Peace and be better able to help others.

**Prayer for Today:** We simple pray for peace; personal peace, family peace and world peace.

# Hitch Hiking

When I was a teenager hitchhiking was one of our primary means of transportation. In my early teens we hitched to the ball field in the next town to see a friend. Wherever the busses did not go we hitched. Even when Mom would give me a nickel for the bus, I would stand there with my thumb out hoping to save the nickel so we could buy candy! There were a lot of fond memories generated by the people I met and the rides we shared.

H. Norman Wright in his book *All My Strength* writes about hitchhikers. His thoughts:

> But consider the hitchhiker for a moment. He wants a free ride. He has no responsibility at all for the vehicle. He doesn't have to buy a car, pay insurance, upkeep or gas. Have you ever had a hitchhiker who volunteered to pay for gas? Not likely. He wants a free ride, a comfortable ride, a safe ride and sometimes imposes upon you to take him out of your way. It's as though he expects you to do this for him.

**No** Servant can serve two masters. Either he will hate the one and love the other, or he will be devoted to the one and despise the other. You cannot serve both God and money.
—Luke 16, verse 13

There are a lot of spiritual hitchhikers today. They know the Lord, but they want a free ride. They want all the benefits of being a Christian but none of the responsibilities or the costs. No accountability, no commitment, no willingness to serve and if it begins to cost, they bail out.

The decision to serve God or serve one's self is a big one. We can't serve both. We can hitchhike in our faith or we can serve our God. The ride is better with Him.

**Thought for Today:** Let us think about the hitchhiker and the driver. The driver is a willing giver. The hitchhiker has a need and thus is a taker. That describes Christians very well and it is OK to be a taker. We do need to decide which we are, which we will be rather than what we want to be. This season let us take a step forward and up. Let us pursue the better ride.

**Prayer for Today:** Dear Lord, today we offer prayers of thanks for the opportunity to serve and contribute to peace on earth. Amen

# Trust

We often try to make things happen in our lives while driving toward human goals and dreams yet conforming to modern society's standards. It is easy to get diverted from a solid spiritual track when we track our or society's way rather than the Lord's way; when we pursue possessions rather than peace of mind.

The question, "How do I know God's will?" has been asked many times. But before this question can be answered, another question should be asked. "Am I ready and willing to do God's will?" If the answer is yes, then the other question can be asked. Remember that in order to do his will, what he has in mind for you may take you by surprise. Perhaps it is best expressed by Isaiah 55, verses 8 and 9:

> "For my thoughts are not your thoughts, neither are your ways my ways," declares the Lord. "As the heavens are higher than the earth, so are my ways higher than your ways and my thoughts higher than your thoughts."

> **Trust** in the Lord with all your heart and lean not on your own understanding.
> —Proverbs 3, verse 5

To know God's will there cannot be any power struggle; he wants our will to be submissive to him. The more we value control and power, the greater a struggle we will have. To be at peace, He needs to be in charge.

**Thought for Today**: Today let's try to do God's will through our daily activities.

**Prayer for Today**: Heavenly Father, today we search for clues to help do your will here on earth. We pray that we can contribute to making your world a better place. Amen

# 1st Commandment

Kent Hughes has written an exceptional book on the Ten Commandments titled *Disciplines of Grace*. He gives a provocative summary of the first four commandments.
He calls each one a word of grace. Let's look at the first commandment.

The First word of Grace, the primacy of God: "You shall have no other God before me." That is, you shall have Me! I must be in first place. If God is first, if there is nothing before Him, you will love Him more and more! Is He truly first in your life?

Frankly there have been times in my life when there was no conscious space for God. That was bad news for me and those around me. I believe that all of us have had those times and they are not pleasant. If you are reading this I suspect you have now gotten through that period and have placed God first. You are blessed.

> **Then** God issued this edict: I am Jehovah your God who liberated you from your slavery in Egypt.
> —Exodus 20, verses 1 and 2

**Thought for Today:**
How may we keep God first in our complex lives? What a question. There is an answer.

**Prayer for Today:**
Heavenly father, help me find a way to keep you first in my life at all times. When the going gets tough, lead me to creativity and solutions; When anger overtakes me, lead me to forgiveness; when things are going great, let me be thankful. Amen

# 2nd Commandment

Kent Hughes, in his book titled *The disciplines of Grace,* gives this summary of the second commandment: The Second Word of Grace. The person of God: "You shall not make for yourself an idol in the form of anything..." That is, you shall not make a material image or dream up a mental image of God according to your design. God wants you to see Himself in His word and in His Son, because if you do, you will love Him more. The clearer your vision, the greater your love. How is your vision?

Often when I arise early in the morning to write, nothing happens; nothing transfers from my fingertips to the keyboard. Is it a temporary lack of vision or just not enough caffeine and sugar? I will never know the answer to that but it is annoyingly inconvenient.

> **So** then, men ought to regard us as servants of Christ and as those entrusted with the secret things of God.
> —1 Corinthians 4, verse 1

None of us seem to have perfect vision to see the way. We seem to lose it and often it is cloudy or blurred. Frankly, that is the mystery of our faith and something we can always work on.

**Thought for Today:** Let us place our vision on our calendar so that we stop and try to clear our vision of God and improve our lives through Him.

**Prayer for Today:** Dear Lord, there are many days that my vision is cloudy. Calendar items block my view, family activity does not give me time to stop and look and often personal items are given priority over you. I pray for the guidance to take the time each day to clearly understand your presence in my life. Amen

# 3rd and 4th Commandments

Kent Hughes, in his book titled *The Disciplines Of Grace,* gives this summary of the third and fourth commandments.

The Third Word of Grace, the person of God: "You shall not misuse the name of the Lord your God." That is, "You shall reverence God's name." Reverently loving Him in your mind and with your mouth will elevate and substantiate your love.

I was once golfing with my pastor and he committed golfing's biggest error; he missed his third putt. I commented that I always wanted to hear what comments he would make while lining up his fourth putt. He stated that he was thinking everything that I would be saying but I would never hear it! I wonder if he took the name of our Lord in vain!

The Fourth Word of Grace, the time for God. "Remember the Sabbath day by keeping it holy." This tells us to keep the Lord's day holy. Are you week by week offering it up in love to Him?

> **Then** God issued this edict: I am Jehovah your God who liberated you from your slavery in Egypt.
> —Exodus 20, verses 1 and 2

When we moved to Minneapolis I was shocked to find stores open on Sunday. We had come from Massachusetts which still honored the "blue laws." Not having them has led to kid's sports on Sunday and Wednesday evenings. Frankly this change has contributed to the wearing down of the family. Few people today honor the Sabbath.

**Thought for Today:** Let us remember in our thoughts and prayers the families of the children, youth and young adults who are struggling with their faith.

**Prayer for Today:** Dear Lord, today we need to slow down and keep you in our sights. We pray for the focus and patience to make it happen. Amen

# Time Out

We are always searching for a better life. When William Longstaff wrote this hymn life was not like it is today here in America; it was during the civil war. It was a bloody time where people did not think a lot about being loving, caring or holy. The world was a troubled place; an ungodly place.

**Take** time to be holy
Speak oft with thy Lord;
Abide in him always,
And feed on His word;
Make friends of God's children,
Help those who are weak;
Forgetting in nothing;
His blessings to seek.
—William D. Longstaff,
George Stebbins
1 Peter 1, verse 16

Longstaff is saying there is a better way; a way to a better peace. My message is that what we do is fine but if we feel a bit empty, that is the message to bring the Lord's holiness into our day. Lincoln put it like this:

"All we want is time, patience and a reliance on a God who has never forsaken his people."

Today in America we are in a better place and have the time if we take it. However, there are many of us who seek but do not take the time. Let's face it, we just finished a long summer; youth sports, at the lake, yard work, vacation trips, ball games, all took our time away. Yes, we relaxed through our activities and many of us are still uptight.

Attendance in Christian churches goes down in the summer and many people go the entire period without recharging their batteries. They get to the end of August tired and feeling empty.

**Thought for Today**: Today let's reach out and show the world our Christ like side.

**Prayer for Today**: Dear Lord, it has been a long busy summer. We are renewing our fall and winter activities. We give thanks for the rest and recreation of vacation times as we move forward into the school year and the fall season. Amen

# Rally Day

As we go through life, we are trained at a very young age that life is easier and more rewarding when we please those around us. I see my eight grandchildren working diligently to do things to please nana and gramps. Helping June in the kitchen, the garden and doing other non-child-like chores. Often they help me with the pool and fixing whatever needs fixing. They love to help and love the approval they receive in return.

When looking at Paul's message to the Galatians, what are we teaching children? To please others gives good feelings. When I think back to my youth, it seems that in my case, I was in my thirties before realizing that being a "people pleaser" was not always in everyone's best interest. Sometimes when pleasing people, honesty is sacrificed and everyone involved misses a chance to be closer to God.

What is the best way to get this message to the next generation?

> **Am** I now trying to win the approval of men, or of God? Or am I trying to please men? If I was trying to please men, I would not be a servant of Christ.
> —Galatians 1, verse 10

Christian education, Sunday school as we used to call it, is probably the best answer. Somehow through the Christian education process, the children learn what is important and meaningful. As they grow they will make a choice to follow Christ and please God rather than people.

Soon it will be Rally Day at most Christian churches. It is a time of coming together for the Lord after a long summer. There will be thousands of children returning and thousands not coming. In one instance we have a friend who was not raised in a Christian environment whose husband enrolled their two children in Sunday school. He sees the need and she is confused and so far a non-participant. Pray for them.

**Thought for Today:** As leaders in our community and family, let us focus on visibly doing God's work in our lives.

**Prayer for Today:** Heavenly Father, we give thanks to the Christian educators that work with children and youth. Those that teach the belief and faith that will guide them throughout their lives. Amen

# Courageous

This passage is one that we need to apply in our daily lives. Our society is a distraction and to get through each day without drifting from our Christian standards seems to be more difficult than it used to be. I guess it is that we have over-complicated our lives in developing our new millennium life style.

In my Friday Bible study there are several who grew up on farms here in the mid-west. They often talk about caring for the livestock before school; going to school for the day (often a long mile walk), and the prize was getting home to help on the farm before doing the homework! That was not my life in Boston or my children's life and is certainly not my grandchildren's today.

Even as a retiree with good calendar control I get waylaid and off target. The easy path is not always the Godly path. It takes a certain amount of courage to say no to a distraction and another bit to do

> **Be** strong and very courageous. Be careful to obey all the law my servant Moses gave you; do not turn from it to the right or to the left, that you may be successful wherever you go. Keep this Book of the Law always on your lips; meditate on it day and night, so that you may be careful to do everything written in it. Then you will be prosperous and successful.
> —Joshua 1, verses 7 and 8

what needs to be done. We need to recognize when our control is slipping away, meditate and pray for guidance. The correct path will always be clear and the courage to take it is available. God is with us but we need to let Him into our day!

**Thought for Today:** Today let us slow down, smell the roses and exhibit our good side. Let this be a relaxing and productive day.

**Prayer for Today:** Heavenly Father, today we pray for peace, love and enjoyment. We pray that we can contribute to each of those things by doing Your will here on earth. Amen

# Daily Diligence

My first real job was a drafting trainee at Bell Labs in Andover, Massachusetts. I look back and think that it may have been the lowest of the lows and the least important position in the company. It was however a great experience working with experienced caring professionals who wanted everyone to grow and succeed.

My mentor, Bob Drew, talked with me a lot about team work and told me something that I never forgot. He came over with an AT&T annual report, opened it to the pie chart that showed their revenue breakdown. He had placed a dot of ink with a quill pen (this was pre-ball point!) and explained that in the big company picture I was smaller than that dot! There were over 50,000 employees during that era. His message was that my dot could only grow when the whole pie grew and that I should

**Whatever** you do, work at it with all your heart, as working for the Lord, not for human masters, since you know that you will receive an inheritance from the Lord as a reward. It is the Lord Christ you are serving.
—Colossians 3, verses 23 and 24

always "…work at it with all my heart." He encouraged me to be a company man and a team player.

In our Lord's world we are one of billions; smaller even than my dot on that pie chart; but in no way are we insignificant. Each of us every day and in every activity has the opportunity to affect those around us in a positive way. We need to be diligent in our pursuit of happiness, love and peace in God's world.

Lincoln said it this way, "The leading rule is diligence. Leave nothing for tomorrow which can be done today."

**Thought for Today**: For today let us remember who our real boss is, our Lord. Let us make every effort to represent him well as we move through the day by having a positive influence on those around us.

**Prayer for Today**: Dear Lord, we give thanks for the opportunities that we will have to help others. We pray that with Your guidance we will have a positive impact on those around us and the world.

# More Grace

We are supposed to be the light of the world; born to give; born to receive graciously; born to accept Grace. Paul's message can be oversimplified by this simple paraphrase: "Through service to others we will find grace and peace." FYI, until I see that written elsewhere we will consider it just one more Pickeringism!

When we give, help, set examples of Grace, we impact those around us in a positive way. That needs to be our mission, our charge and our way of life as Christians: "Thanks be to God for his indescribable gift!"

**Because** of the service by which you have proved yourselves, others will praise God for the obedience that accompanies your confession of the gospel of Christ, and for your generosity in sharing with them and with everyone else. And in their prayers for you their hearts will go out to you, because of the surpassing grace God has given you. Thanks be to God for his indescribable gift!
—2 Corinthians 9, verses 13–15

**Thought for Today:** OK I understand Paul's message for today. Now let us use it!

**Prayer for Today:** Dear Lord, today we desire to serve. We pray that we recognize the chance to help when You place it before us. Amen

# Acceptance

So how do you deal with antisocial, aggressive or opportunistic and generally un-Christian behavior? We encounter it on a daily basis and sometimes we deal like Christians and other times we do not. Wouldn't it be great if we always forgave with prayers and did not cross the line between hurt and anger?

This week, one of my partners in the music business seemed to do something unforgivable. He gouged the company in what seemed to be an attempt to take advantage of his partners. God forgive me, but it was such a surprise coming from him, that my feelings of "hurt" almost instantly crossed into "anger" and near rage. Somehow this turned into a blessing for all of us.

Paul's message asks us to accept rather than judge and I was failing!

**Accept** him whose faith is weak, without passing judgment on disputable matters. One man's faith allows him to eat everything, but another man, whose faith is weak, eats only vegetables. The man who eats everything must not look down on him who does not, and the man who does not eat everything must not condemn the man who does, for God has accepted him.
—Romans 14, verses 1–3

**Thought for Today:**
Today let us all be more accepting of others and their decisions than yesterday!

**Prayer for Today:**
Heavenly Father, today let me accept those things that I do not understand; allow me to trust other people's decisions. Amen

# Judging

Following up from yesterday:

Twenty years ago my knee-jerk reaction would have been to act rather inappropriately; *angry* and un-christian. I would have damaged the relationship, hurt the company and it would have been his fault and I would have been blameless. Have you ever been there while judging someone else?

Instead, I counted to ten (thousand!) a few times and talked with June and Bob over the next few days. Unfortunately, I forgot to pray! However, God works in strange ways and I learned that he was passing on a true cost. The situation to be dealt with as a learning experience rather than a relationship-destroying bit of anger. My first "judgment" was way out of line.

Paul's message asks us not to judge but to let God make the judgments. It is hard to do that in our society, but praying before reacting is a great idea. I wish that had been my immediate reaction. Somehow, God came through and we will all build on His strength together.

> **Who** are you to judge someone else's servant? To his own master he stands or falls. And he will stand, for the Lord is able to make him stand.
> —Romans 14, verse 4

**Thought for Today:** Today we give thanks for the many fall activities: school begins, kids are excited and the formal learning process starts. To some, the start of the fall sports season is meaningful. To others the fall means hunting and being outdoors. It would be easy amongst all the activity to forget God. Let us try remembering that all this is God's work and give thanks for it all.

**Prayer for Today:** Dear Lord, we thank you for Your patient love. We hope and pray that we may use that love to understand this complex world and apply it to everyone's benefit. Amen

# Assertiveness

Several years ago there was a book about being an assertive Christian. It did not promote standing on the corner rattling beads and waving the bible. It asked us to be unafraid to tell people who and what we are through our words and behavior. The simple act of a blessing at the lunch counter, a quiet time during break, a daily meditation on our desk are all subtle but assertive statements.

In the work place today, the human resource departments have declared that religious issues may make someone uncomfortable and therefore are inappropriate.

In fact, many companies' email screens quarantine the Good News as unacceptable. It is not a good idea to be an assertive Christian in the workplace. However, behaving in an ethical Christ-like manner will always improve the chance for success.

Here are three examples of Christian behavior in the workplace. One is a good friend and small business owner who starts each week with a company-

> **For** God did not give us a spirit of timidity, but a spirit of power, of love and of self-discipline.
> —2 Timothy 1, verse 7

wide prayer breakfast. The second has a daily meditation calendar on his desk and says a blessing at all lunches! The third wears a lapel pin of feet from foot prints in the sand. All three inevitably lead to discussions with other Christians and improve the work environment.

We are given power, love and self discipline through our faith. It is important to remember to display and practice it every day.

**Thought for Today**: We Christians spend hours doing good things in society. Many simple things have very little to do with spirituality but come from our hearts through our faith. Let us freely discuss our Christian ethics and beliefs with others so that they may better understand why we are who we are.

**Prayer for Today**: Dear Lord and Savior, we are approaching the time of year when all faiths have special recognition of their beginnings. We pray that through faith we may focus on our similarities rather than our differences. We pray and give thanks for peace and the opportunity to serve humanity through You. We pray that the peace pledged by You spreads through out society. Amen

# Peace Together

Often people tell me they are no longer interested in organized religion. The ritual, rules, money and work did not do it for them; shame on them and shame on their church. There are others that change churches often searching for something they never quite find. They are sad and typically don't know what they are after.

In general those described above are less than happy in their lives.

Jesus' message is clear, He is with us always. When we are searching and restless the ball is in our court; we are the problem. These are the times that we are out of touch with the Holy Spirit; not taking the time to open our hearts. When we are spiritually down and out, we need to look at ourselves first.

There was a song in the '50s that said, "…open up your hearts and let the sun shine in." We need to allow the Lord in so that we may find peace together.

> **Remain** in me, as I also remain in you.
> —John 15, verse 4

**Thought for Today:** Today let us open our hearts to the Lord. Let's find peace with Him.

**Prayer for Today:** Dear Lord, today we thank You for being with us; joining us on our walks, at work, in our cars and in all phases of our day. Today we pray that we may stay in touch with You under all conditions. Amen

# Our Shield

All days are not created equal as we go through our lives. There are highs and lows in life and we have to deal with them.

One day in July 1998, it was way too hot for golf. I did not want to walk the course at 95 degrees but I was the league captain so I begrudgingly went to the course. It was hot and steamy. On the first tee my practice swings made my hands sweat so that the club would slip in my hands. I brought an extra towel just to keep them dry. My confidence was really low and it seemed like a bad idea to be out there.

By the third tee my extra hand towel was already soaked from keeping my hands dry, my shirt was sticking to my body but I had two pars in hand which is a good way for an 11 handicap to start. It was on this par three that my negative attitude changed. I dried my hands, did my set up and put the ball in the cup; my first hole in one! My two partners kidded me because I had been complaining!

> **In** addition to all this, take up the shield of faith, with which you can extinguish all the flaming arrows of the evil one. Take the helmet of salvation and the sword of the Spirit, which is the word of God.
> —Ephesians 6, verses 16 and 17

As I said, things change; that day went from miserable to great!

In our ever changing life there is one constant force available and if you are reading this you more than likely understand. That constant force is our faith. We read that God is always with us. Paul advised the Ephesians to take up the shield of faith. We need to remember that when things are not perfect and give thanks when things are going well.

**Thought for Day:** Today it may rain on the outside or the sun may be hot on our foreheads. Let us keep our faith strong so that we will have a great day!

**Prayer for Today:** Dear God, some days are good, others not so good. Today we know will be a good one because we are thinking about You and know we have You with us. Amen

# Everlasting Faith

We all remember where we were on Nine-Eleven. The physical world changed that day. For several months thereafter, Christian churches experienced a measurable increase in attendance. The best piece of news regarding that is the very high increase in "un-churched" guests that came and the percentage that actually have kept on coming. There is certainly good that comes from bad events.

We will all probably remember that day forever. I would like to share a few memories of my own with you. On November 22nd, 1963, while donating blood in Salem Massachusetts, the nurse told me that she had heard that the president had been shot. I told her that she should not even joke about stuff like that. Many people remember that day.

Solidly burned in my memory is sitting in front of a radio on Haverford Street in Hamden, Conneticut, very afraid, listening to reports of the attack on Pearl Harbor. December 7th, 1941. So what is the big deal? I was only 27 months old.

> I do not hide your righteousness in my heart; I speak of your faithfulness and salvation. I do not conceal your love and your truth from the great assembly.
> —Psalm 40, verses 10 and 11

(I just called my mom to be sure that is all true and we think that is my first memory.) Both those events changed the physical world in which we live. They changed operations, but not our hearts.

In summary, remember the event and accept the changes. Keep the Lord in your heart and share Him with others. He will be with us. Worldly events cannot harm our spirit.

**Thought for Today**: Today let us find a friend and share the story about how September 11, 2001, has not changed our faith or how our faith is helping us through society's changes.

**Prayer for Today**: Dear Lord and Father, today we give thanks for the joyous summer that we experienced and look forward to the fall colors as they arrive. We are thankful for the opportunity to do Your work here on earth and the pleasure we receive from it. Amen

# School Days

In the '40s and '50s, public school in Massachusetts always started with the 23rd Psalm, the Lord's Prayer and the salute to the flag. Wow, by today's standards, that is powerful stuff. Let us take a look at this and see if we can apply it to our lives today.

> **The** Lord is my shepherd, I shall want. He makes me lie down in green pastures; he leads me beside still waters...
>
> —Psalms 23, verses 1–2

The first two lines above lead us to tranquility. Faith will take care of our wants and lead us to that inner peace we desire and lead us to the restful place beside still waters.

> "He refreshes my soul; He leads me in the paths of righteousness for His name's sake"
> —Psalm 23, verse 3

There are always periods when things in our lives need rebuilding. There are temptations to take the easy way. These verses point out that the way to get out of the "dumps" is to follow Him.

"Yes, though I walk through the valley of the shadow of death, I will fear no evil; for You are with me; Your rod and Your staff to comfort me."
—Psalm 23, verse 4

The Psalm points out that the Lord is with us and will guide and support us throughout our lives.

Yes, today our lives get filled with stress. As Christians we are given wonderful tools to work with in our daily lives. The more we let God lead us, the more we will be at peace.

**Thought for Today:** Let us reflect on this fall season. Read the 23rd Psalm and accept the help that God has available to us as we move into the winter and holiday season. It will be a big help in locating those still waters we all seek.

**Prayer for Today:** Heavenly Father, many times stress builds up in our lives. It is a combination of hurts, anger and resentments kept hidden inside of ourselves. I pray that when this occurs, I find a way to let You help and can accept the guidance, protection and support promised through our Christian faith. Amen

# Share Your Spirit

In the early '90s, the pastor at our small church introduced the concept that we were all the ministers. He was just the facilitator or spiritual leader. He used to say that the average Methodist invited a guest to church every 22 years!! He encouraged us to speak our faith, demonstrate our spirituality in our daily lives and reach out to people.

In our wildest dreams we may at some time achieve world peace, resolve world hunger, and become an ethnically and racially blended society. When that happens, it will not happen through the politics that we have today. It will be a Godly event that we cannot perceive.

We are all ministers and have the opportunity to work every day toward an improved society. Language and color divide us into nations and social groups. However there is a common language, "...living words of truth which all may hear; the language all may understand when love speaks loud and clear." We all have a job to do.

> **Teach** us to utter living words of truth which all may hear; the language all may understand when love speaks loud and clear; 'till every age and race and clime shall blend their creeds in one; and earth shall form one family by whom thy will is done.
> —Henry Tweedy, Hymn: *O Spirit of the Living God;* 1935

**Thought for Today**: We can find it easy to get caught up in our activities. Families have the sports programs, school issues and their business stuff. Singles have their way of filling the week. Yes, most of the world's people keep busy. Today let us seek the opportunity to demonstrate and share our spirit with someone.

**Prayer for Today**: Heavenly Father, today we thank You for the people You placed in our lives that have supported and led us to grace. Today we pray for the opportunity to contribute to Your will here on earth. Amen

# Somebody

The Lord works in strange ways. As I write these epistles I never know what will come next. Sometimes it is from an outside source placed before me during the week. This is one of those occasions and it is close to plagiarism!

A pastor and Good News buddy retired last Sunday after 39 years serving the local community. In September of 2009 he wrote "Everybody is Somebody–including you and me." We all know that we are all winners because the Lord is with us. Pastor Mike said it in a similar way that reinforces the thought. Below is a key paragraph from Mike:

"…My theology and values are centered on the conviction that because we are created in the image of God, each of us is valued and has deep within us the potential to reflect the goodness and beauty of our Creator. Therefore, being of Norwegian or German descent,

> **For** it was you who formed my inward parts; You knit me together in my mother's womb. I praise you, for I am fearfully and wonderfully made.
> —Psalm 139, verses 13 and 14

African or Korean, tall or short, gay or straight, rich or poor is not a determining factor in our worth as a human being. We are valued because we are created in the image of God."

My thanks to Pastor Mike.

**Thought for Today:** Today we will have battles we do not expect. With God's help, let us be winners no matter which way the battle turns out! Plus: We have the parts and the image to be of value. Enjoy.

**Prayer for Today:** Dear Lord, today we give thanks for who and what we are; Your image here on earth.

# Start the Day!

Those of you that have known me a long time are aware that I have always been a morning person. In my mind, there is no better time of day than early morning, even sunrise. There is no prettier sight that the sun coming up out of the sea off of Boston, the early light on the first tee waiting for enough daylight to see the flight of the ball or the sun coming up over a mountain when viewed from a canoe while fishing. I am blessed because to me first light is a spiritual event.

Each sunrise starts a new beginning, a new opportunity to do better and a new opportunity to do God's work. Yesterday is gone and cannot be changed and our future is today and beyond.

These Good News epistles that I write started as something to do during the early hours. The news casts on TV were (and still are) depressing. The newspapers are full of bad news. It seems that bad news sells.

**The** path of the righteous is like the first gleam of dawn, shining ever brighter till the full light of day.

But the way of the wicked is like deep darkness; they do not know what makes them stumble.
—Proverbs 4, verses 18 and 19

In Minneapolis, once a week our paper has a half page section called "Faith and Values." It covers all faiths, special events, etc. and does little to offset the many square inches of negativity and promotion of activities disguised as news.

Tomorrow you will see a "first light." It may be at mid morning if you are a late sleeper. It could be a sunrise. Either way, it is a new beginning, a new opportunity. It will be the first day of the rest of your life! Spend it with hope and joy.

**Thought for Today**: There will be seven days this week, each is a fresh start. Let us feel the spirit in the first light, the hope of a new day. Let us live the first day of the rest of our lives with faith and the joy of the Lord.

**Prayer for Today**: Dear Lord, today we thank You for the sunrise; the new beginning; the new opportunity. We pray that we may use this wonderful opportunity to do Your will here on earth. Amen

# Temptations

We will face trials in our lives. Some are simple, some are complex, and all help us become better people when we deal with them correctly. James is exactly correct; tests of our faith develop character and perseverance.

Remember the story read to us as children about the tortoise and the hare? The hare gets overconfident and loses the race. He was the fastest, had all the advantages but lacked commitment and persistence. My favorite poster hung on my office wall for 30 years. It was of a very long windy road, miles long and showed a lone runner. The distance to the horizon appeared to be out to infinity! The caption read "The race is not always to the swift but to those who keep on running!" The title was "Persistence."

James and Jesus knew it; we hear and understand it; we need to persevere in our faith to make the world a better place.

**Consider** it pure joy, my brothers and sisters, whenever you face trials of many kinds, because you know that the testing of your faith produces perseverance.
—James 1, verses 1–3

**Thought for Today**: Today, this week, month and year, let us remember our faith. Each day let us spread our love and joy to make our presence felt in a positive way.

**Prayer for Today**: Dear God, today we give thanks for Your presence in our lives and the ability to resist temptations. Amen

# Whoever Has Ears

This is my first try at using a passage from Revelations and it is scary to me because it is the book that I am least familiar with. Today's passage also appears in Revelations 2 and it is a message from the Angels to several church congregations. However, it hit me because it was used three times in Revelations 3 and it summarizes an article from Sunday's paper entitled, "No religion, too? A recipe for trouble…" written by Katherine Kersten. She states that there is a strong connection between virtue (as taught by religious organizations) and successful self government (democracy).

In her article she points out that the intellectual or "psychological" man is replacing the Christian model of man. Otherwise stated, the soul is being replaced by the "self." Since the Christian model places very high demands on virtue, she fears that our ability to self govern will be sacrificed. My personal thoughts are that this describes many of the issues that are bothering America and the rest of the free world today.

> **Whoever** has ears, let them hear what the Spirit says to the churches.
> —Revelations 3, verses 6, 13 and 22

James Madison, our fourth President said it this way:

"We have staked the whole of all our political Institutions upon the capacity of mankind for Self-Government, the capacity of each and all of us to govern ourselves, to control ourselves, to sustain ourselves according to the Ten Commandments of God."

We have a personal obligation as Christians to demonstrate our faith, to invite others to join us and somehow keep our souls open to inspection. When others learn what we have in terms of happiness and satisfaction, they will join in.

**Thought for the Day:** Today let us radiate our happiness and wear our faith on our sleeves. Let us hear what the Spirit says to the churches throughout our day.

**Prayer for Today:** Lord, today we pray that we may hear the Spirit in our daily activities and can do Your will here on earth. Amen

# Overachievers

In thirty years of sales I have seen many people enter the field "for the big bucks." These people do not become long term overachievers and most seem to underachieve and disappear.

Many of my mentors were overachievers and years ago I thought of them as Boy Scouts. I had not made the connection between them, love and God. Our "Good News" list includes them today. Also on this list are clergy from many faiths and business people from receptionists to CEOs—all successful, primarily through a love of serving.

In business as well as our daily lives love, caring and sharing God with others will lead to success and happiness. Let us follow Nike's lead and "Just Do It."

> **Dear** friends, let us love one another, for love comes from God. Everyone who loves has been born of God and knows God.
>
> Whoever does not love does not know God, because God is love.
> —1 John 4, verses 7 and 8

**Prayer for Today**: Let us search out and focus on the many things we do to "serve." Not just the big things, but the little. The times we allow someone into traffic, open or hold a door, a phone call to say hello, etc. These are all acts of caring. Let us enjoy when someone does these things for us. Let us share our caring spirit and enjoy the day.

**Prayer for Today**: Heavenly Father we need to understand Your "love." The world is full of hate, distrust and doubt of others. Personally each of us shares these at some level. This week we pray that we learn to "love" the way Jesus did and can apply that love in our daily lives as an example to others.

# Rejoice Always

In our very active, overcrowded lives, we are often "stressed out." Often conversations start out with how busy we are. Fitting things in seems to be the norm. Even retirees like to say that they do not know how they ever had time to work! Then they go home and take their blood pressure medication.

Several years ago, a very good friend had both serious back problems and high blood pressure. She had tried too many chemicals to work on the problems and was addicted to the pain killers. The addiction upset her tranquility and effected her blood pressure. A very common and visious cycle for a young lady.

In desperation, she and her physician reduced the chemicals and substituted hypnosis and meditation. The meditation evolved into prayer! Well, I can't say that

> **Rejoice** in the Lord always. I will say it again: Rejoice! Let your gentleness be evident to all. The Lord is near. Do not be anxious about anything, but in everything, by prayer and petition, with thanksgiving, present your requests to God. And the peace of God, which transcends all understanding, will guard your hearts and your minds in Christ Jesus.
> —Philippians 4, verses 4–7

all her problems were solved. She had a bad back disease and a family history of high blood pressure. This is not a story of healing.

However, most of her problems went away. The meditation and prayer brought her peace and relaxed her back muscles and her blood pressure went down. The disease did not leave, but the symptoms were relieved. She found peace and a better life.

The effect of slowing down and taking time out for prayer will make God's peace be yours.

**Thought for Today:** Slow down, pray for peace, pray for the tranquility and serenity that God has for you when you are willing to let it in.

**Prayer for Today:** Heavenly Father, with these words we pray for the ability to live serene and peaceful lives doing Your work:

> God grant me the serenity
> to accept the things that I
> cannot change.
> The courage to change the
> things I can.
> And the wisdom to know the
> difference.
> Amen

# Always Joyful

Joy is in the heart and our heads seem to want to control it. Does that make sense? What I mean is that the holy spirit is always with us and sometimes we do not recognize its presence. This is being written in the seaside village of Torquay in Devon and the rain is pelting down for the eighth or ninth day of this visit. We just had breakfast with 50–60 other hotel guests—some joyful and others sorrowful.

One fellow was looking forward to his round of golf wearing his wellington boots and slicker. He loves his golf and was very positive about the day. Another was going to catch up on his reading in the lounge and then take a walk to a restaurant for lunch. I am writing and then walking in the expected rain! We are the positive force in the room! The spirit of joy and peace is with us.

Several others have long faces and are complaining about the rain. Their heads have taken control and they are missing out on their joy. Yes, there will not be any sunning on the beach, sitting under the palms and the umbrellas will be used to stay dry rather than protect us from the sun. They are missing the point. We are in a beautiful place with great people. The views are magnificent; the food great and there is always tomorrow!

This is the day the Lord has made, let us rejoice and be glad in it!

**Thought for Today**: Today let's recognize that we can be full of joy or worry. Let's choose to be joyful.

**Prayer for Today**: Dear Lord and Father, today we give thanks for people; the individuals that make up humanity. You created them all different but somehow in your image. They come in all sizes and shapes, worship you in many different ways but are overwhelmingly great to know. Amen

> I have told you this so that my joy may be in you and that your joy may be complete.
> —John 15, verse 11

# Peace

Today is a great day here in Minnesota. The sky is blue, the temperature is in the mid seventies (That's twenties for my Euro-friends) and I have had a swim, a jog and played some golf. I am tired and at peace as I write this. I am hoping that world peace (which includes family, city, county, national and any other peace!) is like the weather. It will come someday!

After World war two there was the famous picture of the soldier kissing the nurse in Times Square. After all, that was the war to end all wars. In the fifties a friend from New Hampshire received the Silver Star for his contributions to "keeping peace" in Korea. At my fiftieth high school reunion the list of deceased was overwhelming male. It had a lot to do with Vietnam and of course, agent orange. All of these people contributed to peace, protected our country and I have a great appreciation for their efforts.

**N**evertheless, I will bring health and healing to it; I will heal my people and will let them enjoy abundant peace and security.
...they will be in awe and will tremble at the abundant prosperity and peace I provide...
—Jeremiah 33, verses 6 and 9

The prophet Jeremiah talked about peace 2600 years ago. We are all hopeful and pray for it to come and most of us are willing to help it along. For all of us reading this today, let us contribute a bit of love to the situation. Let us enjoy our peace and hope that it spreads.

**Thought for Today**: Think how peaceful life really is and appreciate it.

**Prayer for Today**: Dear Lord, today we pray for world peace; peace in our families, communities, cities, nations. We recognize that is a lot to ask but we ask you for help. Please show us how we can apply your will in our lives toward this lofty goal. We pray for the safety of the world's soldiers through the end of hatred and war. Amen

# Values and Consideration

Last Sunday was my 72nd birthday and it was a great celebration of fitness, friendship and family. Oh, for some reason I could not resist doing a sprint triathlon in the morning with my brother, granddaughter and daughter. At the race there were several old time fitness friends, triathlon and running buddies to visit with as well as the race staff who knew me well. But the subject for today is not about that. It is about being Christ-like.

When several hundred people are swim racing across a lake, consideration of others is often not visible, tenderness often does not come to mind and selfish ambition seemed to be everywhere. Most people were racing for themselves and if you were in the way most did not share their grace with you!

The good news is that *most* is not *everyone*. The Lord was with me and he sent me plenty of Christ-like people to support me in crises. You see, I had an asthma attack about five minutes into a 20 minute swim. Rather than being one of the strongest swimmers, I was trying to figure a way to survive, keep my head up, and get oxygen into my blood stream. Yes, there were even prayers.

> **Do** nothing out of selfish ambition or vain conceit. Rather, in humility value others above yourselves, not looking to your own interests but each of you to the interests of the others.
> —Philippians 2, verses 3 and 4

Several swimmers heard my rather loud wheezing exhales and offered assistance. Macho me advised them that I would be OK. Lifeguards in kayaks asked if I needed help. Yes I did but my answer was not yet; finishing was important to me. In the last 200 yards a life guard wanted to pull me from the race. My comment to him was that I was a good swimmer and just couldn't breathe right now. He looked concerned and kept close by in his kayak. By the Grace of God in all my bad judgment things worked out well.

The summary of it all was the great support and encouragement other swimmers had for me. One fellow swam alongside me for several hundred yards, the officials in the kayaks were concerned but gracious, and, when in the transition area, a spectator offered me her inhaler! People are wonderful.

**Thought for Today:** Today let us look out for others. Let's lend a helping hand in Christ's name.

**Prayer for Today:** Dear Lord and Father, we give thanks for Your followers; those Christ-like people who are there every day when people need them. We are blessed with our beliefs and more so by those You send to help.

We give thanks to all who are blessed by their beliefs. Amen

# Success

In our democratic society, we are pressed into a competitive marketplace for our goods and services. That is supposed to be what makes America great. Success is often a matter of having more "stuff." We are building 5, 6 and 7,000 square foot houses, owning bigger boats, luxury cars abound, etc. All this is very good for the economy, but is it good for our souls?

Aristotle Onassis' definition of success was to "... keep climbing higher and higher–just for the thrill."

Barbra Streisand said, "success for me is having ten honeydew melons and eating only the best part of each."

Because you are reading this Good News today, I pray that your definition is more closely represented by Dr. Gary Rossberg's perspective:

> Success is not just a matter of money, power and ego, but also issues of the heart–like compassion, bravery, generosity and love. It is an issue of character, not performance. ...of being the person God wanted you to be, not how much salary you can pull down....

> **I** saw that wisdom is better than folly, just as light is better than darkness.
> —Ecclesiastes 2, verse 13

If we sit in our homes surrounded by our "stuff" and still feel underachieved; if we sit on the couch next to our spouse and still feel lonely; we need to go back to the simple things we learned growing up and search our faith for the definition of success. We will find that Rossberg is very close to the answer.

**Thought for Today:** Today let us look at our calendars and try to evaluate where our efforts are taking us. Let us review our goals and our interactions with others. Let us fit our lives into Rossberg's perspective rather than the more material views of success.

**Prayer for Today:** Dear Heavenly Father, our world has changed. Terror seems to be taking over well beyond faith and love. Somehow we pray for an answer to how it all fits Your plan. We pray for Your guidance and somehow for the ability to keep the power of Your light above the darkness that seems to be closing around

# Trust

It always amazes me and reinforces my faith when something Paul said 2,000 years ago applies directly to today's world. For several years our free world economy has been flaky. Trust in government has faded as the leaders of America and the world have become polarized. The advent of Ponzi schemes and fraud by high powered executives have hurt the trust we need in our financial markets for them to be strong. Even at low levels of government, doubt in their ability to perform is stronger than ever. Frankly, it is scary to me because our country is built on trust. Look at your money: "In God We Trust."

My Good News is not meant to be political and that seems to be the case

I rejoiced greatly in the Lord that at last you renewed your concern for me. Indeed, you were concerned, but you had no opportunity to show it. I am not saying this because I am in need, for I have learned to be content whatever the circumstances. —Philippians 4, verses 10–13

today but I promise to turn this around! You see, Paul is pointing out a simple truth and we need to pay attention to it. In a recent telecast, televangelist Joel Osteen put it this way, "We do not know what the future holds but we do know who holds our future." Hmm, there is something to think about.

**Thought for Today**: Today and always let us take time to focus on our savior. Let's take a few minutes to appreciate and welcome Him into our life.

**Prayer for Today**: Dear Lord and Father, today we give thanks for Paul's words and encouragement. We pray that we may accept his advice graciously and lean on You to get through our daily stresses. Amen

# Positive Christian 1

It is another early morning. I am thinking back to a summer where June and I moved into our seventies and deeper into over 40 years of marriage. It is great to celebrate; it is great to reminisce about the victories and challenges we have worked through over the years. June and I are truly blessed.

The story is not all that positive however, we are getting older and as my mom who is in her '90s says, "Growing old is not for the faint of heart." It comes with its own set of challenges. We get tired easier, recover slower, can eat less. Several years ago June and I set a goal of not becoming grumpy senior citizens. We decided to pray and always try to be positive Christians. It is not always easy.

> **He** gives strength to the weary and increases the power of the weak.
> —Isaiah 40, verse 29

**Thought for Today:** Today will be a milestone; things will happen we do not expect. Today let's recognize the blessings we will have, even if they seem like challenges.

**Prayer for Today:** Heavenly Father, today we thank you for our many fond memories. As we face today's challenges we pray that we accomplish Your will, deal with issues Jesus' way and generate more fond memories for tomorrow. Amen

# Positive Christian 2

For the last several years I have exercised with an older retired physician, Phil. We walk, jog, waddle 15–20 miles a week and we have a lot of time to talk. He has completed over 25 marathons, 20 ultra-marathons and most of you know my triathlon history; we talk about those youthful days. We have determined that we just do not recover as fast as we used to. In fact we think that it takes three times as long to get our strength back from a good day. During that time, we feel a bit sluggish and it is hard to stay positive. June can tell you what I mean!

At our age Phil and I have several friends who have lost their spouses. I believe that they are faced with the ultimate challenge and half of us will face it. They are facing different challenges in different ways. Each has shown great growth and seems to be recovering through the grieving process. Each shows a faith and spirituality that they rely on. They seem to be staying positive under the most difficult conditions.

> **Even** youths grow tired and weary, and young men stumble and fall.
> —Isaiah 40, verse 30

All of the above sounds a bit negative and that is not intentional—it is just data. The reality is that it is great to be a Christian. We have a great perspective on life and a lot to share with future generations. In our later years we have the support of our Lord and have time to help others, time to share, time for ourselves, and time to recover from our ills. We need to be positive Christians, set an example on how to live and be happy. As we struggle through our many challenges, we need to remember the following:

> …but those who hope in the LORD
> will renew their strength.
> They will soar on wings like eagles;
> they will run and not grow weary,
> they will walk and not be faint."
> —Isaiah 40, verse 31

**Thought for Today:** Be happy, be positive and share our enthusiasm with others.

**Prayer for Today:** Dear Lord, today we thank You for our blessings and the ability to focus on positive feelings through Your love. Today we pray that we may be positive and radiate joy to those around us. Amen

# Busyness

Those of you that have been Good News buddies for a while know that I relate closely with the many race analogies used by Paul in his letters. They are meaningful today because I have a sense that the events around the world have thrown us in to a high state of *busy*ness. (Spell-check hates that word but I like it!). In Paul's message above he is not talking about a marathon, a work week, getting to the children's activities; it has nothing to do with our *busy*ness. It has to do with keeping our faith peaked during the process of life.

This was triggered today because retired old Bob is too busy with fun stuff, business, helping others in need, increasing my exercise program and generally being Bob. For the second day in a row I woke up before the sun with activities and obligations pushing my spirituality from the forefront. I can tell when that happens because I am not at peace during the day and I generally start reading the newspaper with my coffee; back to my old ways.

> **For** I am already being poured out like a drink offering, and the time has come for my departure. I have fought the good fight, I have finished the race, I have kept the faith.
> —2 Timothy 4, verses 6 and 7

Here is a story that impressed me yesterday. My business associate and Good News buddy has five children and one was in a basketball tournament this weekend. The dreaded event occurred; he made it to the championship game on Sunday morning—oops, there goes the Lord into the back seat. *No*, that is not the story. The game was 40 miles away, it was a Minnesota winter day with freezing rain (June and I had trouble going three miles to church.). This family left several hours early and attended services in the tournament city before the game. They took the time to recharge their spiritual batteries when they could. That's a story worth telling and a family with great priorities.

**Thought for Today**: In a counter to Paul's message about the race, I also read the following from the 23rd Psalm: "He makes me lie down in green pastures, he leads me beside quiet waters, he restores my soul." Take a prayer break today and every day.

**Prayer for Today**: Dear Father, today we pray for personal peace.

# Brotherly Love

Paul is saying that at any moment in time the person closest to or standing next to you deserves dignity and honor. In many cases that is not how it works. We are an overloaded society and rarely give the person near us enough of our thoughts. We are thinking too far ahead rather than in the present. We need to slow down.

My point is that we should not forget to give consideration or care to everyone; even when we do not have time. Christ served everyone; He made time for lepers, prostitutes, tax collectors and all of the "unclean" and destitute as well as his disciples. We are often called or approached by a friend or acquaintance for advice or help at an inconvenient time. Often when that happens we look at our watch while they talk, space out and not listen and then brush them off as quickly as possible. Wow, WWJD on that one!

> **Be** devoted to one another in brotherly love. Honor one another above yourselves.
> —Romans 12, verse10

The above is a real problem faced by all of us almost daily. We have deadlines in our lives and people that matter long term: our families and career colleagues. With that in mind, how do we deal with the others; those who come for help when we do not have time. We need to pray about that, about how we can be considerate and tolerant.

**Thought for Today:** Let's focus on being caring when we are interrupted by a friend. When we are asked for support, let's find a way. Let us ask how Jesus would deal with the telemarketer!

**Prayer for Today:** Heavenly Father, today I will meet someone in need and I won't have time to listen. Today when that happens I pray and listen in Your name; as Jesus would. Amen

# The Prisoner 1

We are often too busy to stop and pray. In fact that is why I write at 5 am– there are few if any interruptions or distractions. It is quiet, still, the coffee is hot and the sugar is sweet. How great can it get?

> **Set** me free from my prison, that I may praise your name.
> —Psalm 142, verse 7

By 8 o'clock my calendar kicks in and prayer and spiritual thoughts will have to fit in between my daily activities. On a lot of days they just do not quite get on the agenda. In a sense we are victims of our own busy schedules trying to meet the needs of family, friends and business associates. That leads to a good life and there is certainly nothing wrong with that.

In the late '70s I had an evangelical tennis partner, Ken, who would not shut up in his attempts to recruit me into his congregation. One day he advised me that I was not saving enough time for the Lord and he was praying for me. That bothered me a lot.

You see, he was not very successful in business and had to do everything on a shoestring. I had a business, reasonably high cash flow, worked 60-hour weeks, ran marathons and played tennis three times a week. My calendar was so full that June and I met at the tennis club Saturdays after my tennis and her workout to visit with each other! It was a full life, very rewarding and there was very little spiritual growth involved.

We were happy as clams and did not realize that we were prisoners of our calendars.

**Thought for Today:** Today let's try to notice how our schedules entrap us.

**Prayer for Today:** Dear Lord, today we give thanks for our family, our friends and our loved ones. We are blessed with them through You. Amen

# The Prisoner 2

That schedule mentioned yesterday led us to counseling and a new set of family rules and priorities. It took outside help for us to get out of our self-imposed prison. Yes, we were still busy because four kids had to go to college and needs had to be met, but we established new rules. Somehow spiritual growth became part of our family equation.

Our prison walls were our calendar items and obligations. When Paul wrote to Timothy, he was in a real prison with real walls. That allowed him a lot of time to write and pray. He was blessed with the Lord inside him to do that. In our self-induced prison of activity, the opposite happened. We did not take enough time for the Lord.

Over the years June and I have learned not to judge others. But today I will ask you to look at yourself and your lifestyle. Is your calendar getting in the way of your spiritual growth? If so, think about altering your long range plan.

Spiritual growth comes with a get-out-of-jail-free card.

> **I** thank God, whom I serve, as my forefathers did, with a clear conscience, as night and day I constantly remember you in my prayers.
> —2 Timothy, verse 3

**Thought for Today:** Today let us react to pressure in a positive way and take a prayer break. When the going gets tough, cool it, count to ten, take a deep breath and take control. Give thanks for having the ability to slow down.

**Prayer for Today:** Dear Lord, we have woven a web of activity into our daily lives. Often we leave You out and seem to be in a prison of our own design. Today we pray that we can keep You with us and that You will guide us and be our get-out-of-jail-free card!

# Help

In 1912, C. Austin Miles was asked to write a hymn that would "… bring hope to the hopeless, rest for the weary and downy pillows to dying beds". The above reminder that we are never alone, that we walk with the Lord at our side is the result of that request.

It is easy to try to be independent when things get tough. After all we are humans and in control of our world! Let me share something with you all. As I write this, my brother is undergoing chemotherapy and my mom who lives with him in Massachusetts, is approaching her 88th birthday. That totals up to two concerns and a joy; the concern of aging, the concern of serious illness and the celebration of 88 years of love. I cannot control any of that. (see Note)

June and I both want to fix the concerns while celebrating the joy. We need to remember that "…he walls with me, and he talks with me," We need to let go and let God take control and sometimes we, especially me, forget who is in control.

He speaks and the sound of his voice
is so sweet the birds hush their singing
and the melody that he gave to me
within my heart is ringing.

And he walls with me,
And he talks with me,
And he tells me I am my own,
And the joy we share as we tarry there,
None other has ever known"
—C. Austin Miles, The Hymn In The Garden, Verse 2, 1913

Yes, all of us have a tendency to take control.

**Thought for Today**: Today let us simply remember that we do not walk alone. When we are confronted with stress, loneliness and the every day events that distract us, let us remember that God is with us.

**Prayer for Today**: Dear Lord, many of us have rejected your help. We were sometimes angry, often controlling and occasionally selfish. We succumbed to the pressures that surround us. This week we thank you for being there and pray that we may take the time to allow you to walk at our side and accept your help. Amen

Note: My brother passed in 2006 and at press time my mom will be 95 and doing great!

# Special Days

There are 365 days every year. Our goal and challenge is to enjoy them all. We can not allow our finances, boss or other outside influences to steal the pleasure from any day. God put us here to be happy and we need to do that for Him.

OK, let's get real, some days are just a drag, things go terribly wrong, God rains on our parade, our back goes out again, etc. When negative things get in the way we can choose to have a bad day or chose to trust our faith and give thanks for what went right. Some days it seems that the only thing to give thanks for is that it is over. Well, that's enough to make it a good day.

A friend of mine recently was on a driving vacation and had her son fill the tank to go from Duluth to Brainerd. She only got a mile from the gas station and her new Caddy died. Oops—Patrick filled it with diesel fuel. A bad day began; they did not get to Brainerd; the repair for cleaning out the oil was over 600 dollars; they had to find a place to stay. Now, there is some good news. The hotel they found was great, her

> **He** who regards one day as special, does so to the Lord.
> —Romans 14, verse 6

insurance covered the repair and they had a very enjoyable evening.

We all have problems and challenges that will take longer than one day to resolve. We need to remember when we live one day at a time, we simplify our solutions. If we do not get it today, we can work on it tomorrow. When an issue is unsolvable, the Lord is with us and He can change the rules. We need to pray and turn unsolvable issues over to the Lord.

**Thought for Today:** This will be a great day for all of us. We will walk through the challenges and bless the Lord for the experiences and lessons that we learn one day at a time.

**Prayer for Today:** Dear Lord, today we give thanks for the many things that go well and the blessings that we have. We give thanks and pray that we may contribute to Your plan in a cheerful and blessed way.

# Don't Fake It

One of my favorite themes has been being true to our faith by being open and honest. It is something that we all desire, but it also comes with some social consequences. There are way too many people in the world that have a different reality than Christians.

> **Woe** to you ...you hypocrites!...on the outside you appear to people as righteous but on the inside you are full of hypocrisy and wickedness.
> —Matthew 23, verse 27

In America and throughout most of the world, life is competitive. It is as if the resources are limited. As Christians, we are taught that the world has an abundance supplied by God and I believe that is true. But there is a major distribution problem in the world.

Dealing with the wealth of Western civilization and how it relates to Christianity is scary. Recently, when talking about a stewardship campaign at our church. it was mentioned that, if all Christians would tithe, we would not need the government to run social programs. That would be "way cool." A pastor in the group commented that when the church had that kind of money, corruption ran rampant and the job did not get done. Sounds like government to me.

Each of us needs to be as good as we can be to contribute to the positive factor in society. We need to take the social risks to reach our real rewards.

He who has clean hands and a pure heart, who does not lift up his soul to an idol or swear by what is false. He will receive blessing from the LORD and vindication from God his Savior.
—Psalm 24, verses 4 and 5

**Thought for Today:** We will have to make a choice this week; to be straight and true or hold back a bit. As we go through the week. We need to make the tough choices that improve the world around us. We need to keep a pure heart.

**Prayer for Today:** Dear Heavenly Father, we give thanks for the many blessings and opportunities You bring to us. This week we pray for the chance to demonstrate our faith to others to help. We pray to be able to do Your will here on earth. Amen

# Family 1

Every day as Christians, we are giving. In the '60s the expression was "giving off vibes" (That probably came from the Beach Boy's "Good Vibrations"). What we give has an overwhelming effect on our lives, our social environment and those around us. Whether we are in the work place, the family arena or driving alone down the street, we are participating and giving to those around us.

**Treat** others as you want them to treat you... Never criticize or condemn or it will all come back to you. ...If you give you will get. Your gift will return to you in full and overflowing measure, pressed down, shaken together to make room for more and running over. Whatever measure you use to give, large or small, will be used to measure what is given back to you.
—Luke 6, verses 31, 37 and 38

anger when we should stop and meditate. Perfection is our goal, perhaps not our reality. When we are down, it is important to remember that we are the children of God, and we have His support in both the good and testing times. He wants us to work with Him to bring peace and good while sharing His love with others. Sharing His love instead of "our frustrations" with others is a lofty goal.

Let's take a look at the place where being positive is the easiest; the family, where love is the strongest. Certainly, within each of our families, we have always been positive, loving and real cool. If you say that, you better take a reality check and be sure your other family members see it the same. Most of us do not meet that standard.

Sometimes we are tired, sometimes the career is not working well, sometimes we

**Thought for Today:** When we feel stressed out, let us focus on not bringing it home. Let us remember that it is OK to ask the family for support during stressful times, but unfair and destructive to pass our stresses on to them.

**Prayer for Today:** Heavenly Father, through your love, we are truly blessed. We stand before you covered with your love. We pray that during tough times, we can reach out to you and feel and share that love. Amen

# Workplace 2

Within the workplace, there are often stresses that have a negative effect on the overall environment. Deadlines that need to be met, projects that are underfunded, professional jealousies that have developed, a lot of issues that are passed on to us that we cannot control. It is easy to be negative and act different than a child of God.

Very early in my career, a very senior engineer at Bell Labs advised me that as an employee, I would always receive a percentage of what I was worth, never 100 percent. His explanation was that the difference was required to have a profitable company. After 40 years of working, that seems to have been very accurate advice. In the business environment, when thinking dollars and cents, his equation seems to work.

A challenge to me personally is the people that are sharks in the business environment and Christians on Sunday.

> **Treat** others as you want them to treat you... Never criticize or condemn or it will all come back to you. ...If you give you will get. Your gift will return to you in full and overflowing measure, pressed down, shaken together to make room for more and running over. Whatever measure you use to give, large or small, will be used to measure what is given back to you.
> —Luke 6, verses 31, 37 and 38

What I mean is, those that are opportunistic, somewhat misleading (I won't say dishonest) and practice ways that are not part of good Christian ethics. My question has always been, "Can you function outside Christian guidelines Monday through Friday, and then consider yourself a Christian?" The most successful business people that I know live only by good Christian ethics.

In the real world, giving is rewarded many times over. I believe that the business world is part of the real world and that we are to act and follow God's guidelines there if we are to live to our full potential.

**Thought for Today:** Today let us be positive and contribute to solving problems rather than spreading them.

**Prayer for Today:** Dear Lord, during our lives we are often tempted to forget Your ways and work out problems in a human rather than a Godly manner. Please give me the strength and foresight to let You work through me when trying to help, both at home and in the workplace. Amen

# In Public 3

These verses remind us that the measure we use to give will be used to measure what is given back. Then what do we get back when we are impatient and angry in public? What did the doctor who exercised his road rage by punching the elderly woman get for his efforts? What did the lady who flipped me off on 394 last week teach the children who were riding with her? Yes, we all have frustrations and bad days. We can choose to be angry—or we can choose to live in God's image and do His work on earth.

It seems that every day we read of some manifestation of a person's anger against those around them, against society. How do we as Christians avoid getting so far down that we cannot control our emotions? We have the tools, then it must be as simple as using them in our lives.

When we think of our life plan, our goals, we think of peace, tranquility and wealth. In Luke we are told that when we share our peace, etc. we will receive

> **Treat** others as you want them to treat you... Never criticize or condemn or it will all come back to you. ...If you give you will get. Your gift will return to you in full and overflowing measure, pressed down, shaken together to make room for more and running over. Whatever measure you use to give, large or small, will be used to measure what is given back to you.
> —Luke 6,
> verses 31, 37 and 38

more back than we gave. As Christians we have the tools and an obligation to use them. As NIKE (my favorite philosopher) says in it's slogan, "Just Do It."

**Thought for Today**: We will all have high and low times, peaks and valleys, frustrations and celebrations. Let us recognize the lows and repeat today's prayer. Let us be peacemakers rather than facilitating the stresses of our society.

**Prayer for Today**: In January I used the Serenity Prayer and suggested that we all use it when stressed.

> God, grant me the serenity to accept the things that I can not change. The courage to change the things I can. And the wisdom to know the difference.
> Amen

# Encouragement

In our every day lives, we encounter negativity, anger and difficult situations. When encountering this negative force, we make a choice in how we will respond. In our society, often we stand up to be counted rather than be perceived as weak, wimpy or undecided. We can meet the challenge head on or take the Godly course and work out the problem through love, through our hearts. We can demonstrate our love of God through our responses.

When we encounter anger, what happens when we show love? ...caring? ...calm logic? ...prayer? A few years ago, I had to deal with a very angry neighbor. She was upset with the world and wanted my advice. She had cut herself off from several friends to the point that it was affecting her family and her overall lifestyle. I was part of her anger equation and saw no real need for what seemed to be misplaced or secondary anger. I could not even figure out what to apologize for! She was irrational.

> **Let** us consider how we may spur one another on toward love and good deeds. ... Let us encourage one another ...
> —Hebrews, verses 23–25

I told her that I appreciated her concerns, could not understand her reaction to her friends, but would pray for her in two ways. First, I would pray that God would lead me to a better understanding of her will. Second, I would pray that God help her find a way of dealing with her resentments without choosing to be angry and lashing out at others. The room filled with silence, we hugged and I left. Our relationship is different today.

**Thought for Today:** Today let us deal at our own level to encourage others to be positive through prayer.

**Prayer for Today:** Let us pray for the unfortunates that are homeless, starving and trapped in a place without shelter. The refugees from society; not just the civilians trapped in a war zone or the poor in remote places, but those homeless in our towns. Let us pray for all of them. Amen

# Ethics

Every day we hear of issues where those involved have chosen to be vengeful, upset or angry. My next door neighbor has a property line dispute with another neighbor over a few inches of dirt. In the work environment, changes at my company have upset several employees to the point of anger. This week a local woman was assaulted by another because she had too many items in an express check out line. It is interesting what causes anger and stress in our society.

Is it too much to "Love your neighbor" and show respect and tolerance? It is it too hard to turn the other cheek? Or are people getting so opportunistic we have no choice other than to retaliate? We live in a complex society that seems to have changed over the last several decades.

When I grew up, there was the expression, "It is not whether you win or lose, but how you play the game that counts." Since the Vince Lombardi era,

> **You**, my brothers, were called to be free. But do not use your freedom to indulge the sinful nature; rather, serve one another in love. The entire law is summed up in a single command: "Love your neighbor as yourself."
> —Galatians 5, verses 13–14

his famous quote "Winning isn't everything, it's the only thing." seems to be a more popular style. That is a sad state of affairs and does not leave a lot of room for love and Christian ethics.

Yes, we all seek freedom. Our country's constitution guarantees it for us. Paul's letter tells us how to use this freedom so that we may all enjoy life to its fullest. It is important for us to show love and consideration for all.

**Thought for Today**: Today, let us focus on our freedoms. When we drive past a church, note its affiliation. When we notice a person that is different, make note of their nationality. Notice all the different makes of cars, different shaped houses and note that we are diverse in all ways. Give a thought to diversity that demonstrates our freedom and enjoy it all.

**Prayer for Today**: Heavenly Father, we pray that we may focus on the parts of our lives that practice love, patience and caring. We pray that in our small piece of the world, we may show Your love through our behavior. Amen

# Be the Best You Can Be

Last evening I sat alone with a friend who is in the middle stages of MS, the part where the disease is starting to really take hold; starting to win. The discussion was not about having an end of life experience or about being disabled. It was about doing things differently, but doing them. It was about being more tired than before and taking longer to recover, and being OK with it. It was about waking up sore and trying to use massage, heat or cold to feel good enough to function for a while. This lady has heart.

In our apartment complex there are several people that went from walkers to electric wheelchairs or scooters. Afterwards we observe that people rapidly lose physical capabilities when they find it necessary to trade up in technology and no longer use their bodies. Recently, a lady traded her scooter for a walker and now crutches! She makes it to the indoor swimming pool at nine every morning and swims

> **David** found strength in the Lord his God.
> —1 Samuel 30, verse 6

for an hour. She is determined to recover what she can from a back surgery. I see weekly improvement and pray for her recovery every time I see her and note the intensity in her eyes.

I do not know where each of the above is in their spirituality. In one case the lady is in a twelve step program with my daughter and is into spiritual growth through prayer and meditation. I believe that the Lord is with them whether they feel Him or not. You can see it in their attitude and the results of their efforts.

**Thought for Today**: Today we will all have a chance to observe people with handicaps or terminal illnesses. Let us take a few seconds when we do and say a prayer for them and contribute to their quality of life through our God.

**Prayer for Today**: Dear Lord, today we pray for those with disabilities and illness. We pray that they recognize Your love and that You are with them. We pray that they work through You to be the best they can be. Amen

# I Yam What I Yam

Was Popeye a philosopher? Cartoonists often are. When Popeye was confronted with difficult situations he would state, "I yam what I yam," gulp down his spinach and defend right!

We are not all Popeyes and we are expected to conform, often to standards below those of our Christian faith and may face difficulties if we do not. In any case it is necessary to understand who we are, what we are and keep the Lord in our daily lives. We need our "spinach."

In many ways we are continually fighting an image syndrome. Conformity is the word, and clones are the result. Quite often we get flack because we don't fit.

If there was a right way to be, how would some of the prophets or John the Baptist fit in with the rest of their society? Probably not too well at times.

The truth is you are you. You are who God created you to be. He wants you to know who you are and understand your

> **You** made all the delicate, inner parts of my body and knit them together in my mother's womb.
> Thank you for making me so wonderfully complex. ... Your workmanship is marvelous.
> —Psalm 139, verses 13–14

unique characteristics. You were created by God and then the mold was broken. No one else is exactly like you.

You are unique. You are special and it is all right to be you. Don't let others shape you. That is God's task. He started with you, He will finish with you and He will be with you. He is our spinach.

He really does want you to be you.

**Thought for Today:** Let us search for the person that God wants us to be so that we may serve Him better.

**Prayer for Today:** Heavenly Father, as we travel through our weekly chores, we need to see a way to help You. We often lose track of Your plan. Sometimes we are too busy and do not understand it. This week we pray that each of us may find a better way to serve You and make life better for everyone. Amen

# Living Lean 1

Life is very interesting and as we grow older we can always look back at our good times and the not so good times. As senior citizens, June and I have plenty of both in our lives. The interesting piece is that the good times happen when our faith is at the forefront of our lives and the not so good tend to be when materialism has taken over. Apparently life is not about things, it's about love and caring. Let me share a story with you.

We have a friend that is a successful entrepreneur. Frankly, he has his own plane, three homes, a political career and a collection of things that is exceptional. His constant pursuit of things has been of epic proportions. My involvement with his family has let me see the other side. His family does not speak to each other. It is brother versus sister, dad versus mom in a near totally dysfunctional way. As individuals, each is a friend and all

I rejoice greatly in the Lord that at last you have renewed your concern for me. Indeed, you have been concerned, but you had no opportunity to show it. I am not saying this because I am in need, for I have learned to be content whatever the circumstances.
—Philippians 4, verses 10–11

are very neat people. However, they are a great example that love of things does not bring peace of mind or a strong family.

**Thought for Today**: Today let us focus on our spiritual needs rather than our material needs.

**Prayer for Today**: Dear Lord and Father, we live in a glorious world with great opportunities. There are opportunities to serve, opportunities to help others and opportunities to demonstrate Your love through our actions. Many here forget to do that and choose a material and whimsical lifestyle. We pray for them and for ourselves. We ask for the opportunity to do Your will here and support others with our love. Amen

# Living Lean 2

Following up on yesterday, we know several families with five to fifteen children. They all have good jobs, but do not generate millions. They are surrounded with love and caring, they live life as a family team. Yes, they face the problems of everyday life as we all do. God did not give us a perfect world or a fair world. However, when crises are met with caring and love at the forefront and a belief system that allows help from the Lord, the difficult times seem to pass and happiness always prevails.

My first running buddy here in Minnesota is 83 as I write this. He had six sons and lost his wife several years ago. The dad and two sons live in the family home; one son is disabled and the other is struggling to get a business off the ground. They have worked out a cooperative sharing of talents to be a team. The Lord is with them.

> I know what it is to be in need, and I know what it is to have plenty. I have learned the secret of being content in any and every situation, whether well fed or hungry,
> —Philippians 4, verse 12

Paul's message to the Philippians was clear. You can be happy when you recognize the spirit of the Lord that is always available to you.

**Thought for Today:** Today let's recognize that we are never alone.

**Prayer for Today:** Dear Lord, we give thanks for Your presence in our lives. Knowing that You are with us is great and satisfying. Amen

# Living Lean 3

In recent years, large segments of our economy have fallen on hard financial times. The airline and the automotive workers are the most obvious. Many of the financially stressed decide to save face by increasing debt. They choose not to live lean; they keep all of their things. Others make adjustments to survive and pull together as a team.

The stories of wealth without happiness are many. Mickey Rooney and Liz Taylor had multiple marriages (six or eight?) and everything money could buy, but perhaps not happiness. Are Donald Trump, Britney Spears, and others happy? We cannot answer that question and we need to focus on our own needs.

We are often required to live within our means when we feel we deserve more. There is always a temptation to put on a false front. We need to remember, "I can do everything through Him who gives me strength."

> **Whether** living in plenty or in want. I can do everything through him who gives me strength.
> —Philippians 4, verse 13

**Thought for Today:** Today let's use our true strength to help get through the day.

**Prayer for Today:** Some prayers are worth repeating: Dear Lord and Father, we live in a glorious world with great opportunities. There are opportunities to serve, opportunities to help others and opportunities to demonstrate Your love through our actions. Many here forget to do that and chose a material and whimsical lifestyle. We pray for them and for ourselves. We ask for the opportunity to do Your will here and support others with our love. Amen

# Testimony

Paul travelled the world in a constant testimony for God through Christ. He did easy time in prison once, followed by what could only be stated as hard time. This message was written while on a kind of death row. Paul knew the end was near and even then he was testifying and true to his faith.

We had a pastor who used to say that the average Methodist invited a guest to church every 22 years! I feel that he was being critical of our ability to testify and invite. He wanted to start including an occasional personal testimony in the Sunday service so he extended an open invitation to the congregation. No one responded. Oops! That was a hint as to why we were a declining church. We are very nice but private people.

Those of you that know me personally know that I love to talk (often way too much!). However, that's in my world, of family, business and especially sales. I was way to quiet regarding my personal faith journey and had a spirit of timidity

> **For** God did not give us a spirit of timidity, but a spirit of power, of love and of self-discipline. So do not be ashamed to testify about our Lord,
> —2 Timothy, verses 7 and 8

in that area. Pastor Rick changed that. Thus you are reading my regular messages.

In our world today, we are often in places where testimony regarding our faith is a challenge. At work we are hushed by rules; at school, scouts, sports and just about everywhere we go, talking trash is in, talking faith is out. There is hope and we need love and self discipline to testify and invite people to join us.

The best thing is *We can do it.*

**Thought for Today**: Let us look for an opportunity to talk about our faith. If we are uncomfortable with that, let's find an opening to invite someone to join us this week.

**Prayer for Today**: Heavenly Father, we pray for the strength to represent You, Your ideals and Your will here on earth. We thank You for the opportunity to be at peace and do Your work. Amen

# Eisenhower

We are in some way the light, ministers of the gospel or promoters of the Holy Spirit. That is a part of the covenant we make when we join the Christian church. That is awesome responsibility and I for one certainly don't feel like a spirit promoter every day.

Those of you that know me are aware of my propensity for relaxing through exercise. It is a daily piece of my life and pursuing it often shows my selfish streak. In my late twenties I made a covenant with myself to be as good as I could be. I wanted to be a good dad and husband and believed that fitness was a piece of the equation.

Later in life, June and I decided together that fitness was more than physical; i.e. it was spirit, mind and body! Oops—that decision meant three times as much work. We agreed that we would work on the spirit and mind together but she had no interest in joining with me on my swims,

> **He** has made us competent as ministers of a new covenant—not of the letter but of the Spirit; for the letter kills, but the Spirit gives life.
> —2 Corinthians 3, verse 6

bike rides and runs. (She was always a bit smarter.)

Our 34th president Dwight David Eisenhower was a strong believer in this. Whenever possible he kept his calendar open for an after lunch nap and when at the White House he would spend time chipping and putting before his afternoon meetings. His colleagues considered him eccentric and selfish. He felt he needed a scheduled break to be the best he could be for himself and his country.

We all need to be the best we can be, for ourselves, our families and to serve the Lord. Be a bit selfish so that you can help.

**Thought for Today:** Today let's do something for ourselves that will help our spirit, mind and body.

**Prayer for Today:** Dear Lord and Father, today we pray that we can keep our covenant we made to you; we pray that we are shining your light as bright as we can. We pray that we are the light of the world so others may find You through us. Amen

# Trust in the Lord

We, June and I, just enjoyed four weeks of vacation. It was not easy to do that when surrounded by the world events. While staying in Pyrford, south of London, there were concerns regarding a serial rapist that had just struck for the ninth time. A sniper started shooting in Washington. There was a bomb in Bali and then a plane crash Friday. It is easy to ask, "Where is God in all of this?" It is logical, by human standards, to be concerned, or feel concerned and helpless. It is common to feel guilty while enjoying a vacation amongst the tragedies.

Somehow, through prayer and understanding, we need to keep the faith we have in the Lord. He does not expect us to understand everything, just to love and trust Him to put it all together. Together we need to demonstrate this trust and love to others through times of

> **But** blessed is the man who trusts in the LORD, whose confidence is in him. He will be like a tree planted by the water that sends out its roots by the stream. It does not fear when heat comes; its leaves are always green. It has no worries in a year of drought and never fails to bear fruit.
> —Jeremiah 17, verses 7–10

stress and tragedy. We need to be like the tree whose roots are planted by the stream. We need to be fresh and always bear the fruit of the Lord. We need to have this fruit available when others need it.

**Thought for Today:** Today let us focus on our fruit and understand what our faith can do for others with less understanding. Let us pray and keep our spiritual fruits fresh so that we may share them with those in need.

**Prayer for Today:** Heavenly Father, we come to You confused by world events. We are concerned about our own personal issues; unemployment, depleted retirement funds, sickness and many other issues. Throughout all of this, we pray that we may recognize our role as servants and that we make our spiritual fruits available to those in need. Amen

# Winning

Who in our lives are the winners? Some say the one with the most toys wins. That materialistic one-liner that gives me goose bumps. However, in our society today, we tend to pursue things instead of happiness and peace. So who are the real winners and how do they win?

God placed us here to be His stewards with our first priority to be sharing the gifts we received from Him with others. That seems to be a very tall order. However, we always feel great when we have reached out and helped a friend or stranger. This reward is explained in Paul's message to the Romans, Chapter 2, verse 6, "God will give to each person according to what he has done."

**Praise** be to the God and Father of our Lord Jesus Christ, the Father of compassion and the God of all comfort, who comforts us in all our troubles, so that we can comfort those in any trouble with the comfort we ourselves have received from God.
—2 Corinthians 1, verses 3 and 4

God gives us resources in many different forms. We have money that we earn and knowledge that we have learned. We graciously share these things with our families and children and that makes us feel good. We also reach out beyond our own family units and share. We share at work, in church, through volunteer activities and in too many ways to list. We share and sow the seeds that God has given us to plant, and we are real winners when we reach out and share our gifts.

**Thought for Today:** Let us look for an opportunity to help someone; perhaps someone who is sick, someone hurting or someone lonely. Let us see if we can share a bit of ourselves to make someone else feel better.

**Prayer for Today:** Heavenly Father, today we pray for an opportunity to help and share with someone, an opportunity to demonstrate Your Grace through our actions. Amen.

# Whose Law?

In Civics 101 we are taught that in America we follow a version of the English common law. Our official motto mixes things up by declaring "In God we trust" and then separating church and state. What a conundrum. We have to deal with the duplicity.

Somehow each state legislature and the congress write thousands of laws and they seem to change them yearly. We spend a lot of time adjusting, ignoring or being unaware of the changes.

Governments seem to want to legislate what we know as good Christian ethics; caring about each other, helping each other and developing community. There is no allowance in law for unconditional love and caring for our fellow man.

> **Clearly** no one who relies on the law is justified before God, because "the righteous will live by faith."
>
> —Galatians 3, verse 11

Fortunately, as Christians, when we follow God's law, we are in alignment with most manmade laws and we coexist very well. In fact, the most successful people that I know of follow God's law first and man's law second. There is a connection with faith and success.

**Thought for Today**: Today let us practice God's law. Let's demonstrate our caring and love of humanity in our actions. Let's demonstrate unconditional love in our daily activities.

**Prayer for Today**: Dear Lord, today we pray that in our toughest moment and most challenging time, we may be strong and follow Your law. Amen

# Indian Summer

In Minnesota we are experiencing a wonderful autumn. An "Indian Summer" as it is called. Our first heavy frost was followed by a freeze and now we have warm temperatures. Certainly this is a gift to us by God. It is something that we all appreciate and offer our thanks.

During this time, the crab grass has died; there is color in the leaves; the lawn does not need to be mowed as often; the evenings are cool; the garden does not need weeding.

There are many blessings about "Indian Summer" and they are easily recognized. In our daily lives there are also many blessings but we often do not see and acknowledge them. We try to control our lives and often do not turn enough over to God. The more we allow Him to take over, the more blessed our lives become.

The Psalmist says, "...But may all who seek you, rejoice and be glad in you...." As we give thanks for good weather, we need also to give thanks and recognize God's role in our daily lives.

**Thought for Today:** The fall season is upon us. The busy holidays are approaching us all too swiftly. This week we have the opportunity to relax and enjoy the lull in activities between the end of summer and the holidays. Let us enjoy by allowing God's will into our daily lives. Let go and let God and appreciate the things He will do for us.

> **This** is the day that the Lord has made, Let us rejoice and be glad in it.
> —Psalm 118, verse 24

**Prayer for Today:** Father, we pray specifically for those in the world that need food, shelter and a quality of life. In our country there are too many people out of work or threatened by unemployment. In many countries the Holy Season approaches many desperate people. We pray for them and that somehow the prosperous peoples of the world can find a way to do Your will. We pray that we may find a way to contribute. Amen

# Positive Attitude

It is interesting to think about what makes us happy, excited and pleased with our lives. Each of us is different, but I suspect that in Paul's letters he had certain things in mind. I doubt they were what we consider life experiences.

> **I** know that there is nothing better for people than to be happy and to do good while they live.
>
> —Ecclesiastes 3, verse 12

Yesterday on the golf course, on the very first tee, I was very nervous because my game has been suffering all summer. It was in England with my nephew Matt and I wanted to do well. My drive went long and straight and stopped exactly where I wanted it, and my approach held the green less than 20 feet from the hole. Yes, I was happy, but that is not what Paul meant by "do good."

Recently while talking with a friend, Dave, about a sporting event that we both were interested in, we were joined by Don who's dad has recently passed away at age 101. The subject changed as Don processed some of his grief. We were silent (you know that is not my normal style) and let him talk for 20 minutes. We heard about being a volunteer fireman for 60 years, early days on a farm in Windom, Minnesota, hunting trips with dad, etc. Don was in his glory telling us these stories and both Dave and I listened intently. We were helping in a silent way.

Paul was a teacher with a mission. We have been given the task of carrying on his mission in our faith. The Lord has not given many of us the ability to be preachers or to talk the talk every day. We are not all evangelists. However, if we are Christians we are all ministers of the gospel. Knowing that, how do we preach the word? We preach every day through our actions and the example we set in our daily lives.

We need to "…be happy and do good…" every moment we can.

**Thought for Today:** Today we will be tested. Things will not all go well. We need to find a way through our faith to be an example to those around us, an example of good living and happiness.

**Prayer for Today:** Heavenly Father, today we pray that we may help Your cause. We pray for the opportunity to help. Amen

# Operating Style

This is not a political statement. It is just a story. Recently I mentioned the following quote, often attributed to John Madison, to a non-believing friend:

> **Walk** in his ways, and keep his decrees and commands, his laws and requirements, as written in the Law of Moses.
> —1 Kings 2, verse 3

> We have staked the whole of all our political institutions upon the capacity of mankind for Self-Government, the capacity of each and all of us to govern ourselves, to control ourselves, to sustain ourselves according to the Ten Commandments of God.

His comment was something like, you were doing all right until you got to that last part! So I asked him if he would accept the quote if we substituted "ethical behaviors" for the commandments. He was OK with that.

I missed an evangelical opportunity here but he was looking for an argument and I was not in the mood.

My two points today are:

Political rhetoric is un-godly, self serving and often malicious and the Ten Commandments and common courtesies of human nature are often left aside. We need to pray about that.

Second, I find it interesting that my non-believing friend was happy when I removed God from the quote but was still accepting of the ethics clearly specified in the commandments.

My conclusion is that we need to keep on keeping on! People like my friend are closer than they think! Accepting the ethics of the commandments is just one step away from accepting the Spirit!

**Thought for Today**: Today let us lead by example through obedience to our Lord's commandments.

**Prayer for Today**: Dear Lord, we thank You for the opportunity to lead and demonstrate that Your way is the correct way. We pray that today we will overcome the many temptations set before us and follow Your laws to the letter. Amen

# Operating Results!

Yesterday we talked about operating within God's laws and Christian ethics. They are important to us and when we function within those limits we feel good. Feeling good is important.

> ... **you** may prosper in all you do and wherever you go.
> —1 Kings 2, verse 3

Beyond feeling good, in my forty years of doing business, I have observed that ethical business was good business. The bad guys seem to get all the publicity; Ponzi schemes, Enron, and fraud generate headlines. Many of the younger generation have the opinion that profitable business is ripping off people. It certainly is not and none of us would have careers in America and we would not be a great nation without the profit motive.

My point is that yesterday the quote was about self-governing and the Commandments. My point today is that successful businesses also follow and meet those same standards. When they do we are all blessed.

**Thought for Today:** Today let us follow those same standards, the Commandments, in all of our business and personal activities.

**Prayer for Today:** Dear Lord, we thank You for the opportunity to lead and demonstrate that Your way is the correct way. We pray that today we will overcome the many temptations set before us and follow Your laws to the letter. Amen

Note: The prayer is repeated because I felt it is especially important!

# Faith And Life

*Written in October 2001*

Since September 11th, Americans have been living in a changed world. For the very first time in history, we realize the fear of attack. Malls are empty, travel is light, people are cautious and church attendance is up. We all realize that we are not immune to attack. Our nation is at its highest level of security.

June and I flew to the UK on the second international flight out of Minneapolis. That was on September 18th—it was an interesting feeling flying on the same type of aircraft that the terrorists had used. For whatever reason, neither June nor I was concerned. It was a routine flight.

June and I have developed a strong faith during our lives. We often quote the Psalmist who wrote the 23rd psalm—those familiar words, "Even though I walk through the valley of the shadow of death, I will fear no evil, for you are with me." The Psalmist does not say that we will not have to walk through the

> **The** Lord Almighty is with us; the God of Jacob is our fortress.
> —Psalm 46, verse 7

darkest valley or that evil does not exist. Rather, the Psalmist reminds us that we need not fear or be overwhelmed because God is present with us at all times and in all places. God will see us through. The ground and content of our hope is the promise that nothing in all creation can separate us from God's love.

**Thought for Today**: Since those who walk with God are never alone, then let us focus on our faith and try to live a normal life.

**Prayer for Today**: Almighty God, when the foundations of our lives are shaken, hold us close to You and remind us that You will never leave or forsake us. You alone are our hope and security. Amen

# Courage

Often we are tempted to take shortcuts to success. Perhaps we leave someone out of the loop because we do not want to deal with their point of view. Sometimes we take action on our own out of some sort of arrogance; we just know it is the right thing to do. That is an operating style of many successful people. The word is control.

Another way to operate is to delegate that control. People that delegate often seem uninvolved. Some are and some are not. Successful delegators trust others to make decisions and operate with a minimum of control. In our homes and at work this is often a successful way to get things done.

Now I have to ask if our style is what works? Or is it our beliefs? People with strong spirituality, a God-like manner,

**Be** strong and very courageous. Be careful to obey all the law my servant Moses gave you; do not turn from it to the right or to the left, that you may be successful wherever you go. Do not let this Book of the Law depart from your mouth; meditate on it day and night, so that you may be careful to do everything written in it. Then you will be prosperous and successful.
—Joshua 1, verses 7 and 8

tend to be the successful players in life. They build trust with their peers, are liked and generate a comfortable environment within their relationships. Successful people are "...strong and very courageous...do not turn from it to the right or to the left...meditate on it day and night...." When people follow those laws, they succeed no matter what their operating style.

**Thought for Today**: We all have read, heard and recited God's laws many times. We have slipped a few times and broken a few! Today let us focus on being "tough and courageous" in our efforts. Let us focus on keeping our spirituality and beliefs in the forefront of our activities.

**Prayer for Today**: Heavenly Father, we are approaching the great season of joy and thanksgiving; a season when You are worshipped and thanked by many religions and in all languages. We pray that we may have the courage and strength to do Your will during this time of great thanksgiving. Amen

# Harvest

This is the third season that June and I have not had the benefit of the gardens that we had at our home before we downsized. We worked very hard evenings and weekends and always had a bountiful harvest to have and share. We do not miss that very much. We have other harvests.

Since we "downsized" and became non-landowners, we have had 40-45 days to fill that used to be spent gardening. Many of those days are spent together sowing seeds in our relationship. Some of those days are taken up by spending time with others that we did not have time for in the past. As a result, we reap a closer relationship with each other and with many other people.

We are blessed by our deepened

> **Remember** this: Whoever sows sparingly will also reap sparingly, and whoever sows generously will also reap generously. Each man should give what he has decided in his heart to give, not reluctantly or under compulsion, for God loves a cheerful giver. And God is able to make all grace abound to you, so that in all things at all times, having all that you need, you will abound in every good work.
> —2 Corinthians 9, verses 6–8

relationships with each other as well with others. You see the analogy of reaping crops used by Paul in his message in Corinth is still valid today. We need to sow seeds every day in relationships, our minds and with each other so that we may reap the harvest of love and friendship.

**Thought for Today**: For today let us take a quick look at our calendars and see where we can sow seeds for our future. Look for the opportunity to sow seeds selfishly for our worldly future as well as seeds for the Lord. He is our real future.

# Healing

There are diseases that require medical treatment and some that need to be cured by other means. All diseases are helped by spiritual treatment, especially mental and chemical issues. When I say helped, please do not substitute the word "cured." But, doing hospital visits, spiritual people seem to deal with serious illness better than people who ask, "Why me?"

Where I want to go with this is to have a discussion on depression; a disease that seems to be growing in today's fast moving society. My experience is that those diagnosed have mostly lost touch with their spiritual side. They feel alone, hopeless and incapable of dealing with life. They cannot recognize that God is with them!

> **But** for you who revere my name, the sun of righteousness will rise with healing in its rays.
> —Malachi 4, verse 2

They are most often impatient with God.

A case in point is a friend who is clinically depressed but deeply religious. That seems like a Catch 22 but it is true. You see, many people in church on Sunday are searching for something; seeking peace and coming away empty. They leave it behind by having a closed mind. That's the disease.

As Christians we need to learn to recognize our friends, reach out to them and help them grow to know the spirit of Christ. Spiritual growth is the answer and we are the tools placed here to help.

**Thought for Today:** Today let's call or talk to a friend in need; let's just help!

**Prayer for Today:** Dear Lord, today we are thankful for our many blessings; of the spirit, the mind and the body. We appreciate what You made us. Amen

# Sincerity

Love versus evil and hanging on to what is good sounds very simple. In life and relationships the definition of good and evil have a variety of meanings and are analog terms. Those meanings are often personal and evolve through relationships, based on a person's point of view. They change from personal to business and become confused based on each individual's socialization.

I am not talking about evil in the sense of murder, rape and criminal stuff—just simple things that are often unacceptable at certain times. In business there are sociopathic managers (that's from Kurt Vonnegut) and in our personal life different lifestyles are considered "evil" or unaccepted by others. For today let's take a few standards from my life observations.

In divorce cases there are often issues of abusive behavior that are by any definition truly evil. There are also issues that are defined within a couple's relationship, considered "evil" by some, totally acceptable to others. I remember stopping at a friend's house at 9 am on a Saturday and sitting in his kitchen listening to him complain because his wife was still asleep and had not yet made the morning coffee. That standard was unbelievable to me. In his mind he

> **Love** must be sincere. Hate what is evil; cling to what is good.
> —Romans 12, verse 9

was suffering abuse—in my mind he needed to make some coffee. (Oh, and maybe bring her a cup in bed!)

Through the years we have all heard stressed couples express their spouse's evils: too much time at work; too much golf, hunting or fishing; shopping, spending etc. These are all not evil but negotiable in a healthy relationship. These are communication issues rather than good versus bad.

In summary, Paul's message works in all phases of life—clinging to and living to acceptable standards generates happiness and long term success. Even in today's world.

**Thought for Today**: Today let us be sincere in every activity. Amen

# Our Rock

Growing up in New England we often fished in streams and frequently crossed them by stepping from rock to rock. When we stepped on a loose one or slipped from one, we got cold and wet. The analogy I am getting at is we chose the wrong rock! That is not an option with God.

The Lord is the rock of our life; our foundation and always with us. There are times when we forget that simple truth; when we feel lonely; when we will not let Him in to help. During those times we can feel cold and lonely. (Hopefully not wet!)

Prayer and devotionals will help that situation. If you are reading this today you are probably sitting squarely on the rock.

**There** is no one holy like the LORD; there is no one besides you; there is no Rock like our God.
—1 Samuel 2, verse 2

**Thought for Today:**
Today let's be aware of our foundation, our rock!

**Prayer for Today:**
Heavenly Father, today I recognize You and give thanks for being my rock and foundation. Today I pray that I may recognize someone who has slipped from Your rock and help them through You. Amen

# Fear No Evil

As Americans, fear seems to have become a resident in our neighborhoods, living rooms and our daily lives. Not the instantaneous fear felt when we have a close call in an accident or other one-time event, but a subtle, hollow fear about our security. That's right, since 2001 our society has come to the realization that we can be harmed at home!

Right after 911 our neighbor canceled a bicycle trip to the south of France. My doctor canceled a vacation trip to Italy. June and I went to the UK for a visit and our children were concerned. People generally feel different when going downtown to a high-rise building. Church attendance has steadily increased. Yes, fear has found a place in our lives in a different way than ever before.

The fear that used to be most common was that one time event, usually over in seconds, an automobile scare, a fall on the ice—that type of event. In 1991, while leaving the U.S. Open golf tournament, a driver going the wrong way on a one way road came within a few car lengths of hitting us head on at high speed. He missed. With this one kind of event, God seems to follow it up because there is no time to pray. The

**But** now, this is what the Lord says, "Don't be afraid, for I have ransomed you; I have called you by name; you are mine. When you go through deep waters and great trouble, I will be with you. When you go through rivers of difficulty, you will not drown. When you walk through the fires of oppression you will not be burned up, the flames will not consume you.
—Isaiah 43, verses 1 and 2

fear we feel today is different from that.

Read Isaiah 43 carefully. Understand the message. As Christians, we need not let fear change our lives. We are blessed with the ultimate protection plan. It is through our Lord, God. Yes, we have fear today. And yes we have a tool to alter that fear and convert it to a concern. It is our faith through meditation and prayer.

**Thought for the Day:**
Let us all focus on our new-found fears. Let us recognize them as real. Let us pray about them and ask God for guidance. Let us change our fears and move them down one level to concerns. Remember the 23rd Psalm, "Even though I walk through the valley of the shadow of death, I will fear no evil, for you are with me...."

**Prayer for Today:** Dear Lord, the world has become a violent scary place to live. The events of the last few months are beyond our comprehension. We ask Your guidance in all of this. We ask that we may understand it all. We ask that somehow throughout the fear, terror and war, there will emerge a global understanding, peace and a world where love and respect are at the forefront. Amen

# Hide?

What about when we want to be alone, when we desire solitude and we just need to withdraw? Yes, there are those times

> **Can** anyone hide from me? Am I not everywhere in all of heaven and earth?
> —Jeremiah 23, verse 24

when solitude is desired; no prayer, no pressure, just quiet time. I guess we may all relate to that. Often when we feel the need to rest, the desire to chill out and recharge our batteries, solitude is a positive experience.

There was an Easter Sunday in the early '90s when I felt this need. The company I was working for was being sold, we were behind on our yard work, we were going to have a large family dinner in mid afternoon and there was a lot of stress. That day I decided to do a long run between early church and dinner to shake the stress. Usually, when overstressed, exercise is not the way to go, the blood does not seem to flow freely, the heart rate is already elevated and mentally there is little strength available. However, on this particular day, I went out alone, but somehow had friends.

The first thing that happened is that at two miles I met up with a neighbor who was also taking a jog. The first words out of his mouth was what a great way running was to relieve stress. Then he told me about his issues. I chose not to share mine that day because they were minor compared with his. Another

factor that faced me was he was faster than me and running further than I had planned and I was pushed past my limits. But we were staying together and enjoying each other's company.

At six miles, a point when he would usually pull away, he started singing to me! He is a known nut case. He created his own words to an Easter hymn and sang, Bob the Runner has risen today! We laughed alot, had a great experience and I ran ten miles better than I can ever remember doing it. You see, I had two friends with me that day; we can not hide from Him.

**Thought for Today:** There will be times when we want to be alone; times of fear, concern, grief and others. We can seek solitude and we can go off by ourselves. However, we will never succeed. We cannot ever hide from the Lord. He will be there for us.

**Prayer for Today:** Dear Lord and Father, we give thanks for Your presence in our daily lives and Your persistence in caring for us. We are often adrift and think we are challenging the world on our own. However, You always seem to show up when we need and least expect You. Thanks again for Your faith in us and Your presence in our lives. Amen

# God is Ready

How do we do God's work here on earth? How do we make sure that what we are doing follows His plan? These are questions that are often in our minds. When we awake, we often just dive into our daily routines, off to the office, to school or whatever. We rarely set a goal to "follow the Spirit" but somehow we experience the fruits mentioned by Paul in his letter to the Galatians.

In September, a friend asked me about a career opening that he needed to fill for his non-profit company. As I thought about it, all the people that fit were not available and those that were available did not fit. God was not ready yet.

Several weeks ago I called to console an application engineer who had been laid off that week. She mentioned that her dream would be "to find a career where she would be working for more than just money. Perhaps a non-profit." Wow, was God ready?

> **But** the fruit of the Spirit is love, joy, peace, patience, kindness, goodness, gentleness and self control. Against such thing there is no law. ...Since we live by the Spirit, let us keep in step with the Spirit.
> —Galatians 5, verses 22–25

The parties are together now and we are all praying that God's will has been done. The Spirit is present, the fruits of "love, joy, peace and patience" somehow all came together because three people were willing to follow the Spirit.

Life is good when we do.

**Thought for Today**: As we go through this week, let us think about the millions of people in transition during this economic slowdown. Let us each make a call to someone and console them. Let them know that we care, that we are available to talk and ask them their thoughts. If they will talk, let us listen. You never know where the discussion may lead.

**Prayer for Today**: Heavenly Father, we are living in a confusing and angry world. People are feeling economic pressure. There is terrorism, war, conflict and deceit everywhere we turn. We look at all this and challenge Your plan and wonder how it all fits. Somehow we pray that we can continue to follow the Spirit and experience its fruits. Amen

# Halloween 1991

Halloween in 1991 was a significant event in the northern part of the United States. In our neighborhood we had two significant events to prepare for; children trick or treating and June's departure for a family visit on November 1st. Mother nature also had a plan that she had not consulted with me on; the great Halloween three-day blizzard in Minnesota which was a piece of what is now known as "The Perfect Storm."

Paul told the Philippians "Do not be anxious about anything…" but millions of Americans were anxious that weekend! People died on lost ships on the Grand Banks and Minneapolis had 30 inches of snow. But it was not all bad on our end. Let me explain.

In the early afternoon we had a temperature drop and a snow squall started. That is not unusual in Minnesota in the fall and we did not expect it to be anything but a fun Halloween! You see, I had already decorated the outside of the house with Christmas lights so we turned them on. The lights drew a large group of Halloween revelers. We met them with a special greeting, "Ho Ho Ho, Happy Halloween." There was six inches of snow on the ground and we did pray for the safety of the children.

> **Do** not be anxious about anything, but in everything, by prayer and petition, with thanksgiving,
> present your requests to God…which transcends all understanding.
> —Philippians 4, verse 6

In the morning there was 15 inches of snow and the visibility was near zero. A trip to the airport seemed impossible. Prayers were needed. We decided to depart after lunch for a 6:30 flight and the 20 minute trip took over two hours and was very dangerous. June's flight departed 3 hours late and I had a three hour ride home. Happy Halloween.

I assume you all know about the perfect storm and sinking of the Andrea Gail from Gloucester. Our trials are minor when compared with the loss of a ship and lives. When we heard the story, it put everything into perspective. We were stressed and blessed at the same time.

Today is Halloween, enjoy it with your neighborhood goblins!

**Thought for Today:** Today is a special day and we should enjoy it with the revelers. We should also think back to 1991 and be prayerful.

**Prayer for the Day:** Heavenly Father, today we pray for children on a day they look forward to each year. We pray that they be safe and have a great evening. We give thanks for their presence in our lives. Amen

# Be Real

Open and honest is a great way to go through life. Where did Jesus end up when he tried it? There are two answers. One is "On the cross." The Christian answer is "At the right hand of God."

In our society we are often afraid to be real and share our thoughts. In some organizations being real will cost you. In the work place differing from the opinion of the leadership can hurt your career. In church, differences are often divisive and we need to pray about that.

Recently, in the workplace, I had the choice to be open and honest with a new vice president of the company that I represented for thirty years. My openness probably accelerated my retirement by three years. It is something that is OK at age 66 but would have been a crushing blow at age 55. It is an issue that all faithful Christians have to deal with.

> **Love** must be sincere. Hate what is evil; cling to what is good. Be devoted to one another in brotherly love. Honor one another above yourselves. Never be lacking in zeal, but keep your spiritual fervor, serving the Lord. Be joyful in hope, patient in affliction, and faithful in prayer. Share with God's people who are in need. Practice hospitality.
> —Romans 12, verses 9–13

As we travel through life we always need to work to keep bread on the table. In many areas we will be tempted to hold back for the purpose of self preservation. We do need to:

Never be lacking in zeal, but keep your spiritual fervor, serving the Lord. Be joyful in hope, patient in affliction, and faithful in prayer.

In the long run, we work for the Lord.

**Thought for Today:** We often have to make decisions regarding "being real." Today let us focus on demonstrating sincerity, zeal and joy through the patience we are blessed with through Jesus.

**Prayer for Today:** Dear Lord, we are surrounded with the love of Jesus as we approach the holiday season. It is a time of social pressures as well as great joy. Today we pray for those who have a problem experiencing this joy. We pray that they find the belief and experience the circumstances that will give them everlasting peace. Amen

# Bill's Big Book

Many twelve step programs are based on Dr. Bill's Big Book that was written for Alcoholics Anonymous. It is a guide to spiritual growth through twelve steps and a way to let go of negativity. It has been adapted to weight loss, drug use and numerous other difficult personal challenges that are faced by the human race.

A strong piece of it is admission of past wrongs and recognizing that we can be forgiven. That is an important piece of life that we need to recognize. (Or at least I do.) You see, we were not and will not live perfect lives, our humanness gets in the way. As an example, a senior pastor in our Bible study keeps talking about his thoughts regarding Sophia Loren, another younger man mentions JLo, and there are lawyers in the group that need to represent clients who need protection from an unknown truth. These issues can lead to guilt.

Growing up, my church did not have confession at any level. Massachusetts

> **As** Jesus was saying these things, a woman in the crowd called out, "Blessed is the mother who gave you birth and nursed you." He replied, "Blessed rather are those who hear the word of God and obey it."
> —Luke 11, verses 27–28

was a Catholic-dominated state so I had a lot of Catholic friends that were required to go to confession weekly. I did not even understand why. I do now. Accumulating wrongs or guilt at any level is dangerous and leads to creating a negative personality and inhibiting spiritual growth. Our faith is sure, we have a guarantee, but in our weakness we sometimes fail. Recognizing our mistakes in a simple way and learning to accept Christian forgiveness keeps us on a path to spiritual growth. That is the real reason for confession.

# Deal with Worry

We are in the holiday season, a time of great joy, thanksgiving and love. We share with others, we give more freely than we do at other times of the year and often it is a time when we miss loved ones that are not with us. We need to pray about that.

Yes, the term "blue Christmas" applies to everyone to some degree. It is easy to mask sadness during this period of celebration. Each year in our family, we follow a tradition started by my mom. The children and grandchildren come help trim our tree. It is chaotic with the excited grandchildren. It is a blessing and a joy that my mom started when we were in Massachusetts. She is 1500 miles away and we miss her every year.

We have several friends who have lost loved ones this fall. They will be "celebrating" with an empty place at the table, a gift missing under the tree and an empty pew beside them at church. The "blue" in their Christmas will be a sadder "blue" than us missing Mom. We can call Mom.

> **Do** not worry about anything, but in everything by prayer and supplication with thanksgiving let your requests be made known to God.
> —Philippians 4, verse 6

There is a temptation to mask or bury the blue piece of Christmas. Bury it in celebration, cover it with a smile and a "Merry Christmas." It is important to acknowledge it with prayer. Through prayer, focus on the blue and "...with thanksgiving let your requests be known to God."

**Thought for Today:** Let us focus on the spiritual piece of the holiday season. Take an honest look at our whole selves. Acknowledge the many blessings we are experiencing and also the sadness of things and people we will miss. Let us pray to God giving thanks for the blessings while asking for relief from our sadness.

Let us use prayer to help fade the color "blue" in our celebrations.

**Prayer for Today:** Heavenly Father, we are in a joyous season of celebration. There are many of us who have lost loved ones. We pray that they will find peace knowing that they are with You. Amen

# He Comes Through

Every day the Lord gives us blessings. In our busyness it is easy to forget the role He plays in our lives, there were a lot of events that made me think of the Lord this week. Here are three of them.

Early in the week when with a very good friend, we were talking about the things that we prayed for. They were guidance, support, internal peace and several others. It was obvious that neither of us prayed for favors or help. We realized that through prayer, good things would happen.

Later in the week, a young athlete competing for a chance to compete in next summer's Olympics collapsed and was taken from us. Why? That is a big question and certainly something that makes people doubt. When the final reports are in on this, somehow goodwill will come from his young life. It is too soon for mortals to understand.

The third event that brought the Lord to the forefront was a correspondence from a Good News buddy from San Diego

**Praise** the Lord, I tell myself, with my whole heart I will praise his holy name.

Praise the Lord, I tell myself, and never forget the good things he does for me.
—Psalm 103, verses 1 and 2

about his return home after a fire storm that ravaged his neighborhood. There were 15 of 47 houses destroyed on his street and the sanctuary of his church on the next block was lost. Here are the words he used in closing his correspondence:

Truly God is good. There are many lessons to be learned and many prayers have been answered. To God be the Glory.

**Thought for Today:** Today will be just like many others. Our calendars are full, we will have unreasonable demands on our time and we will need to focus to make it all happen. With that in mind, let us take a few minutes and think about the Lord's role and in our lives. Let's let Him in to our day also!

**Prayer for Today:** Dear Lord and Father, today we pray to see the results of your participation in our lives and the ability to accept what we do not understand. We trust that good things will happen. Amen

# Personal Care

We are all having our lives adjusted since the World Trade Center attacks. There are concerns regarding out safety, travel is more difficult, we are more tense and restless, we are changing our style of operation and the way we live our lives. Many of us have some deep-seated resentment regarding the changes.

One of the reasons that Good News exists is exactly this quote. Meditation works and helps bring us back to reality. There is a Good News recipient whose wife has had chronic degenerative back problems for over 15 years. She is tired of pain killers and muscle relaxants. A few years ago she started meditation classes and learned to meditate almost to the point of self hypnosis. She reduced her drugs to one quarter of her previous dosage. The stress and worry about her disease was causing the tension and many problems that added to her symptoms.

Reducing stress, taking time to pray and to love will improve our lives.

> **Love** bears up under anything.
> —1 Corinthians 13, verse 7

**Thought for Today:** Let us take time with our families and with God. Let us contribute to peace and tranquility rather than helping increase stress.

**Prayer for Today:** Heavenly Father, somehow please guide us to contribute to peace and friendship; give me the good judgment to stop and pray rather than to react. Help us do Your will through our presence here on Earth. Amen

# Home Care

Following from yesterday:

One of the things they teach us in sales is to always be ready for the "sales call" or meeting. Sit in the car before entering the building and review in your mind why you are there and what you hope to accomplish. It works in sales and in life. We always need to be ready for the events of the day.

Many of us bring our daily problems into the home at night and let our frustrations affect our family life. The children bring home their frustrations from school, mom and dad from their jobs (or from a bad round of golf) or from the evening traffic. What for? Tonight when you go home, try sitting in the driveway and read today's passage and leave the stress behind. Pray that you can go into the house in a loving and caring mood and contribute to the peaceful and loving environment called home.

> ...**and** everything that comes, is ever ready to believe the best of every person, its hopes are fadeless under all circumstances.
> —1 Corinthians 13, verse 7

**Thought for Today:** Someone once said that at times we are all salesmen. My example of preparing for a meeting is a serious part of business life and success. Let us all focus on "preparing for the meeting" with our families and with God. Let us contribute to peace and tranquility rather than helping increase stress.

**Prayer for Today:** Heavenly Father, in our world today there is war, fear of attack, theft and many negative forces. Somehow please guide us to contribute to the peace and friendship, somehow show me how to act when stressed, somehow give me the good judgment to stop and pray rather than to react. Help us do Your will through our presence here on Earth. Amen

# Protect Our Hearts 1

Today we need to protect ourselves from our own self-induced stress as well as the negativity in the world that we cannot control. As Mac Hammond from the Living Word Christian Center puts it, "We need to protect our hearts." The question is how?

Over the years I have often heard the expression "When the going gets tough, the tough get going." In business and sports this meant to me that when the pain sets in, run harder; when it is break point, put the ball away; when the order is being lost, dig deeper. In each instance, "I" assumed the full responsibility for correcting "my" problem. My male ego would come into the issue and apply pressure to the situation. This has worked very well over the years, but it is not how I have acted since the late '80s.

I needed help from someone with more power!

> **Finally**, be strong in the Lord and in his mighty power. Put on the full armor of God so that you can take your stand against the devil's schemes...
> —Ephesians 6, verses 10–18

**Thought for Today:** Today is the first day of the rest of our lives, let us move forward through daily prayer and let the Lord help us through it.

**Prayer for Today:** Heavenly Father, life is good. The kids have food and shoes, there are two cars in the garage, and TV sets in every home— we are truly "fat cats" living under Your domain. Today we all want to give thanks to you for the physical needs that we have met and ask for help daily, meeting our spiritual needs. Amen

# Protect Our Hearts 2

Continuing from yesterday:

Like many parents, when my two youngest were in private colleges, my ego driven logic failed me. The financial pressure combined with the desire to service the educational needs was too much to get through. This independant guy needed help and it came through the simple saying, "Let go and let God." Funny how that works, everything turned out OK.

When we are deeply involved with our loved ones, we need to protect our hearts. We need to keep our feet on the ground and make caring decisions through love. If we allow the Lord to help protect our hearts, if we listen to Him and accept His part in our lives, our lives will be better and simpler. Keep on asking for support through prayer.

**Stand** firm then, with the belt of truth buckled around your waist, with the breastplate of righteousness in place, and with your feet fitted with the readiness that comes from the gospel of peace... And pray in the Spirit on all occasions with all kinds of prayers and requests. With this in mind, be alert and always keep on praying ...
—Ephesians 6, verses 13–18

**Thought for Today:**
Today each of us has a chance to renew ourselves, forgive others, and move forward with positive thoughts.

**Prayer for Today:**
Heavenly Father, life is good. Today we all want to give thanks to you for the physical needs that we have met and ask for help daily, meeting our spiritual needs. Amen

# Global Peace

There are over 300 million people in America and billions worldwide. As individuals we are not "statistically" significant overall. But we all know that statistics can be manipulated and are often misrepresented. Certainly within our Christian faith, each of us is significant to God. In many of Paul's letters he advised that "God will be with you." I will add, "...personally, up front and close."

As statistically insignificant as the mathematicians make us, God gives us meaning, power and faith. We are the power of one. As Christians, we can impact the world one individual at a time through our faith. When we demonstrate that we are at peace, we infect those around us. When we demonstrate good Christian ethics, we lead others to follow us. When we are at peace, others want to join us.

We all know of pyramid schemes and chain letters. We have an opportunity through our faith to be at the top of a

> **Whatever** you have learned or received or heard from me, or seen in me—put it into practice.
> And the God of peace will be with you.
> —Philippians 4, verse 9

living chain. Each day we are at peace through our faith we will positively affect our environment. Our challenge as people of faith is to work our peace so others will join us.

**Thought for Today:**
It is challenging but exciting to think that we can affect others with our positive actions. Let us consider others and by example, share our hope regarding our future.

**Prayer for Today:** Heavenly Father, we see and hear ugliness in the world on a daily basis. The Mid-East is in turmoil, many of our streets are not safe and there are too many negative financial issues within our institutions. It is hard to understand where You are when we are bombarded daily with these issues. We pray for understanding of Your role and that we may participate in an overall solution. Amen

# Spiritual Gifts

Often the Bible mentions the gifts given to us by the Lord. However, in every case the same spirit is mentioned. Think about what that means to all of us. Think about us as a team, a Christian body, placed on earth to do God's work. Not alone but as a team.

> **Now** about spiritual gifts, brothers, ...There are different kinds of gifts, but the same Spirit. There are different kinds of service, but the same Lord. There are different kinds of working, but the same God works all of them in all men.
> —1 Corinthians 12, verses 1–6

So we all "have different kinds of gifts but the same spirit." We can all participate and use these gifts to do God's work but we do not have the gifts to do it all alone. We need each other; we need our Christian family to get the job done.

**Thought for Today:** Llet us focus on our talents, God's gifts to us. Let us recognize our gifts and use them to do God's work.

**Prayer for Today:** Heavenly Father we ask, "What is it all about?" We pray to You for the ability to better understand it all. We pray for the ability to recognize our gifts and the knowledge on how to utilize them to help. Amen

I have always preferred working with a partner. My belief is that two people working as a team are four times better than the best of the two working alone. If that is true, then how powerful is a small congregation working together doing God's work?

In their first Super Bowl, New England Patriots came out to play without the TV network's usual fanfare of individual introductions. They came and won as a team. Last week in the paper there was a page dedicated to the state girls' soccer championship. It listed the rosters of the two finalists as well as the state all star team. There were no all stars listed on the rosters of the two teams playing in the finals. There is a message here somewhere.

# Always Friends

Most of us have a problem with feeling like one of "God's chosen people." The control freak in us wants to believe that we chose to follow Him. That is ego-centric and introspective. We all know that we chase Him until He catches us. In our lives, who are "God's Chosen" and what do they do?

This month is Thanksgiving and one of my traditions is to do Christmas cards. Each card that gets addressed is to someone special. The addressees have all played a role in my life. Each in some way has been a friend, advisor, mentor, coach, etc. What a wonderful feeling it is to sit there and think about each of them (you). Are they God's chosen people?

There is a priest in the UK who included me in his daily prayers during my cancer period, another is a running buddy of over twenty-five years duration, and several former pastors who were spiritual advisors... the list goes on. The holiday season is a great opportunity to celebrate

**Therefore**, as God's chosen people, holy and dearly loved, clothe yourselves with compassion, kindness, humility, gentleness and patience. Bear with each other and forgive whatever grievances you may have against one another. Forgive as the Lord forgave you.
—Colossians 3, verses 12–14

Christ's birth and life. It also is a chance to think of the many people God has placed into our lives that have demonstrated to us "... compassion, kindness, humility, gentleness and patience."

**Thought for Today**: Let us simply think about our friends. Let us remember why they are, who they are and what they mean to us.

**Prayer for Today**: Dear Lord and Father, we have many blessings that You have given to us. Among them are our friends and contacts. Each of them is in some way a blessing. We offer our prayers for their health and happiness and thank You for presenting them to us. Amen

# Love

In our over forty years of marriage, one of the discoveries that June and I made is:

As we developed our spirituality, we became spiritually intimate. We had a deeper understanding of each other than I personally thought was possible. It minimized walking on egg shells, the fear of raising questions and it allows us to live in confidence.

Somehow we learned to share our hurts, concerns, frustrations and joys together. Worshiping together and sharing ourselves with others has created a special bond. This bond, in my mind, is a gift from God that we were somehow open to receiving and did not recognize it when it arrived.

We are glad and thank God that we received it.

**Many** waters cannot quench love; rivers cannot wash it away. If one were to give all the wealth of his house for love, it would be utterly scorned.
—Song of Songs 8, verse 7

**Thought for Today:** As we take our personal and corporate walk through life, let us keep the Lord a priority and a commitment.

**Prayer for Today:** Dear Lord we pray that we can let Your love and spirit in to our hearts; we renew our commitment to Christ so that we will be his sister or brother. Amen

# Unseen 1

Life is not a sprint; it is an endurance event. Endurance athletes pride themselves on doing events from two hours to three days long. That is certainly commendable. I do not mean to sell them short, but all of us need endurance and focus to get through a 168 hour week, a four week month and a fifty-two week year.

Marathon runners do not get to the end of the race by being discouraged by the next hill, they focus on the finish; that which they cannot see. An interesting piece of that is the pain suffered when nearing the end almost always subsides when the finish line comes into view. That was always true for me in my triathlons.

**Therefore** we do not lose heart. Though outwardly we are wasting away, yet inwardly we are being renewed day by day. For our light and momentary troubles are achieving for us an eternal glory that far outweighs them all. So we fix our eyes not on what is seen, but on what is unseen. For what is seen is temporary, but what is unseen is eternal.
—2 Corinthians 4, verses 16–18

When we are travelling through our years there will be peaks and valleys. Sometimes the hill out of the valley seems too steep to climb. One step at a time we will get to the next peak when we keep our focus on the unseen prize.

**Thought for Today**: Today let's think about what the prize is we want in life. Let's focus on it.

**Prayer for Today**: Dear Lord, today we pray for a vision; Your vision for us. We pray for the understanding of what Your will is so that we may focus on it. Amen

# Unseen 2

Following on from yesterday:

Each of us needs focus and endurance to get through our lives. My friend and colleague will celebrate a significant birthday this summer. To celebrate she is going to Colorado and run the Pikes Peak marathon. Not only is that a challenge, it is one that can keep her focused on the prize "…that far out weighs them all." She has shown me tenacity and an example of excellence in life style in her athletics that carries over to her personal and business life. Of course, although many people are secretly jealous, some think that she is nuts!

We cannot see around the corners of our lives and must live one day at a time. Each day's challenges and problems dealt with properly is a step toward peace. Living each day in a Godly manner with our eyes on the eternal prize will bring us peace.

> **So** we fix our eyes not on what is seen, but on what is unseen. For what is seen is temporary, but what is unseen is eternal.
> —2 Corinthians 4, verses 16–18

**Thought for Today:** Today let us look ahead in our families (in some cases think back about), to our elders. In some ways that gives us a preview of our future. However, there are no guarantees, positive or negative. Let us think about our dreams, fantasies and goals. Let us remember what we see every day is "…temporary, but what is unseen is eternal."

**Prayer for Today:** Heavenly Father, today we thank You for the blessings that we have and can see. We pray that through You we have the endurance to reach the unseen; the ultimate prize. Amen

# The Dalai Lama

June and I have been blessed with the ability to enjoy our lives; both the pitfalls and the pleasures. We strongly believe that somehow the Lord has been involved in our lives and lead us to enjoy the simple pleasures. We both believe that the ability to put the events of our life into perspective is our greatest blessing through our faith.

Several weeks ago a Good News buddy forwarded this to me. I believe that this is not describing a person of faith but is right on for those that have not developed a spiritual lifestyle.

The Dalai Lama, when asked about what surprised him most about humanity, answered,

> Man. Because he sacrifices his health in order to make money. Then he sacrifices his money to recuperate his health. And then he is so anxious about the future that he does not enjoy the present; the result being that he does not live in the present or the future; he lives like he is never going to die and he dies having never really lived.

**Can** any one of you by worrying add a single hour to your life?
—Matthew 6, verse 27

**Thought for Today:** Who in our circle of friends resembles the Dalai Lama's description? It could be family, neighbor, friend or even someone in our church. Today let's think about that and find a way to share our faith with them.

**Prayer for Today:** Dear Lord, today let us pray for those who have not included Christ in their lives; those who are spiritually weak, worried about physical rather than Godly issues. We pray for them and ask You for a way to help, a way to share and a way to contribute to their spiritual growth. Amen

# Standing

This is one of June's favorite hymns that covers a lot of issues in our lives. What do we stand for? What is the promise? They are simple questions that I will oversimplify today.

First, we stand for ethical Christian behavior that will benefit ourselves and everyone around us. We stand for living by following the Ten Commandments. Examples of being good are needed in our world and we are designated to show our stuff!

Second, the promise is Grace; given to us by Christ when He died on the cross. We want to think there are more promises than that. When we need more money, more self control, more time; more… etc! Somehow we feel deserving. We want what we want when we want it! We already have what we need–Grace!

> **Standing** on the promises of Christ my King, through eternal ages let his praises ring; glory in the highest, I will shout and sing, standing on the promises of God.
> —R. Kelso Carter, *Standing On the Promises,* verse 1, 1849–1926

We need to show off, stand for our faith!

**Thought for Today:** Today let us stand out in the crowd; stand for our Christian beliefs.

**Prayer for Today:** Dear Lord and Father, we find it easy to sit and watch. Today we pray for the opportunity and courage to stand up and be counted in Your name. Amen

# Doubt

It is not our reality to get through this life without having crises. In fact, every day has potential pitfalls. It is our job to focus on the ultimate promise and work our way through those challenges to our faith. Doubt will be with us and how we deal with it is our challenge. It is OK to doubt and to recognize the challenge. If I was a retailer I would call my store "Temptations R Us." That's a business idea without a market; people would not have to come in and buy what they find daily for free.

In a recent Bible study that includes several retired ministers (ministers never really retire!) the concept of Grace was the subject. If you have accepted our savior, you have it; it is yours; accept it. It is our blessing.

> **Standing** on the promises that cannot fail, when the howling storms of doubt and fear assail, by the living word of God I shall prevail, standing on the promises of God.
> ——R. Kelso Carter, *Standing On the Promises,* verse 2, 1849–1926

**Thought for Today:** Today let's walk around with a smile realizing we have recognized our Grace.

**Prayer for Today:** Heavenly Father, today we give you thanks for our individual peace and grace. We pray that we may go through the day standing on our beliefs, doing your work. Amen

# Success

Faith and mystery are two words that weave their way throughout discussions regarding Christianity. People who do not believe use modern day logic to negate Christian beliefs. That is their choice, their way, and certainly not my way.

> **Standing** on the promises I cannot fall, listening every moment to the spirit's call, resting in my Savior as my all in all, standing on the promises of God.
> ——R. Kelso Carter, *Standing On the Promises,* verse 4, 1849–1926

The collection of stories called the Bible are too many and too often repeated and confirmed to be ignored. Truly the prophets advised people 2500 and 3000 years ago of future events that would occur. That is why when the Bible was configured they were listed as prophets!

Yes, people can challenge any one story. Did David really go up against Goliath with a sling? Did Noah really build an ark and save two of each species? There is the burning bush, the tablets with the commandments, etc. Logisticians can challenge each story; but why?

My choice is different. There is a totality in the good news stories repeated around campfires for thousands of years. There is a common thread that certainly would have died if it were not a truth. They are wonderful promises; an optimism; a kindred spirit and Grace. Stand on these promises and you will have success!

**Thought for Today:** Today let us appreciate the mysteries of our faith. Let is stand on the promise and have success.

**Prayer for Today:** Dear Lord, today we give thanks for the promise of your Grace. We appreciate the mystery of it all and stand by the promise. Amen

# Prosperity

Prosperity is generally the result of good work; some are prosperous and some are not. The world economy works that way. It is competitive and there are winners and losers.

Today ask yourself where you are in this regard and become a guaranteed winner. You see, real winning is not a financial thing at all. In our competitive business world, growth has been difficult. Regarding our physical selves, growth in fitness, weight loss, and staying healthy are challenges that few actually change from year to year. That is why New Year's resolutions go by the board.

One area where we can always grow healthier and have plenty of help is spiritual growth. If you are reading this devotional you are on the right track. You

> **After** Job had prayed for his friends, the LORD made him prosperous again and gave him twice as much as he had before.
> —Job 42, verse 10

see, there is no limit to God's love and the benefits of being a spiritual being. Spiritual growth is always available, unlimited and beneficial. That is where true prosperity is found.

**Thought for Today:** Today let us ask if we have had spiritual growth this year? ...and why?

**Prayer for Today:** Lord and Father, today help me grow in You, grow in my faith so that I may be a better servant. Amen

# Open Up To Joy And Love

What does it take to be positive and happy? When we are sad, blue or hurt, what is the best way to fix ourselves? That's correct, "fix ourselves." We choose our moods and often hang on to our hurts and remorse. We are responsible for our attitudes and can work to adjust them.

Several years ago while doing volunteer work in treatment facilities, it was common to see patients carrying a plastic garbage bag. It was called a "pity bag" and used to symbolize the emotional garbage that was being carried by the patient. I hope that those bags did well for the patients because they did me a lot of good. It is a helpful concept to know that we can choose to throw away our troubles. The tough part is learning how.

There are two messages that we need to remember to keep on the positive side of life. First is to remember that God is with us and second is to "Fling wide the

**Lift** up your heads, ye mighty gates; behold, the King of glory waits;… Fling wide the portals of your heart; make it a temple set apart from earthly use for heaven's employ, adorned with prayer and love and joy. —George Weissel, *Lift Up your Heads, Ye Mighty Gates,* Methodist Hymnal 213, 1642

portals of our hearts…" and let Him help out. With His help we can throw away most garbage and stay positive.

**Thought for Today**: Our lives and days are full of choices that we need to make, routine and difficult. Let us allow God to help us with the tough decisions. Let us pray about them.

**Prayer for Today**: Heavenly Father, this is a time of Thanksgiving and prayer, the start of the holiday season. We pray for the peace and hope promised through our faith. We give prayers of joy for Your gifts and the many blessings in our lives. We pray that through our example of love and joy we may influence those around us. Amen

# Universal Hope

The holiday season is a time of hope. The Psalmist notes that there is one clear message from the heavens, one God with one message in all tongues to all peoples. Clearly, this encourages us to believe that there is hope for universal understanding and some day world peace.

We live in an often troubled world. This year there have been natural disasters, terrorism, attacks in schools, layoffs and all sorts of ungodly events. They capture the headlines. Certainly there many who question God's role in all of this.

We need to remember that "The heavens declare the glory of God; the skies proclaim the work of his hands." The press and news media report on other issues. It is up to each of us to focus on the message. With our example, we can infect the world with faith, peace and hope.

> **The** heavens declare the glory of God; the skies proclaim the work of his hands. Day after day they pour forth speech; night after night they display knowledge. There is no speech or language where their voice is not heard. Their voice goes out into all the earth, their words to the ends of the world.
> —Psalm 19, verses 1–4

The parable of the seeds points out the greatness of a well planted thought. John F. Kennedy said it this way, "One person can make a difference and every person must try."

**Thought for Today:** There will be bad news and we'll hear it, see it and sometimes feel it. We need to overcome it with the faith and hope of the Lord. Let us show others our hope for future generations.

**Prayer for Today:** Dear Lord, this is the time of year when all faiths celebrate You. We celebrate Your presence in different ways with the common thread of thanks, love and peace. This season we pray for the guidance to share our faith so that we may sow a seed in Your name. Amen

# Spiritual Strength

If you have read this devotional from the beginning you will recognize that I have said this before; it is important but the final time! We need to keep up our strength, spirit, mind and body! June and I just returned from an after-the-early-service walk at the zoo. We observed several things.

First we observed the physical fitness of the people in line. It looked like a group of people waiting to get into their first Weight Watches meeting; obesity was clearly visible. There were people enjoying themselves, a coffee in one hand (probably a 750 calorie mocha!) and breakfast in the other. This was not a physically fit crowd and they were half of our age.

Secondly, there were lots of excited children bursting with energy; running around the lawn. They were having a great time anticipating their trip to the zoo. Throughout the morning, June and I enjoyed watching these children as they visited the animals. There is nothing that makes June and I happier than observing families as they enjoy themselves and spend time together. That is always a beautiful scene on a warm sunny morning.

> **He** will keep you strong to the end, so that you will be blameless…
> —1 Corinthians 1, verse 8

One question that I asked June was, "Do you suppose that even one of these families considered taking these kids to Sunday school today?" You see, we arrived there at 10:15 and there were hundreds of children. There would have been many faiths represented in the crowd but I suspect that many were not charging their spiritual batteries. Also many faiths worship on Friday and Saturday and I apologize to them and pray for the others.

As you know, I preach about physical fitness a lot; June says way too much! I am hard to live with because of it. Paul is preaching about Spiritual strength, fitness. We need to exercise to keep our bodies feeling good and moving. We also need to exercise our minds to keep up the spirit!

**Thought for Today**: Today let's allow time for our spirit to recharge, let's grow in the Spirit!

**Prayer for Today**: Dear Lord, today we pray for fitness. We pray that we may keep our spirit, minds and bodies strong and serve you well. Amen

# Thanksgiving

June and I are especially thankful for a family running event we started in 1990, now called the Turkey Day 5K. Each year we are tearfully proud when 10,000 plus runners, walkers, pets and wheel chair participants enjoy their Thanksgiving morning in downtown Minneapolis. An aside, but probably more important, will be the contributions of food and hard cash that will be received by the Second Harvest food shelf. We both feel blessed that the Lord gave us the inspiration start this event and placed people in our path who have made it special.

Thanksgiving is the traditional start of what we call the holiday season. While giving thanks we must be aware and focusing on the good rewarding parts of our lives, focusing on the positive.

I like the way H. Norman Wright put it:

> Thanksgiving is not to be limited to only the times when we are aware of blessings. Let us give thanks even when we have a problem to solve, when there are difficulties to be met. At these times, we give thanks to God for unconditional love and goodness, for unlimited wisdom and abundance. When we give thanks continually, we are rejuvenated— spirit, mind and body.

**As** therefore you received Christ Jesus the Lord, so live in him, rooted and built up in him and established in the faith, just as you were taught, abounding in thanksgiving.
—Colossians 2, verses 6–7

Let us hold those thoughts and be thankful for all of our blessings.

**Thought for Today:** Let us focus on giving thanks to God for the love we have for each other and the support we both give and receive.

**Prayer for Today:** Dear Lord and Father, we give you thanks for our friends, our families and our troubles. Yes, we give You thanks for our financial crises, our family stress and the ripples in our personal seas of tranquility. Through our troubles we learn to pray and appreciate the many blessings that seem greater when compared with the ripples of life. We give You thanks for our lives, Your love and Your Grace. Amen

# Thanksgiving Concept

This is just a short prayer of Thanksgiving today for all of you. The best part of Good News and Spinach is the many of you who contact me that I have never met. Our Good News list of friends includes four CEOs (at least two take time to share the Good News with staff), many salesmen (because that is my world), several clergy in several countries, many retirees and all sorts of others. Thanks to you all because you each enhance my life at some level.

Several years ago my pastor spoke of "returning thanks" to God this week rather than "Giving Thanks." It was something his grand father used to do three times a day. His basis was that God gave us the things we are thankful for and he wanted to hear from us but that we were really giving back or returning thanks.

> **As** therefore you received Christ Jesus the Lord, so live in him, rooted and built up in him and established in the faith, just as you were taught, abounding in Thanksgiving.
> —Colossians 2, verses 6–7

This day I return thanks to you all, as well as to God, and share my love of people and life with you.

**Prayer for Thanksgiving**: Dear Lord and Heavenly Father, we return blessings and thanks to you today for the many wonderful experiences we have, the love that we feel from our friends and acquaintances and for the guidance that you give us in our daily lives. We pray that throughout the world people learn to appreciate Your blessings and to live the life that You desire for us; one of peace and good will for all. Amen

# Thanksgiving

Thanksgiving Day, but wait a minute, very day is a thanksgiving day. Every day of our lives can be a day of gratitude. Thanksgiving is more than a day of football games, reunions and eating.

Have you ever made a list of all you have received that you are thankful for; an extensive list compiled over time and added to as you feel appreciative? A great family activity for the holiday is to share this type of list with each other and recognize God's contributions that are on the lists.

The Pilgrims knew what gratitude was—at least those who were still alive. Many had died on board ship and the survivors were wintering in a harsh new country. Those that had left in that fall were grateful because they were now free and not oppressed for what they believed; they had a new beginning and there were two babies born that were a symbol of new life. They faced hardships, but being thankful doesn't happen without difficulties; it happens in the midst of difficulties.

> **Enter** into his gates with thanksgiving and his courts with praise. Give thanks to him and praise his name.
> —Psalm 100, verse 4

In the past year we made a choice to remember the good and the bad events. On this day we are asked to focus on the good. God gave us a grateful heart and wants to hear about our gratefulness to him through prayers of Thanksgiving.

**Prayer for Today**: This is a week of Thanksgiving. Let us give thanks for the blessings that we have received and pay close attention to what we mean to others. We are blessed and you are all on my list.

**Prayer for Today**: Heavenly Father, let me be more aware and thankful for Your presence in my life. Let me share my gratitude with others and contribute positively to the world in which we live.

# Love

Love is a choice. Yes there are many feelings of love at times, but they come and go. It is a choice, especially agape love. This word is used over 200 times in scripture. It is the type of love that will make your marriage come alive. It is difficult and you cannot do it on your own. You need God infusing you with this love and the strength to be consistent with it. There are three words that describe how Jesus loves us and how we are to love others.

We are loved unconditionally. He loves us whether we are bad and no matter how bad we are. That's unconditional love. To be like Jesus, we must also love others in this way.

We are loved willfully. Do you understand what this means? He wants to love you. He was not forced to go to the cross for you; He chose to. How do we love others? By choosing to.

We are loved sacrificially. Sacrificial love gives all, expecting nothing in return.

> **Love** the Lord your God with all your heart, with all your soul, with all your mind and strength. Love your neighbor as your self. There is no commandment greater than these.
> —Mark 12, verses 30 and 31

**Thought for Today:** Let's focus on two or three individuals who cause us angst. How can we find forgiveness and love for them?

**Prayer for Today:** Let us pray that through some miracle there will be a loving peace in our lives and around the world.

# Thanksgiving Prayers

The Holiday season has arrived. Thanksgiving just passed and surely we all spent four days meditating and offering prayers of thanks for our blessings. *What?* That's not what we did in my house! What we did was have a wonderful gathering with both friends and family. Yes, there were prayers and thanks combined with some outside games, football, Christmas shopping and a 5K race. Put the weekend's activities on a list and most of us would realize why we were tired the following week.

As Christians, we are coming to a very special day; a day to celebrate the birth of Jesus Christ. Our focus however is often placed on gifts, parties, getting our acts together for the New Year. Our calendars are full with many special events: holiday parties, Winter sports, Christmas pageants and services, shopping, year-end business meetings. Sometimes it just gets out of control. Is all this activity a bad thing? I think not,

**Come** to me, all you who are weary and burdened and I will give you rest. Take my yoke upon you and learn from me, for I am gentle and humble in heart and you will find rest for your souls. For my yoke is easy and my burden is light. —Matthew 11, verses 28–30

especially if somehow we can get through it all by keeping Christ at our side and on our minds.

Christianity and spirituality are wonderful allies during busy times.

**Thought for Today**: Let us focus on finding more time for ourselves during this busy period. Let us be selfish once a day and take time out from our obligations to society. Let's find a few minutes each day to let Christ help us enjoy the season.

**Prayer for Today**: Heavenly Father, we are overburdened with problems. There are people dying at war and on the streets of our cities. We are busy with year-end business activities and planning for Christmas. Many of us will be traveling over the holidays. Please give me the power to be aware of Christ's presence through all of this. Help me find a way to walk through this activity with God as my co-pilot. Amen

# Expressing Yourself

As Christians we need to demonstrate our goodness every day in every event. That does not mean walking around handing out roses hugging everyone we see. That would scare a lot of people off if I did it!

Therefore there must be another way.

Greeting people in biblical times included a hug, a cheek kiss and sometimes water to wash off dusty feet and cool the head. I am pretty sure that if I did that people would be uncomfortable also. Times have changed over 2000 years. However, expressing our faith through love still works.

There are simple things that you may do that will help and you can see the effect immediately. When you open a door for someone, make eye contact and smile; they will almost always smile back and seem more relaxed. When in public we

> **The** only thing that counts is faith expressing itself through love.
> —Galatians 5, verse 6

often see a crying child with a frustrated mom. Don't look away or walk away! Try to make eye contact and wave to the child; say something nice. Inevitably if you do, both the mom and child will relax. You would have expressed love in a simple way.

In photos and movies Jesus is generally portrayed with piercing loving eyes; often a stare. No one really knows if that is a truism but it works. We are to be the light of the world; we can be through simple acts of consideration and love!

**Thought for Today:** Today let's smile at people and see the difference they have; they will be more comfortable with us!

**Prayer for Today:** Heavenly Father, today I pray that I may demonstrate Your love and my faith through my behavior toward others. I pray that I shine Your light brightly. Amen

# Invisible Qualities

This is a very busy time of the year. There are next year's budgets at home and at work, the snow needs to be shoveled (for us northerners!), and increased activity at church, holiday parties and all the holiday sports tournaments are added to our month's activities. It is easy to get caught up in all the human activity and leave our spirituality behind: Merry Christmas.

It is interesting that activity surrounding Christ's birthday celebration may often deprive us of the time to meditate and appreciate the wonders of his gifts. It is a glorious time of the year, full of memories of our youth and the excitement of growing closer to our families. Where is God in all of this?

First and foremost, God is with us, even when we are too busy to be conscious of His presence. His "…invisible qualities, his eternal power and divine nature" are available to us all, every day. All days are not created equal! We all have our ups and downs. On those days when we are out of touch, where is the Lord? He is exactly where we left Him, waiting to support us.

> **For** since the creation of the world God's invisible qualities, his eternal power and divine nature, have been clearly seen, being understood from what has been made, so that men are without excuse.
> —Romans 1, verse 20

**Thought for Today**: We are faced with the holiday activities that are added to the norm. It is a blessed time of the year. Let us focus on being sure that we bring the Lord with us every day. Yes, He can go shopping, to a youth holiday tournament, to a business meeting or any place we will take Him. Let us silently recognize His presence through meditation and prayer.

**Prayer for Today**: Dear Lord and Father, today we thank You for the gift of grace received through Your son Jesus. We are blessed this time of year through the memories of His life and the celebration of His birth. We give thanks for Your presence in our lives and the ability to reach out to You when we are stressed. Amen

# A Day of Joy

The holiday season is here. The obligations are building and if you are paying attention you can feel the stress building: at work, at home, in the kids' schools. Often I talk about being the best you can be and refer to the YMCA logo: Spirit, Mind and Body.

> **For** in six days the Lord made the heavens and the earth, the sea and all that is in them, but he rested on the seventh day. Therefore the Lord blessed the Sabbath day and made it holy.
> —Exodus 20, verse 11

We need rest physically and mentally. There is rhythm to the seventh day of rest that is a good balance of work and rest. Many people put themselves out trying their own plan. God is saying that once a week we need to take a break. He is saying there is more to life than work. He is also urging us to follow His pattern.

Spiritually we need this time to refocus our lives. God wants us to spend one day looking to him and thanking him for being liberated. Listen to what the Lord said to Isaiah: "If you keep your feet from breaking the Sabbath and from doing as you please on my holy day... then you will find your joy in the Lord."

There is a Good News family and former neighbor of ours that showed more respect for the Sabbath than any other modern family that I know. Mom does not even have to cook on Sunday. They are a family that has a lot of love and joy. That is really our life-long goal.

**Thought for Today:** Take some time to meditate and pray for rest and peace in our lives. Take some time to recharge your spiritual batteries. Take some time to find the joy.

**Prayer for Today:** Dear Lord, today we pray for people who just can't take time to rest and meditate. May they somehow grow to find joy in the Lord. Amen

# Happiest Season

It is a great time of the year when we look forward to celebrating Christ's birth. We are blessed because we believe and are warmed by His presence in our everyday lives. Amongst the daily stresses that our society places on us, we have a God-given relief.

I find it interesting that 30 plus years after his birth he was asking who they believed he was. My thoughts are that the Christmas story would be enough. But then, nothing in this world is ever easy; not then and certainly not now.

So what is Christmas really about? Gifts, material giving and a recharging of our spiritual batteries. It is a great time of the year, the happiest time of the year. We need to enjoy the season while we recharge our batteries, reinforce our beliefs and prepare for the New Year ahead.

Katharine McPhee said in her song:

> "Have yourself a merry little Christmas
> Let your heart be light.
> From now on our troubles
> Will be out of sight."

**Jesus** and his disciples went on to the villages around Caesarea Philippi. On the way he asked them, "Who do people say I am?" They replied, "Some say John the Baptist; others say Elijah; and still others, one of the prophets."

"But what about you?" he asked. "Who do you say I am?" Peter answered, "You are the Messiah."
—Mark 8, verses 27–29

Blessings to you all for a great season of joy!

**Thought for Today:** The Christmas season is not all joys. We will encounter stress, financial hardships, bad weather and all the events of winter life. They are all blessings that are part of our lives. We need to keep Christ as our focus and our stresses will be overcome.

**Prayer for Today:** Heavenly Father, we give thanks for Christmas and all the festivities. We give thanks that "our troubles will be out of sight" through prayer. Amen

# Relaxing

If this passage sounds familiar, you read it on November 27th. This is a strong message worth repeating during such an active time. It suggests that we have tools through our faith that can help us enjoy the season. However, just like the tools in the garden shed, they will not help us if we don't reach out and pick them up.

The many tools of Christianity are available to us all, and "picking them up" just takes the time to allow them to work. Here are some suggestions.

Try changing your daily routine for the season. In the morning shut off the news, put down the paper, and sit alone with your beverage and just think about the season in quiet. That may change your outlook for the day.

When you feel out of control or stressed, keep today's message in your presence; take a break and read it. Give your faith a chance.

Something that I do is wear my lapel pin, the pair of feet from "footprints in the sand." They constantly remind me that I am not alone.

> **Come** to me, all you who are weary and burdened and I will give you rest. Take my yoke upon you and learn from me.
> —Matthew 11, verse 28

There are many options and God is available to us, but we have to let Him into our lives.

**Thought for Today:** The Christmas story is one of wonder and genius; the genius of the wise men to read and follow the signs shown to them. They took the time to go and answered a call. They took a leadership role. As we go through this busy time, let us understand our roles as Christians and be leaders in spirituality.

**Prayer for Today:** Heavenly Father, we are experiencing unusual times. The weather is confusing and there is unrest in our society. We are approaching a New Year with hesitance and in many cases fear. We need You beside us in times like this. We pray for the presence of mind to stop and let You come with us. Amen

# Endurance And Encouragement

Instant gratification is something that we always seem to want and often expect. We have national lotteries around the world and people become instant winners. (They may have played for twenty years!)

> **May** the God who gives endurance and encouragement give you a spirit of unity among yourselves …
> —Romans 15, verse 5

The desire is clear; we want what we want when we want it!

If that is where you are at in your life, you need not read any further today. That is not my message! Paul's message to the Romans is about endurance and encouragement; two things given to us through our faith and prayers that will make us successful. There will be no lightning bolt that makes us winners.

In the years that June and I were associated with my son's music business, we dealt with hundreds of starry-eyed musicians who were waiting for their big break. Some actually made it but all that did, earned it. The ones that worked at it 24/7, the ones with undying passion for writing and performing; those who were too serious about it to enjoy the party atmosphere were the successful ones.

In our own lives we need to endure. Life is not a sprint, it is more like a marathon and there are no days off. We will feel weary and need encouragement.

We need a place that we can find the encouragement; we have it because God is with us. We do need to reach out and grab it through prayer.

**Thought for Today:** Today let's think who we could reach out to for encouragement: our pastor, significant other, child, bartender. There is always someone.

**Prayer for Today:** Dear Lord, we thank you for your support and pray that we can let you in when we are tired. Amen

# Recovery

Not all Good News buddies are believers. The following is a story about a close associate that has had over fifty years of hardship. He was a star college hockey player, married a beautiful lady and it did not work. Tried marriage again two more times and failed. Worked his way out of a career over six years ago and was nearly living on the street. He tried everything but living a faithful lifestyle and was addicted to alcohol and gambling. At his bottom he Recognized that a power greater than himself could restore him to sanity. That person is God."

Stories of recovery are common and many of you recognize that quote as the second step of a twelve step program. At age 60, my friend went to AA rather than a sports bar that facilitated both of his destructive habits. He took a step that I took in March of 1977 and never looked back. Read tomorrow for more on him. It is a blessed story.

**The** LORD is gracious and righteous; our God is full of compassion.
—Psalm 116, verse 5

**Thought for Today:** Let's think about who we know that needs to allow the Lord into their life. Let us reach out to someone and see if they are ready.

**Prayer for Today:** Dear Lord and Father, we are blessed to have You in our lives. We pray that we honor Your presence and help others let You into their lives. Amen

# Hockey Players

More from yesterday:

That was less than three years ago and we do not have enough time to tell the whole story of his spiritual growth and so you get the short version. Last year after four years without a job and one year after finding a higher power, a former business associate sought him out for a six month contract; his first job using his degree and experience in five years! That was a good thing and recently they talked about hiring him for real—with benefits.

Well, now comes one of those coincidences that in my mind are God moments. He needed to meet the VP of operations before he could be hired. He was a bit nervous to say the least but by now he knew how to pray. He walked into the office and the 15 year younger VP had a photo of Bobby Orr, the great Boston Bruin defenseman, on his wall. The conversation started with him asking the VP, "Did you ever see him

> **The** LORD protects the unwary; when I was brought low, he saved me.
> —Psalm 116, verse 6

play?" They got to talk hockey and they had both grown up on the north shore of Boston and the VP was a former college hockey player. Hey, this was in California where hockey players are scarce. I do not believe in coincidences. He got the job.

In three years our Good News buddy has bounced off of the bottom, become a believer and recognizes the benefits of our faith. The Lord is always with us and available when we let Him in!

Today's thought and prayers are repeats of yesterday. They are important!

**Thought for Today:** Let's think about who we know that needs to allow the Lord into their life. Let us reach out to someone and see if they are ready.

**Prayer for Today:** Dear Lord and Father, we are blessed to have You in our lives. We pray that we honor Your presence and help others let You into their lives. Amen

# Why Fear

The terms shaky ground and solid ground generate strong visual images that are easy to understand. Growing up in Massachusetts we played in the grassy marsh lands alongside the tidal rivers north of Boston. The land was around six inches above what was called "mean high tide." We often ran into shaky ground, ground that was virtually floating. That was always scary because several times one of us broke through the sod and had to be helped out. Breaking through could be fatal.

Solid ground is also something very definable: a rock or piece of ledge. When we went fishing in these tidal streams we would fish from the rocky corners where we would be safer. The tidal flows had eroded the mud bank back to solid ledge and often the water was deeper there. That's where we felt safest.

In life, we are safest when we are strong in our faith, when we have time for God, when we remember our rock. Our rock protects us emotionally and physically. Our rock is eternal.

**You** will keep in perfect peace him whose mind is steadfast, because he trusts in you. Trust in the LORD forever, for the LORD is the Rock eternal.
—Isaiah 26, verses 3 and 4

**Thought for Today:**
Today let us remember to stand on our rock!

**Prayer for Today:**
Heavenly Father, today we pray that when we have issues we can stay grounded in our faith. We pray that we remember our rock when we are stressed. Amen

# Infamy

Today is a famous day described as a day of infamy. It is one of the most famous days in the history of war. There are a lot of famous battles described in our history books: David and Goliath, Troy, Gettysburg…and the list goes on. I need to wonder and ask why. Most wars since WWII have been un-Godly, nobody wins, situations that do not seem to resolve anything. In fact, after the treaties are signed there has been as much tension as before and does not make a lot of sense to me.

So where is God in all of this? What would Jesus do? How come both sides can think God is with them? These are great questions and I am not even going to try to answer them. I will refer them to Abraham Lincoln as he analyzed God's presence in war.

In Abraham Lincoln: A History by Nicolay and Hay, Lincoln is quoted:

> **Surely**, as I have planned, so it will be, and as I have purposed, so it will happen.
> —Isaiah 14, verse 24

"The will of God prevails. In great contests each party claims to act in accordance with the will of God. Both may be, and one must be wrong. God cannot be for and against the same thing at the same time. In the present civil war it is quite possible that God's purpose is something different from the purposes of either party—and yet the human instrumentalities working just as they do, are of the best adaption to effect His purpose…God wills this contest, and wills that it shall not end yet. …He could give final victory to either side any day. Yet the contest proceeds."

Today we need to remember Pearl Harbor, a day in infamy. We also need to pray for an end to all conflicts, we need to contemplate world peace.

**Thought for Today:** Contemplate world peace.

**Prayer for Today:** Dear Lord and Savior, today we are wondering where it will all end. Throughout history the world's people have found ways to battle. Today we pray for some understanding as to your role in all of this. We pray for understanding so that we can represent your will in search for peace. Amen

# Slow Down and Enjoy

This Saturday morning it is obvious to me that the Christmas season has definitely taken over my life. Yesterday I was booked from 7 am to 3 pm with no breaks or items on my list that I was not going to get to. Thursday evening I was so tired that I only skimmed through my Bible study. On Friday I had a meeting set up with a friend to tour his robotics lab at his school. It was going to be fun and following that I had two business appointments.

The day did not go as I had it planned. At 6:45 am in 10 degree F. temperatures, a tire blew out as I entered the freeway. Fortunately there was an immediate exit leading to a strip mall that included a Caribou coffee shop. (It could have been worse!). Oops, there goes the men's breakfast and bible study and the tour of the lab.

After a trip to the tire store, I made a quick stop at the office to check email and do a few of the things on the list. There was a message cancelling my tour. So, I did not miss anything and had time to be better prepared for a meeting over lunch. Everything worked out.

> ...**give** thanks in all circumstances, for this is God's will for you in Christ Jesus.
> —1 Thessalonians 5, verse 18

I do not like to think that God works at the daily line item level because that would make Him very busy. But I carried some guilt as I waited for AAA to change my tire. Just maybe I was being punished for skimming over the Bible study material. Then when I saw the cancellation that came in after I left for the day, it looks like God was just keeping me from making an unnecessary trip! Thus, no more guilt.

My summary is: God is with us and God is good!

**Thought for Today:** Today and throughout the holiday season, let us shed the stress, pray for the moment and find the joy.

**Prayer for Today:** Heavenly Father, today we ask that we may find the joy of the holiday season. We ask so that we may share it with others and be leaders in our faith. Amen

# Yule Fire

In Minnesota where I live, the holiday season is cold. In fact there is a cable station that stops programming and runs a Yule log burning as a symbol and backs it up with holiday music. It is very peaceful and meaningful.

The symbol of the Spirit's fire warms our hearts during this season and up here in the northland it is very welcome. This is a blessed season and we all need to focus on the spiritual blessings as we work our way toward the year end.

**Do** not put out the Spirit's fire; do not treat prophecies with contempt. Test everything. Hold on to the good.
—1 Thessalonians 5, verses 19–21

**Thought for Today:** Let us think about our spiritual goals. Let us carry the joy of Christ's birth with us and the materialistic pieces of the season will fall into place.

**Prayer for Today:** Dear Lord and Father, we give thanks to You for the love that we feel when You are in our hearts. Today we pray for a chance to help serve You after the season. We pray that we find opportunities to do Your will here on earth; a chance to contribute to a loving peaceful world. Amen

# Joy

Christmas is a joyful time. The joy of the celebration generally pushes the stress and negativity into the background. A friend recently commented that he wanted to bottle up the holiday spirit for later use. He needs to learn that the bottle he needs is the Bible on his bookcase. The Bible is more than a bottle; it is a large jug of joy. A drink a day will keep miseries away and you can take as many drinks as you want!

Ok, so that's enough analogy for today! If you are reading this "Good News" you know where to go when in you are in need. You know to seek out a spiritual mentor, a sponsor or even to grab your favorite prayer guide and pray. That is truly what spirituality is all about; having the faith to snatch joy from the heat of the moment rather than getting bogged down in negativity.

> **Be** joyful always; pray continually; give thanks in all circumstances, for this is God's will for you in Christ Jesus.
> —1 Thessalonians 5, verses 16–18

**Thought or Today:**
Today and throughout the holiday season, let us shed the stress, pray for the moment and find the joy.

**Prayer for Today:**
Heavenly Father, today we ask that we may find the joy and spirit of the holiday season. We ask so that we may share it with others. Amen

# **P**roblems?

Every day is a day to rejoice. We are between our formal day of Thanksgiving and Christ's birthday celebration. Most of us are enjoying what we call the holiday season. Today's passage tells us that God wants us to rejoice, to be happy. We need to pay attention to that.

**From** them will come songs of thanksgiving and the sound of rejoicing. I will add to their numbers, and they will not be decreased; I will bring them honor, and they will not be disdained.
—Jeremiah 30, verse 19

**Thought for Today:** Today we will be happy! We will work through the busy schedule, deal with holiday stress and at the end, let us rejoice!

**Prayer for Today:** Dear Lord and Father, today we rejoice in Your name and thank You for giving the Grace and spirit of Your son, Jesus. Amen

# Service

I like the term, measure of faith, in any context. It causes us to stop and wonder exactly what scale we would measure it with, yards or meters? Euro vs dollars? Pounds vs. kilograms? Faith, of course, can not be measured in such easily quantified terms. The measure that probably matters is probably how well we use God's gifts.

When serving others is done as a passion it is truly a gift from God. The warm feeling of having helped is always worth the efforts. Many people are famous because of this gift and some have been raised to sainthood. In our generation, Mother Theresa was certainly blessed with it. The best part of the gift of service is we all have it and can feel it at some level. We all at some time will have the opportunity to be the "good Samaritan." We need to use this gift when we can and enjoy the feeling that God gives us as His reward.

> **For** by the grace given me, I say to every one of you: Do not think of yourself more highly than you ought, but rather think of yourself with sober judgment, in accordance with the measure of faith God has given you.
> —Romans 12, verse 3

**Thought for Today:** Today let us think about how we may help. Is there someone with an ill family member that could use a visit? Can we make time for coffee with a friend? If we can't, let's plan an opportunity to serve.

**Prayer for Today:** Dear Lord, service to You is important. Violence seems to invade our lives at all levels. We need and want to help. We need and desire to serve our families, others around us and somehow contribute to Your will here on earth. We pray for an opportunity to help others in a way that will benefit all.

# Purification

Somehow Love seems needed in our world today. Business has become cutthroat. The unemployed scramble en mass for what few jobs are open. There is competition for what seem to be limited resources. There is a scramble for the top. What is it all about?

Well, I suppose we need that second SUV, the lake home, the 60-inch TV for Sunday's game. Yes we have surely become very material. But is it all necessary?

We all know the answer to that is no, but somehow we all participate at some level. Many people have "things" but are not at peace. There is a need in our society for spiritual growth that is as important as the need for economic growth. We need a strong faith community to support an economic and political system that seems in need. We need to demonstrate through our own behaviors that we are at peace.

**Now** that you have purified yourselves by obeying the truth so that you have sincere love for your brothers, love one another deeply, from the heart. For you have been born again, not of perishable seed, but of imperishable, through the living and enduring word of God. For "All men are like grass, and all their glory is like the flowers of the field; the grass withers and the flowers fall, but the word of the Lord stands forever."
—1 Peter 1, verses 22 and 23

This is a special season when we are reminded of Christ's birth. We may be bombarded with materialism, but we are also reminded of our Christian roots. This time of year is our opportunity to refresh our spirituality; it is a great chance to grow in faith.

**Thought for Today**: Let us demonstrate through our behaviors that we are at peace. Let's deal with the demands placed on us in the way that Jesus would advise us; through forgiveness and prayer.

**Prayer for Today**: Heavenly Father, the world still seems to be suffering many ills. The lack of love, trust and the violence of terrorism seem to dominate the news. We pray for some understanding of the situation. We pray for a way to bring your love into the equation of international and interracial differences. Amen

# Refresh

Almost every night we go to sleep without fear; knowing that we will awaken refreshed and ready to make it through another day. We walk one step at a time, we live one day at a time and sometimes the days break down into minutes and hours. But we get through them.

> I lie down and sleep; I wake again, because the LORD sustains me.
> —Psalm 3, verse 5

In AA programs the expression "one day at a time" refers to another day without using alcohol or drugs. As an endurance athlete I assure you that you try to avoid thinking about the distance and keep up that one step concept. That is harder than you think because your focus needs to be on the balloon arch that covers the finish line. That's a conundrum because you need to visualize the finish without thinking about the distance!

Making it through a day without addiction, running miles, just getting through a day are always easier when you have faith. You need to believe you can make it and the best way to believe that is through the spirit of the Lord. With His help we will be sustained and succeed!

**Thought for Today:** Today we awoke refreshed. Tonight we will be tired. Let us go to bed proud of what we did today!

**Prayer for Today:** Dear Lord and Father, today was a day of progress. Tomorrow we pray that we may believe that You are with us as we walk through the pitfalls of life. Amen

# Encouragement

Life is never a sprint and often it takes courage to stay the course, to do what is right. During the holiday season we are blessed with great memories and the thoughts surrounding Christmas. There are also temptations that arise during the many celebrations.

My single biggest temptation is at what my friend calls grazing parties; I overeat. Prior to 1977 the temptation was to drink too much alcohol; it was almost a tradition in my family! It seemed that the women cooked and the men drank too much. They were not the greatest of days.

People are also tempted to overspend. The credit card society we live in is difficult to control and peer pressure to be sure the kids have what they want can be extreme. We need to be careful in all cases and meet our needs and separate them from our wants. Sometimes that takes bravery!

> **Be** strong and let us fight bravely for our people and the cities of our God. The LORD will do what is good in his sight.
> —2 Samuel 10, verse 12

During the month between Thanksgiving and Christmas we tend to burn the candle at both ends. Often it takes strength and sometimes feels like a battle. We need to keep the Lord in sight as he keeps us in His!

**Thought for Today:** Today let's fight bravely as we deal with the issues of life!

**Prayer for Today:** Dear Lord, we pray for the strength to do Your will here during this busy season. Amen

# Faith And Illness

Holiday cheer is a great and wonderful thing. It is a time when it is easy to be happy in our society; there are bright lights, merry music and more smiles and eye contact as we walk along the streets. Yes, the holiday season brings us great joy.

There are, however, those that are experiencing tough times. There are events that just cannot be ignored. There are those with critically ill loved ones who are fearful that this is their last holiday together. There are those that are experiencing their first holiday season alone after losing a loved one. There are many who are ill and fearful. These are friends of ours that are experiencing a "Blue Christmas."

Many of us do not know how to deal with people in this kind of emotional need. We would love to help but do not want to interfere. I pray that all of us think about that. This is a time to share; a time to listen; a time to pick up the

> **Humble** yourselves ... under God's mighty hand, that he may lift you up in due time. Cast all your anxiety on him because he cares for you.
> —1 Peter 5, verses 6 and 7

phone and just say hello; a time to ask someone if they would like to share a prayer. This is a time when we can reach out to someone out of love and share God's faith.

**Thought for Today**: Let us focus on those around us that are experiencing a blue Christmas. Let us identify them. Let us reach out to them with love.

**Prayer for Today**: Heavenly Father, we pray for ourselves, our friends and loved ones. Many are ill and experiencing fear, uncertainty, loneliness or hurt. Many need you in their lives and have not found You. We pray that we may be the conduit that strengthens their faith and eases their anxieties. Today we pray for a way to do Your will in this way. Amen

# Christmas Love

The holiday season is a time of great joy. It is full of symbolism. There are bright lights in almost every neighborhood. Stores are full of shoppers buying gifts for their loved ones. Christmas trees light up our homes. Special carols that we sing only once each year sound pleasing to our ears. Yes, the celebration of Christ's birthday is a wonderful experience.

As Christians, we proceed through this season each fall. In general, love abounds within our society. When we donate to the food shelf; to Toys for Tots; serve at a shelter; or just say Merry Christmas or Happy Holidays, we feel good because we are demonstrating our love for each other—through Christ. Love is wonderful gift we have been given through our faith.

> **If** I have the gift of prophesy, and can fathom all mysteries and all knowledge and if I have a faith that can move mountains, but have not love, I am nothing. If I give all I possess to the poor and surrender my body to the flames, but have not Love, I gain nothing…
> —1 Corinthians, verses 3 and 2

**Thought for Today**: As we go through the week before Christmas, stress tends to build. Year-end activities pile up on top of holiday parties, annual budgets and all the "to do" about Christmas.

As we go through the day, let us focus on why we are doing all of this. Not because we have to, but out of love for each other, those around us and the love of Christ.

**Prayer for Today**: Heavenly Father, we are all wrapped up in the season's activities. We are concerned about all of the "hate" in the world. The Mid East, Afghanistan, northern Ireland, all seem to be embedded in it. In America and throughout the free world, there is confusion and fear of terrorism. We pray that somehow love can shine through all of this and that we as people may see through the negative forces and learn that love is possible. Amen

# Blue Christmas

Each year our former pastor had a special service for people having a sad time over the Holidays. Pastor Rick must have been an Elvis fan because he called it a Blue Christmas Service. It was one worth attending whether you were sad or not. We can always find reasons to be blue over the holidays and it is good to take a look at those feelings, put them in perspective and pray to God for the support that is available to us.

This year there are Good News friends without jobs, others who recently lost their spouses to cancer, several fighting serious illness and others in severe career and financial crises. I ask you all for prayers.

Several years ago we met a young gentleman at the Blue Christmas Service, John, who had visited during the summer. He was in tears during the service. He was despondent because his parents were having a problem with his sexual preference and he was not being welcomed at the family celebration. In another year both June and I were having some doubtful health issues and attended for ourselves.

> **Have** mercy on me, O God, have mercy on me, for in you my soul takes refuge. I will take refuge in the shadow of your wings until the disaster has passed.
> —Psalm 57, verse 1

Each year there are people in attendance who are experiencing their first holiday season after losing a loved one. Many are experiencing the angst of serious illness. There are many reasons to feel pain during the season of joy. It is important to take refuge in the shadow of God's wings.

**Thought for Today:** Let us take note of our sad feelings over the holidays. Let us recognize that they exist. Rather than mask them with joy, let us pray about them, and turn them over to God so we can enjoy the celebration of Christ's birth.

**Prayer for Today:** Heavenly Father, today we have special prayers for the holidays. We pray that the reminder of Your presence brings trust and love to the world. We pray for people who have lost loved ones and are spending their first Christmas with an empty place at the table. We give thanks for the role that you play in our lives and the help you give us. Thank you for being available for us each and every day. Amen

# Bottle?

Today we awaken with a week before the Christmas celebration. We are tired, weary and excited. Our hearts are full of the joy and spirit that this wonderful season creates. It would be great if we could bottle it all up so we could drink it year round.

Our Good News friend Paige said it well on her Facebook site this week, "I wish it could be Christmas every day..... I'm getting the best present of all this year." She will be moving in to a new home near her daughters and grandchildren and they will celebrate Christmas together. You see, she was widowed last year and this is a great gift and the result of hard work, planning and having a strong faith.

In our family we will experience Bennett's first Christmas. Born in October he is our ninth grandchild. There is something very special about a Christmas with a new baby. I guess like everything else, there is only one first!

> **There** is a time for everything, and a season for every activity under the heavens.
> —Ecclesiastes 3, verse 1

I have said many times that one of my best gifts is you; what I like to call my Good News buddies. You drive me to read, write and consider what Christ means to me and the world. Wow, that is a great gift. Thanks.

> Down in a lowly manger
> The humble Christ was born,
> And God sent us salvation
> That blessed Christmas morn.
> —John W. Work Jr., *Go Tell It on the Mountain*, Verse 3, 1907

**Thought for Today:** Today let us all enjoy the celebration. The birth of Christ is fast approaching. Today let's focus on the excitement, blessings and spiritual meaning of it all. Also let us remember that this spirit can be with us all year long—we do not need a bottle, it is in our hearts!

**Prayer for Today:** Today we pray for peace and give thanks for our friends. Amen

# Midnight Clear

Living in Minnesota the idea of clear air at midnight on a sub zero evening is a great set up to think peaceful thoughts. I was just outside in that exact setting and the amazing feeling of quiet, beauty, freshness and the wonders of the evening seem endless.

The stars are so bright that I wonder why we need the Hubble telescope. The freshness of the air was tremendous. It makes me feel like cold air has more oxygen; it was almost intoxication. The feeling of the air on my face must have increased the blood flow to my cheeks and felt great. It brought back memories of days spent sledding with my friends many years ago. Yes, God has created a great place for us.

The following is what one of our Good News buddies had to say,

> I'm officially embracing winter (though it took a while). Snowshoeing at Murphy in the early morning and breaking paths was great fun and cross-country skiing this afternoon was awesome…

**It** came upon a midnight clear, that glorious song of old, from angels bending near the earth, to touch their harps of gold: "Peace on the earth, good will to all, from heaven's gracious King." The world in solemn stillness lay, to hear the angels sing.
—Edmund H. Sears, *It Came Upon the Midnight Clear,* Methodist Hymnal 218, 1849

This is a beautiful time of year and the beauty, stillness, invigorating atmosphere are gifts for us all. It is easy to sense how the three Wise Men must have felt while following that star many years ago.

Luke put it this way:

Suddenly a great company of the heavenly host appeared with the angel,

Praising God and saying, "Glory to God in the highest heaven,

and on earth peace to those on whom his favor rests."
—Luke 2, verses 13 and 14

**Thought for Today:** We live in a wondrous world; let us enjoy it, appreciate it and protect it.

**Prayer for Today:** Heavenly Father, today we give thanks for our worldly blessings and the bountiful lives we have through You. Amen

# Universal Hope

The holiday season is a time of hope. The Psalmist notes that there is one clear message from the heavens, one God with one message in all tongues to all peoples. Clearly, this encourages us to believe that there is hope for universal understanding and some day world peace.

We live in an often troubled world. This year there have been natural disasters, terrorism, attacks in schools, layoffs and all sorts of ungodly events. They capture the headlines. Certainly there are many who question God's role in all of this.

We need to remember that "The heavens declare the glory of God; the skies proclaim the work of his hands."

The press and news media report on other issues. It is up to each of us to focus on the message. With our example, we can infect the world with faith, peace and hope.

> **The** heavens declare the glory of God; the skies proclaim the work of his hands. Day after day they pour forth speech; night after night they display knowledge. There is no speech or language where their voice is not heard. Their voice goes out into all the earth, their words to the ends of the world.
> —Psalm 19, verses 1–4

The parable of the seeds points out the greatness of a well planted thought. John F. Kennedy said it this way, "One person can make a difference and every person must try."

**Thought for Today:** There will be bad news and we'll hear it, see it and sometimes feel it. We need to overcome it with the faith and hope of the Lord. Let us show others our hope for future generations.

**Prayer for Today:** Dear Lord, this is the time of year when all faiths celebrate You. We celebrate Your presence in different ways with the common thread of thanks, love and peace. This season we pray for the guidance to share our faith so that we may sow a seed in Your name. Amen

# In the Bleak Midwinter

Often here in the northland the weather during the holiday season can make one weary; ice scraping the windshield, brushing off the car after a long day at the office, stuck in traffic on the way home and then try to be smiling for the family at dinner! It can be trying, even depressing. Merry Christmas, Ho, Ho, Ho!

Well, it is a season to be jolly, to be spiritual, to be with family and friends and we certainly compound the issue. There are extra events in all areas of our lives; sports tournaments, holiday parties, shopping, gift wrapping and cooking! Through it all we recognize the fun and spirit of the season.

Within our Christian faith there is an entity that cannot be conquered by all this activity. That is the love that is in our hearts. It seems to swell up in magnitude

**In** the bleak midwinter, frosty wind made moan, / Earth stood hard as iron, water like a stone; / Snow had fallen, snow on snow, / In the bleak midwinter, long ago. / What can I give him, poor as I am? If I were a shepherd I would bring a lamb; / If I were a wise man I would do my part; / Yet what I can I give him: give my heart.
—Christina Rossetti, *In the Bleak Midwinter,* 1872

during Christmas. Our energy levels increase and through all the activity we can say Merry Christmas and mean it— we have an embedded passion and love.

And the child grew and became strong; he was filled with wisdom, and the grace of God was on him.
—Luke 2, verse 40

**Thought for Today**: For today let us feel the wonders of the season– The love in our hearts for Jesus and those around us. Let us share it with others.

**Prayer for Today**: Dear Lord and Father, today we pray for people who are overstressed by holiday activity. We pray that they may find peace through it all. Amen

# There's a Song In the Air

There is a lot of joy around the Christmas season. I am somewhat reluctant to use non-carols as a lead-in but the pop songs do create joy. Songs of Rudolph, Jingle Bells, White Christmas, Grandma Got Run Over by a Reindeer, (My personal favorite for a Christmas laugh) and many more usually do not help increase the spirituality but do certainly add to the happiness of the season.

Several years ago at lunch with a pastor, the restaurant was playing pop Christmas music. He did not want to hear about Rudolph, Santa or Grandma. I spent a good part of the lunch applying my considerable sales skills trying to manipulate the mood to positive and in the spirit of the season. I could not do it! I realized later that he was having a bad day and grabbed on to the music as a symbol of his angst.

> **There's** a song in the air!
> There's a star in the sky!
> There's a mother's deep prayer and a baby's low cry!
> And the star rains its fire While the beautiful sing,
> For the manger of Bethlehem cradles a king.
> —Josiah G. Holland,
> *There's a Song In the Air,*
> Methodist Hymnal,
> number 249, 1905

My view on Christmas pop music is non-critical; it adds to the joy, the event and maybe even brings someone to church. It gives people an opportunity to think about what it is all about and adds to the season.

Glory to God in the highest heaven, and on earth peace to those on whom his favor rests.
—Luke 2, verse 14

**Thought for Today:** For today as we wrap up our last minute preparations for Christmas, let us take a few moments, forget the stresses and enjoy the moment.

**Prayer for Today:** Heavenly Father, today we approach the celebration of Jesus birth. It is a wonderful season and we are blessed. We thank you for the Grace guaranteed us through Him. Amen

# Joy to the World

There are a lot of one liners that can be taken from Christmas carols. The opening of "Joy to the World" says it all to me. It summarizes our Christian lives. Lives of joy through the forgiveness of our faith and our Christian peers. Let us all feel the joy of the season, the love for each other and keep our faith strong throughout the season.

> **Joy** to the World, the Lord has come.

With blessings, have a great Christmas eve.

# Good Christian Friends, Rejoice

This is the day the Lord has made, let us rejoice and be glad in it. Christmas is a special day in our faith and our society. The public displays that represent our faith, the music, the crowded stores and many special events impact the world, as has Jesus.

June and I lived for several years in a complex that was over half occupied by Jewish families. In the lobby there was a Christmas tree alongside a menorah. Several of the Jewish families put up lights and had Christmas trees. Recently, one of June's friends, Cheryl, invited her to see her first Christmas tree. Religion was not the issue. Happiness, sharing joy and a beautiful tree was what it was about.

My Jewish tennis friend Bobby has a daughter in college. Every year since she was very young, they would set up a tree for Christmas and Bobby and his wife would share gifts to celebrate Christ's birthday. He and his wife wanted to acknowledge the spirit of the Christian celebration and it gave them the chance to discuss openly the differences that exist in the world. Bobby also attends Bible study and often contributes with stories from his Older Testament knowledge.

> **Good** Christian friends rejoice with heart and soul and voice; Give ye heed to what we say: News! News! Jesus Christ is born today! …Jesus Christ was born for this! …Jesus Christ was born to save!
> —John Mason Neale, *Good Christian Friends, Rejoice,* Methodist Hymnal, number 224, 1855

My family is Unitarian and my mom's grandparents were both Unitarian ministers. They view Christ as a great teacher and philosopher. They do not recognize the Holy Trinity. However, Christmas is certainly the most important day on their church calendar. They share in our Joy of Christmas.

So they hurried off and found Mary and Joseph, and the baby, who was lying in the manger.
—Luke 2, verse 16

**Thought for Today**: This is the day the Lord has made:

Jesus Christ is born today

Jesus Christ was born for this!

Jesus Christ was born to save!

**Prayer for Today**: Dear Lord and Father, today on this joyous day we simply pray that we may follow Jesus' teachings and do Your will here on earth. We pray for a world of peace and love.

# Let Go

I have watched hundreds of people take a step to believe a power greater than themselves would restore them to sanity; people that were so down and out that the concept of God was beyond them. That is how someone who is chemically dependent starts their journey to sanity. It is a process of spiritual growth.

Several people that I worked with were not capable of grasping the concept, even when God was referred to as a higher power. They were too afraid to let go of the control. Most of us try to control too much and do not like letting go.

In a few nights we will experience New Year's Eve and many of us are making resolutions and setting goals. Today I want you to think about something other than exercise and weight. Think about adopting the slogan "Let go and let God." Make that your New Year's resolution and you will have a great year!

> **But** he who unites himself with the Lord is one with him in spirit.
> —1 Corinthians 6, verse 17

**Thought for Today:** Today let us think about what we can turn over to God so that we may have a less stressful New Year!

**Prayer for Today:** Dear Lord, today we pray that we may trust in You and allow your control and spirit into our daily lives. Amen

# Grace

Christmas has passed and we all were caught up in the materialism of it all at some level. The advertising, the gift giving, the holiday cards all tend to lead us away from the real meaning of it all. It is not about the gifts that were given and received by people.

Earlier this year we read about the gifts that God gave us. Paul's letter to the Romans has a very special meaning. When reading further through verse 9, God's many gifts to us are listed. It is important to understand God's gifts to us and recognize which gifts we were given. We need to understand where we fit in God's world and how to apply His gifts in our lives. These are the gifts that really matter. They are not advertised on TV or in the news paper. They are given to us by Him to use. We reviewed some on December 5th through 9th. We need to think about them all between now and the New Year.

**For** by the grace given me I say to every one of you: Do not think of yourself more highly than you ought, but rather think of yourself with sober judgment, in accordance with the measure of faith God has given you. Just as each of us has one body with many members, And these members do not all have the same function, so in Christ we who are many form one body, and each member belongs to all the others. We have different gifts, according to the grace given us.
—Romans 12, verses 3–6

**Thought for Today:** As we approach the New Year, let us think about who we are and what gifts God has given us. Let us learn to use these gifts to make our lives and the lives of others better.

**Prayer for Today:** Dear Lord, at this time of the year, self improvement always seems to be an objective. Each year I focus on "my improvement" and sometimes do not recognize the tasks You may have set forth for me. I pray that this will be the year that "my improvement" is accomplished by recognizing Your gifts to me and finding a way to do Your work with them. Amen

# Renewal

We are in the Holiday recovery mode and are weary. From time to time it is necessary to take a break. It is important to prevent burnout and refresh ourselves. If we are to be the best we can be, do our jobs as parents, employees and citizens, we need to have rest.

Along with rest we need meditation. Ok, if you are reading this I am preaching to the choir again. However, there are some of my friends that rest and renew their minds and bodies without thinking of renewing their spirit. They forget to pray or recognize the Lord's role in their lives.

Others neglect their bodies. It is easy to overeat during the holidays and also easy to skip a workout! That's a double edged sword that I personally am guilty of more years than not! That's what New Year's resolutions are all about. The message from Isaiah is to keep hope in the Lord, keep Him in your life and he will help you soar like an eagle. We will do fine next year!

> **But** those who hope in the LORD will renew their strength. They will soar on wings like eagles; they will run and not grow weary, they will walk and not be faint.
> —Isaiah 40, verse 31

**Thought for Today:** Let us think about keeping God in the forefront of our minds.

**Prayer for Today:** Father, today we ask that You fill us with Your spirit; we ask for strength and guidance. Amen

# Show Off

We are at the end of a year, staring New Year's Eve right in the face. Resolutions and promises abound and we are having thoughts regarding improving our lives. This will be short and sweet, "What will you do next year to improve other people's lives?"

I suggest that you live a Godly life. Make your choices by asking, "What would Jesus do?" That would be something significant; people would notice. It would be a very loud but subliminal testimony of your faith.

Go out and show it off!

> **Go** into all the world and preach the good news to all creation.
> —Mark 16, verse 15

**Thought for Today:** Let's consider our behavior as a subliminal testimony of our goodness and faith. Next year let us demonstrate we are the children of God.

**Prayer for Today:** Dear Lord, today we pray for our pending New Year. We pray that our Christian behaviors and ethics impress others so that they may want to join us. Amen

# Sincerity

During the Christmas season we all share material gifts. It is a time of great love and caring. There are a lot of hugs, kisses and tears of joy. It is a truly wonderful time of year. We are blessed with love and the spirit of Christ.

Now we are faced with a New Year and all of the resolutions that come with it. In most cases, we go back to the grind of daily life and settle into our routine with very few changes. However, we need to continue to share this love, this zeal and this joy. When we do, we all benefit and live better lives. Here are two of my favorite quotes and worth thinking about for the New Year.

John F. Kennedy: "One person can make a difference and every person must try."

John Wesley:

> Do all the good you can,
> by all the means you can,
> in all the ways you can,
> in all the places you can
> at all the times you can,
> to all the people you can,
> as long as ever you can.

**Love** must be sincere. Hate what is evil; cling to what is good. Be devoted to one another in brotherly love. Honor one another above yourselves. Never be lacking in zeal, but keep your spiritual fervor, serving the Lord. Be joyful in hope, patient in affliction, and faithful in prayer. Share with God's people who are in need. Practice hospitality.
—Romans 12, verses 9–13

**Thought for Today:** As we proceed toward the New Year, let us focus on ourselves and our talents. Let us recognize that we have special gifts, given to us by the Lord to use for Him.

**Prayer for Today:** Heavenly Father, we are entering the New Year and we wonder what it will have in store for us. We pray we can apply our talents and gifts in the New Year to pursue Your will. Amen

# New Year's Eve

> **The** Lord Almighty is with us;
> the God of Jacob is our fortress.
> —Psalm 46, verse 7

Today rather than focusing on a new beginning, let's give thanks for the blessed year that has passed. Certainly as we think back there are both positive and negative memories. We may ask why we did some dumb things? ...or why something great happened? Whatever the case, the Lord was with us and we need to be thankful.

**Thought for Today**: Today let us be thankful for last year and prayerful about our future. As we move forward let's remember two of my favorite themes. Keep healthy in spirit, mind and body. Also when in doubt about something remember my favorite philosopher, NIKE and "Just do it!"

# R